# Jesus
# and the Little People
## Gospel Encounters

Michael T Winstanley SDB

*May you journey in peace
and love as a disciple of Jesus*

*Michael*

**Editor's Note**

In this book, footnotes have been converted into endnotes. The main reason being that these notes are too precious to be relegated to the smaller print of footnotes and they provide a valuable commentary on the main text of the book. However when authors have been quoted within the main text they are given the credit of their full name.

**Front Cover Picture**
Title: Christ calling Zacchaeus
Palma, Jacopo (called Palma il Giovane)
Italian; Venetian School 16 Century
© The Fitzwilliam Museum, Cambridge

ISBN 978-1-909080-17-1
November 2012
© 2012 Don Bosco Publications
Thornleigh House
Sharples park
BOLTON
BL1 6PQ
www.don-bosco-pulications.co.uk
joyce@salesians.org.uk

Printed by Buxton Press

For my brothers and sisters
in the GBR Salesian Family,
in appreciation of their kindness,
inspiration and support
over many years,
as we seek to follow Jesus.

# Contents

# Introduction

The *Little People* first came to my attention some twenty years ago. I was reading Rhoads and Michie's groundbreaking book *Mark as Story*, as an introduction to the narrative critical approach to the Gospels. In the section dealing with Mark's use of characters, they list Jesus, the authorities, the disciples, and then the *little people*.[1] They later define these minor characters as individuals who appear briefly on the scene for one incident and then disappear from the story; they lack a continuing or recurring presence in the narrative.[2] Often they are anonymous. Unlike the authorities and disciples, they cannot be considered a group character, because they are not connected to each other. Some are unobtrusive; others simply facilitate the action of an episode; others serve as catalysts. Some play a greater role, standing out for the quality of their faith and trust, or because they convey the meaning of service.[3] Their role is important and memorable, and impacts strongly on the reader, because *in contrast to both the opponents and the disciples,*[4] *minor characters consistently exemplify the values of the rule of God.* (David Rhoads & Donald Michie)[5] I find the designation *Little People* much more attractive and engaging than *Minor Characters.* In a book I was writing at the time, I included a chapter on the *Little People*, and resolved that I would pursue the theme more thoroughly, one day.[6] That project has eventually given birth to this book. The encounters between Jesus and the *Little People* throughout the Gospel story reveal a great deal about Jesus himself and about the nature of genuine discipleship.

From time to time, the Evangelists insert into their narrative short passages which are usually described as *summaries*. Quite early in his Gospel, for instance, Mark, talking about Jesus, writes:

and he went throughout Galilee, proclaiming the message in their synagogues and casting out devils. (1:39)[7]

Proclamation and exorcism are, for Mark, the two major aspects of Jesus' ministry. Later, after the first multiplication of the loaves and fishes, and Jesus' subsequent walking on the lake, Mark notes that:

when they had crossed over, they came to land at Gennesaret and moored the boat. When they got out of the boat, people at once recognised him, and rushed about the whole region and began to bring the sick on mats to wherever they heard he was. And wherever he went, into villages or cities or farms, they laid the sick in the marketplaces, and begged him that they might touch even the fringe of his cloak; and all who touched it were healed. (6:53-56)[8]

In a different context Matthew states:

> After Jesus had left that place, he passed along the Sea of Galilee, and he went up the mountain, where he sat down. Great crowds came to him, bringing with them the lame, the maimed, the blind, the mute, and many others. They put them at his feet, and he cured them, so that the crowd was amazed when they saw the mute speaking, the maimed whole, the lame walking, and the blind seeing. And they praised the God of Israel. (15:29-31)

It is clear that during his itinerant ministry around the villages and small towns of Galilee, and at times further afield, Jesus encountered a large number of people. The majority of these remain anonymous. For most of them we have no record of what exactly happened, how their lives subsequently unfolded, what their long-term relationship with Jesus might have been. We do not know whether they simply got on with their lives, whether they became stay-at-home disciples, or whether later after the post-resurrection preaching they joined the Christian community. Their stories are lost forever. Others, however, met Jesus and the incident was significant enough to be remembered and handed on within the early Christian community, and finally it found its way into the Gospel narrative. These are the *Little People*, who are still remembered, and whose stories we continue to listen to and reflect upon centuries later.

Rhoads and Michie, to whom I have referred, were concerned with the Gospel of Mark, Culpepper with that of John. Whilst also concentrating in the main on Mark, I have chosen to include in this book individuals from the other Gospels too. Consequently, rather than follow Mark's narrative sequence, I have adopted alternative headings under which to group the various stories. After an introductory chapter which addresses the wider context, and therefore has a distinctly different *feel* from what follows, I propose in Chapter Two to examine the stories of people who experienced God's forgiveness through the presence of Jesus. There are a handful of incidents which concern non-Jews, and I have dedicated a chapter to them. Many Jewish women feature in the story of Jesus, and a chapter is devoted to them. Then there is a chapter for other male characters on whose lives a meeting with Jesus had an impact.

During the Passion of Jesus and in connection with his Resurrection, several individuals have a part to play which we need to consider. In a final chapter I attempt to pull together what we may have learned about Jesus and about discipleship, in the hope that this may enrich our own journey of discipleship.[9]

For each passage considered, I have used the same approach and format. In the first place I try to locate the extract in its wider Gospel context, and then make relevant exegetical comments in order to explore and clarify the content of the episode. Secondly, I highlight what the text teaches us about Jesus and about the *Little People* involved. Thirdly, I offer some brief personal reflections arising from the text, which I hope will be helpful to the reader for prayer and pondering.

The English version which I use is the NRSV, which I believe renders the original Greek most faithfully.[10] Whenever I approach a Gospel passage, I tend to do so from three complementary perspectives: the literary, the historical and the theological.[11] The main purpose of the Evangelist is, I believe, theological. As people of deep faith, the Evangelists seek to share that faith vision and conviction with others. They are preachers and catechists; their work has been described as sermons in story form. They set out to tell us about God and God's offer of salvation and new life, about Jesus – his life, ministry, death and resurrection, about the world we live in, about sin and death, and about discipleship. The Evangelists have their own individual theological emphases and perspectives. They tell the story of Jesus in order to elicit from the audience or reader a response of faith, ongoing conversion, love and commitment.[12] And so I believe that the key questions I need to ask when confronted with a Gospel extract are, *What is the theological message, the word from God, which this Evangelist is seeking to communicate here? What aspects of the faith of the early Christian community is the author articulating and proclaiming?* Moving on from there, I seek to discern what the Gospel message is for me, for us today, in our very different world and evolving culture, with its new problems and fresh challenges. It is my belief that the Holy Spirit continues to be present with us in this quest, for the word of God is always a source of enlightenment and fuller life.

I also value the Gospels as pieces of literature, written by competent writers for a particular clientèle, using the literary techniques of their time. They are, I believe, the word of God in human language. Each Gospel manifests an overall general structure, and also a carefully-arranged detailed structure. Structure and context provide clues which help us to discover the author's intention and message.[13] The authors base their narrative on sources, oral and written, and it is instructive to observe the way in which they use and edit them.[14]

The Evangelists have their own individual style and characteristic traits. Literary techniques are employed, like irony, symbolism, inclusion, parallelism. There is a plot, character portrayal, conflict development, the careful use of movement, and of time and space settings. The Hebrew Bible (the Old Testament, as we are wont to describe it) is constantly in the background, implicitly and explicitly. Over the last twenty five years or so there has been a great deal of interest in the Gospels as story (narrative criticism); this has, I believe, injected new life into scriptural research and biblical study, and provided new perspectives and enrichment for the reader.[15]

The Gospels are also historical documents, but not in the sense that every detail is factually accurate. Jesus lived in a particular geographical, social, religious, economic and historical setting, in a predominantly Jewish culture which was also influenced by the wider Greco-Roman culture of the Mediterranean basin. The rich diversity of this backcloth is reflected in the Gospels. Many historical issues arise in the narrative, and require consideration. At times, I will draw attention to these, without seeking to discuss them in detail.[16] Knowledge gleaned from other academic disciplines, such as archaeology and cultural anthropology, can further enrich our understanding of the story.

The written Gospels were the outcome of a complex process of development, from the initial impact which Jesus made on his followers during his ministry, which became the core of the apostolic testimony and preaching. This Jesus tradition, the remembering of *what Jesus said and did*, was handed on orally in a world which was largely illiterate. In such oral transmission of communities, there is inevitably variation, but since its purpose is primarily to recall and preserve what is valued from the past, the nucleus or core content tends to remain stable and fixed.[17] In the light of the Resurrection and the subsequent outpouring of the Holy Spirit, deeper dimensions of the historical ministry and death of Jesus came to be appreciated, this new understanding was reflected in the telling of the story of Jesus. Development occurred over a period of some 40 to 70 years, as the early Christian communities grew, spread and reacted to their own changing environment and to the various challenges which faced them, from within and without. Liturgy, worship and catechetical instruction exerted a significant influence.

Eventually, from a variety of traditions about the teaching and life of Jesus, which were circulating in many communities of faith, Mark composed the first written Gospel, creating with originality, technical skill and theological acumen a connected narrative.[18] Matthew and Luke drew on Mark, their own special sources and oral traditions, and a further written source, no longer extant, known as Q, containing many of Jesus' sayings.[19] John's Gospel was written independently of the others, and has its own very distinctive style, symbolism and theology. Occasionally, there are clear points of contact with similar early traditions.[20] *The Gospels are a wonderful weaving together of history and theology, as they report the events of Christ's life intertwined with later understandings of Christ from the communities of the first century.* (The Gift of Scripture)[21] History and faith are integrated; the Gospels are memory and testimony.[22]

In this book, in my treatment of the different texts in which Jesus encounters the *Little People*, I have sought to be sensitive to these different aspects, issues and approaches, without too much detailed analysis; this would be beyond the scope of this work. My focus is the Gospel narrative in its final form. One drawback of my approach and the way in which I have opted to organise the material is that a sense of the gradual unfolding of the unified story of Jesus in each Gospel is inevitably lost or at least diminished, for the various episodes are located strategically by the evangelist, and the storyline moves systematically towards its climax. In dealing with each passage, however, I have sought to be sensitive to the bigger picture, and have explicitly situated it in the wider context.

In presenting this book, I acknowledge my enormous debt to the writings of numerous scholars which I have consulted over the years, which are summarised in these pages, and to which I make frequent reference in the endnotes. Their learning, insights and integrity have been instructive and inspirational. I hope this book will be accessible to a wide readership, lay, religious and clergy of all denominations, who wish to deepen their understanding of Jesus and his message, and to explore the implications of discipleship for today. It can be used for personal study, prayer and reflection, and also for Christian groups of various kinds: prayer groups, bible study groups, RCIA groups, and also for retreatants, teachers, catechists and students at different levels.

I wish to thank Fr Tony Bailey SDB and the staff of Don Bosco Publications for their patience and expertise in preparing the manuscript for publication, and Fr Kieran Anderson SDB, who read the text and made useful suggestions. Much of the work for this book was done in preparation for or during my recent semester stay in the Don Bosco Centre of Studies, Parañaque City, Manila; I wish to thank the Salesian community there for their hospitality and kindness. Finally, I thank my Salesian confrères and many other friends – contemporary disciples of Jesus, for their encouragement, inspiration and support over many years.

Michael

Savio House,

Bollington, Macclesfield.

July 2012

Introduction

# Chapter One – The Context

The focus of this book is the ministry of Jesus, and the encounters which he had with various people in different situations during that ministry. Through examining these encounters, what happened and what was said, I believe that we can learn a great deal about Jesus and about discipleship.

In all the Gospels, the immediate context for the ministry of Jesus is the appearance of the Baptist, and his prophetic mission of preaching and baptising, his renewal movement. Mark begins his narrative with this figure. Matthew and Luke preface their accounts of the ministry of Jesus with Infancy Narratives, in which they inform their readers about the identity and role of Jesus, and, like musical overtures, give a first airing to some of their key themes. John introduces his Gospel with a hymn-like poetic piece, which is usually called *The Prologue*.

Jesus launches his itinerant mission after his baptism and the desert testing. He preaches in the villages and countryside of Galilee, and shares table with people on the religious periphery; his message is accompanied by acts of healing and exorcism. In this first chapter, before examining individual stories in which Jesus encounters *Little People*, I would like to explore the wider context. I will begin with Mark's presentation of the Baptist. Then I shall take a brief look at the Infancy Narratives of Matthew and Luke, which will provide clues for a better understanding of the later episodes from their Gospels. In like manner, I shall explore *The Prologue* in the Fourth Gospel, which clarifies the deeper dimension of Jesus' identity, and highlights key aspects of his role. Finally, I shall examine the way in which Mark describes the beginnings of Jesus' ministry: the baptism, temptation and initial proclamation of the Good News.[1]

## The Baptist

Mark opens his Gospel rather abruptly with a statement which expresses his faith stance, *The beginning of the Good News of Jesus Christ, the Son of God.* Perhaps echoing the first phrase of Genesis, it serves as a kind of title or heading for the story which is starting, a story which heralds a new creation on God's part.[2] This story is good news, news to make the hearer or reader glad, news which is a cause for rejoicing.[3] In the Greco-Roman world the verb (*euangelizein*) was used for the announcing of royal births, military victories, imperial accessions or political triumphs; in events like these can be detected a nuance of new beginnings. The prophets of Judaism, especially Isaiah, adopted this way of referring to God's saving and vindicating action, especially liberation from the Babylonian exile, *How lovely on the mountains are the feet of him who brings good news.*[4] In Jewish apocalyptic circles at the time, it was used to refer to liberation from demonic powers.[5]

The key figure is introduced immediately. He is the one who brought and proclaimed this news through his preaching and actions. He is also the content of the story, for the author intends to share with his community and others beyond its confines the significance of his presence in the world.[6] This Jesus, Mark confesses, is *the Christ*, the Messiah, *the anointed one*. Rather than his name, the word *Christ* designates his role, his mission.[7] And he is the *Son of God. Like the ideal King of Israel and the chosen People of Israel he can be regarded as son of God, and thus 'Messiah', because of his relationship with God.* (Francis J Moloney)[8]

A scriptural quotation, a prophetic word from God, follows:

> As it is written in the prophet Isaiah, *See, I am sending my messenger ahead of you, who will prepare your way; the voice of one crying out in the wilderness: Prepare the way of the Lord, make his paths straight.* (Mark 1:2-3)

Although attributed to Isaiah, it is actually a composite citation, strategically adapted.[9] Isaiah was the prophet who was particularly significant in proclaiming the hopes for the messianic age.[10] God enters the story, and speaks off-stage to Jesus, indicating that it is *God*, who sends a messenger ahead of Jesus to prepare his way. God is the initiator, the guide and power behind all that will now take place. The term *Lord*, used constantly in the Septuagint for Yahweh, is here applied to Jesus. *Where Jesus is acting, God is acting.* (Joel Marcus)[11] *The way of the Lord* is often found in Isaiah for the route or road by which God will bring the people back from exile. The term *way* will be important later in Mark's story, designating both route and journey; Jesus is to follow a God-directed way; disciples are to follow Jesus on that way too.[12]

The tone and setting change, as, without any mention of his background or earlier history, the messenger then arrives on the scene. In the Gospels, John is naturally viewed in his relationship with Jesus. In fact, he was a significant and important figure in his own right:[13]

John the baptiser appeared in the wilderness, proclaiming a baptism of repentance for the forgiveness of sins. And people from the whole Judean countryside and all the people of Jerusalem were going out to him, and were baptised by him in the river Jordan, confessing their sins. Now John was clothed with camel's hair, with a leather belt around his waist, and he ate locusts and wild honey. He proclaimed, *The one who is more powerful than I is coming after me; I am not worthy to stoop down and untie the thong of his sandals. I have baptised you with water; but he will baptise you with the Holy Spirit.* (1:4-8)

God's messenger is immediately referred to as the *Baptiser.* The verb means to dip, wash, immerse, soak; this is the distinctive prophetic activity through which he is best known.[14] As indicated by God's word, he makes his appearance in the *wilderness.* This setting is highly symbolic. In the hindsight of centuries, the time spent in the wilderness during the Exodus came to be viewed rather idealistically as the period of God's (honeymoon) closeness with the People in covenant love and liberation, the time of Israel's most intense experiences of God, even though it was also a time of testing, rebellion and punishment. This view was then romantically projected into the future, so that, with the years, the expectation developed that God's final saving intervention in the end time would commence in the wilderness, as a kind of new Exodus.[15] So the wilderness setting suggests that God is about to renew the covenant with Israel, to inaugurate the new age. John seems to have moved up and down the lower Jordan river in the barren land east of Jerusalem towards the Dead Sea.

John quickly won the respect of the ordinary people, who came out from the villages and towns of Judea to find and listen to him. He appears as a nomad prophet, and operates independently of institutionalised religion. He seems to have nothing to do with the Jerusalem Temple and its authorities and sacrificial system.[16] Nor does he quote the scriptures. His garb, diet and lifestyle were typical of the Bedouin nomad, and may have reminded the people of their wilderness wandering, prior to entry into the land of promise. Some scholars believe that the reference to his camel-hair clothing and leather belt is intended to evoke the figure of Elijah, who was expected to return as forerunner of the Messiah.[17] John was convinced that the root of the crisis of his people was their sinfulness, which was frustrating God's design. There was need for radical change and a fresh start. His baptism was a rite of conversion and forgiveness, signifying a new beginning and a new future.

John's baptism is part of a larger water picture.[18] In the Old Testament there are many prescriptions for ritual washing, and the prophets and psalmists use such washing as a symbol of interior cleansing.[19] The prophets came to hope for a deeper cleansing and renewal at some future date, when God would pour out his Spirit on his people like water.[20] In addition to the regular lustrations performed by people when they had incurred uncleanness, and the washing prior to praying, in the time of John and Jesus voluntary ritual washing was on the increase amongst the Pharisees and the Qumran community which dwelt near the Dead Sea.[21] Private or public confession of sins was not uncommon in Judaism, and was a standard form of prayer.[22]

There was something special, however, something original and innovative about John's baptism. It was different from the self-administered immersion which some scholars believe converts to Judaism were expected to undergo. It differed also from the repeated ritual washing practised in the elite Qumran community, also self-administered. John's baptism was offered to all Jews. It was a one-off event and not repeated. It was not self-administered, but administered by him. It stemmed from the recognition that Israel had gone astray, the realisation of the need for conversion, both personal and national.[23] There was an urgency about it. Through submitting to John's baptism, people signified their repentance, their commitment to conversion, and they pledged to live a reformed life. They expressed their hope of escaping the threat of judgement, and of sharing in the great outpouring of God's cleansing, forgiving and life-giving Spirit when the day of God's imminent saving intervention occurred.

Repentance and the forgiveness of sins are central to John's proclamation and baptising activity.[24] For him, this forgiveness lay in the future, when the *stronger one*,[25] whose sandals he was unworthy to untie, would come. It is he who will baptise with the Holy Spirit.[26] The outpouring of the Spirit was expected in God's time of salvation, bringing about complete renewal and restoration.[27] For Mark, John's main role is to be the precursor, to pave the way for *the stronger one, the coming one*, the agent of God's salvation – Jesus. John was probably not clear about who was to follow him; there is no hint that John recognised Jesus, as the one whose coming he had proclaimed.[28] John's later question, when in prison facing death, which is brought to Jesus by his disciples, *Are you the coming one?* suggests that the Baptist is struggling with the possibility of having to reshape his expectations in the light of Jesus' different message and his itinerant healing ministry. (Matthew 11:2-6)

Jesus' reply focuses on what is happening in his ministry as a sign that the prophecies of Isaiah are coming to fulfilment, and as an indication of God's loving and merciful action for Israel's salvation. *And happy is he who is not scandalised because of me* is a respectful and gentle appeal that the Baptist should put his faith in him. No response is recorded.[29]

# Before the Baptist

## Matthew

Whereas Mark commences his Gospel with the adult Jesus, Matthew launches his story with what is usually referred to as the infancy narrative.[30] Firstly, he provides a genealogy of Jesus, whom he proclaims as the *Messiah, the Son of David, the Son of Abraham.*[31] Jesus is proclaimed as the fulfilment of Jewish messianic hopes, heir to the promises made to David, and heir to the promises made to Abraham for all the nations.[32] The genealogy firmly anchors Jesus in the history of his people; the dividing points indicate that Jesus is one with them in their highs (the reign of David) and their lows (the exile). The number *fourteen* probably indicates Jesus' connection with David.[33] The names on the list of ancestors suggest that Jesus' lineage is not racially pure or without sin.[34] The providence of God in the unfolding of this long story is evident. The rhythm of the genealogy is broken when Joseph is not said to be the father of Jesus. He is presented as the husband of Mary, *of whom Jesus was born, who is called the Messiah.* The explanation of this change is provided in the subsequent narrative.

The storyteller informs us how the birth of Jesus the Messiah took place. Mary and Joseph were betrothed, but had not yet come to live together.[35] Through the creative action of the Holy Spirit she was with child. Her pregnancy throws Joseph into crisis, for he knows he is not responsible for this. As a devout, law-abiding Jew he feels obliged to divorce her; as a compassionate man, he decides adopt the less-public divorce procedure. But he has a dream, a revelation from God, which changes all that.

Dreams are a feature of Matthew's Infancy Narrative. The five examples follow the same basic stereotyped literary format: the Angel of the Lord appears, gives a message/command, with an accompanying explanation of the rationale behind the action indicated; then Joseph immediately obeys to the letter. The only exception to the template is this first dream, which is more complex because it contains elements of an annunciation of birth narrative; such narratives have their own template or pattern.[36]

Joseph, addressed as *Son of David*,[37] is told not to be afraid to complete the marriage process by taking Mary home as his wife. The angel then explains that her pregnancy is the result of the action of the Holy Spirit. This is the heart of the message. Following the normal pattern of such annunciations, Joseph is assured that she will in time give birth, and he is told what the child's name is to be, with an etymological explanation of the name, which also describes the child's role or mission from God.

The child's name, given by God, is to be *Jesus*. This was a fairly common name in first century Palestine. It was a derivative of the name Joshua, the successor of Moses, who led the people of Israel into the land of promise. Originally the name meant *Yahweh helps*, but in popular etymology the meaning had come to be understood as *Yahweh saves*. The angel links this meaning with Jesus' name. His role in life will be to save his people. *People* is probably to be understood here more widely than simply the people of Israel; it includes both Jews and Gentiles.[38] This salvation, surprisingly for that time in the history of Israel, is not nationalistic liberation from economic or political oppression, which was the common expectation, but *from their sins,* and the consequences of their sin.[39] Saving from sins becomes a way of characterising the whole messianic mission of Jesus.[40]

A scriptural quotation provides further insight into his identity and role.[41] Matthew applies a passage from Isaiah to the virginal situation of Mary's pregnancy; and Jesus is proclaimed to be *Emmanuel*, meaning *God is with us*. The God who was present with Israel throughout its history, is now present with God's people in a new and very special way.[42] On awaking, Joseph follows the angel's instructions to the letter. He takes Mary to his home. She gives birth to a son, and Joseph names him Jesus. Adopted in this way, Jesus becomes a member of the Davidic line.[43] He is Son of David and Son of God.

The next episode takes up the implications of the title *Son of Abraham*. For, as Matthew's story moves on, a group of Magi arrives on the scene, wise men, astrologers probably. They come from the exotic East, possibly from Arabia. Observing a new star rising above the horizon, they interpret it as a sign that a king has been born in Judea. They feel obliged to make the journey to seek him out, planning to do him homage and offer him gifts. Their journey initially takes them to Jerusalem.

At their arrival, and their open, perhaps naive, request to see *the child who has been born king of the Jews,* Herod is said to be *perturbed.*[44]

The Greek verb conveys a strong meaning; it is sometimes used to describe a violently stormy sea; it denotes deep emotional shock and turmoil. Because of current messianic hopes for a true Davidic ruler, and given his own questionable legitimacy, Herod senses his authority to be threatened, his throne to be in jeopardy.[45] The whole city of Jerusalem shares his fear and dismay. Matthew here presents king and city as united against Jesus. Herod summons *all the chief priests and scribes of the people* in what appears to be a formal gathering. The term *chief priests* includes not only present and past high priests, but also members of the privileged families from whom high priests were chosen, and also other significant Temple figures. The *scribes* were the professional exponents and teachers of the Law, Judaism's spiritual and intellectual leaders, its most prominent citizens.[46] Matthew here has the passion in mind, when *all the chief priests and scribes of the people* come together to condemn Jesus, and *all the people* accept responsibility for his death.[47] The end of the story is foreshadowed.

Herod enquires of them the place where the Christ was to be born. He speaks of the *Messiah,* whereas the Magi have spoken of *the King of the Jews,* a title which will not recur again until the passion. The religious elite unhesitatingly provide the answer:[48]

At Bethlehem in Judaea, for this is what the prophet wrote: *And you, Bethlehem, in the land of Judah, you are by no means the least among the rulers of Judah; for from you will come a ruler to be the shepherd of my people Israel.* (2:5-6)

The Son of David theme continues. Once again, the identity, credentials and role of Jesus are emphasised. The child is born in Bethlehem, the city of David the shepherd king. He is the Son of David (as asserted in the genealogy), the awaited Messiah, the King of the Jews, and his mission is to be the Shepherd of his people. This defining of his mission in terms of his shepherding leadership provides the key for our understanding of his subsequent adult ministry; he lives out this shepherding role particularly by proclaiming the message of the Kingdom, and showing care and compassion for the lost, especially by bringing them wholeness and healing.[49] Occasionally he will reach out beyond Israel to transform Gentile lives also.

The covert departure of the Magi creates a situation which demands the departure of Jesus too. Already riddled with fear and threatened to the core of his being by the foreign visitors and their star story and talk of a rival king, and impervious to God's claims, Herod reacts with fury on realising that he has been outwitted by the Magi. In a dream, Joseph is warned about the threat, and is instructed to escape into Egypt, the traditional place of refuge. Once again, Joseph obeys without delay, heading off with mother and child into the night. Matthew, at this point, inserts a quotation from Hosea:

> This was to fulfil what the Lord had declared through the prophet: *Out of Egypt I have called my son.* (2:15)

The original text reads, *When Israel was a youth I loved him; out of Egypt I called my son.* Matthew applies directly to the individual Jesus a verse which unambiguously refers to the Exodus of the people of Israel from Egypt. He is also explicitly claiming that Jesus is God's Son. If the people were *God's Son*, the title is applicable to the one who saves the people from their sins.[50] This claim, the most exalted definition, is the major thrust of the passage,[51] the theological high point of the infancy narrative.[52] The quotation points in the wrong direction, since at this juncture Jesus is en route to Egypt! The probable reason for this is the Evangelist's wish to give a different geographical thrust to the return journey, and to evoke the Exodus before referring to the Exile.[53]

Herod orders the death of all the male children in Bethlehem under two years of age, basing himself on the date of the star's rising according to the information provided by the wise men; he widens the net of slaughter to the surrounding district. A quotation from Jeremiah captures the pain and tragedy of the situation, linking the episode with the weeping of Rachel, the mother of Israel, when her children were deported into exile in Babylon.[54] Rachel becomes the representative of the mothers of Bethlehem. Matthew, with great ingenuity, connects the experience of Jesus with the two nadir moments in Israel's history, Egypt and the Exile.

The final episode of the Infancy Narrative takes place after the death of Herod. Again Joseph is visited by the angel of the Lord in a dream. The pattern follows the usual model. This time, he is instructed to get up, take the child and his mother (the wording carefully avoids any suggestion that Jesus is Joseph's son),[55] and return to the land of Israel, for the child's enemies are dead.[56] God's saving interventions, seen in the return journeys, of the Exodus and Exile are recalled.

Warned again in a dream, Joseph avoids a Judea, now in the power of Archelaus, and heads for Galilee, *Galilee of the Gentiles*, as Matthew will call it later.[57] He settles in Nazareth.

Once again a scriptural quotation is added, *He will be called a Nazorean.* This is probably an allusion to the *nazir,* the holy man consecrated to God by vow from the womb, like Samson and Samuel.[58] There may also be a reference to the messianic branch (*neser*) from the root of Jesse.[59] The two possible *sources* are not mutually exclusive; Matthew could have both in mind.[60] The infancy narrative ends in the place from which Jesus will later go forth to begin his mission.[61]

In his infancy narrative, Matthew provides the reader with a rich Christology: Jesus from Nazareth is the Messiah, the Son of David, the Son of Abraham, Emmanuel (God with us), the Shepherd-Leader, the Son of God, the new Moses, the new Israel, a Holy One. The Evangelist has also outlined different responses to Jesus, acceptance and rejection. As well as looking backwards and recapitulating the history of Israel, the narrative looks forwards and offers a kind of preview of the ministry of Jesus, in which he will be accepted by some, but rejected and done to death by the Jewish religious leaders and the secular power. Killed in Jerusalem, the centre of opposition, he will reappear in Galilee, Galilee of the Gentiles, as the Risen One, and receive the worship of his disciples, whom he will send to all nations. It is also a preview of the history of the Church until the time of Matthew's writing. The good news that Jesus is Messiah and Son of God was preached to the Jews first: some believed and offered him their loyal submission, whereas others refused to accept him. The Pharisees in general, despite their knowledge of the scriptures, were hostile to Christian claims. The Gentiles, however, were turning in faith to Christ in increasing numbers.

## Luke

Luke too begins with an Infancy Narrative, which differs from Matthew's in tone, style and content.[62] For the purpose of the encounters between Jesus and the Lukan *Little People* which I have included in this book, the Infancy Narrative creates a powerful and enlightening context. For, if we take the narrative as a whole, rather than as a series of isolated incidents, made familiar through the liturgy, we become aware that the God whom the Evangelist portrays is a God of faithful and compassionate love, who through Jesus and the active presence of the Spirit, intervenes with great freedom in order to save.[63]

This is particularly evident in the beautiful hymns which are such a regular feature of our liturgical prayer, and which have their origin in this text.

In the *Magnificat,* Mary celebrates God as Saviour, who has *looked upon the lowliness of his servant,* and she praises God because *his faithful love extends age after age to those who fear him.*[64] In the concluding summary of that hymn she sings, *He has come to the help of Israel his servant, mindful of his faithful love – according to the promise he made to our ancestors – of his mercy to Abraham and his descendants for ever.* She recognises that what is happening to her and through her is an expression of God's faithfulness and compassionate love, reaching out to help and to save, and that this is in line with a long history of such love and faithfulness, right back to the time of the great patriarch, Abraham.

In the *Benedictus* too, Zechariah places the birth of his child in the same context of God's promises *from ancient times,* God's *faithful love to our ancestors,* God's *keeping in mind his holy covenant,* again specifically referring to Abraham. At the end of the hymn, when the future Messiah is referred to, Zechariah again mentions the *faithful love of our God,* which has given rise to this saving *visitation.* (1:78)

The God of Luke is also a God who saves. Zechariah is told by Gabriel that his future child *will bring back many of the Israelites to the Lord their God,* (1:16) and that, following in the footsteps of Elijah as extolled by the prophet Micah, he will have a reconciling role. (1:17) The child to be born of Mary is to be named Jesus, which was popularly held to mean *Yahweh saves.* It is precisely as Saviour that Mary praises God in the *Magnificat.* She describes this salvation as including the reversal of many of the unjust and painful situations in society in favour of the poor and lowly ones. The *Benedictus* speaks about God's establishing a *saving power* or *horn of salvation* in the House of David, and refers to God's promise to save the people from their enemies, and *deliver* them from the hands of their foes. (1:71; 1:74) The role of the future Baptist is described as *to give his people knowledge of salvation through the forgiveness of their sins,* a knowledge which is not theoretical, head knowledge, but experiential and vital.

In Luke's well-known presentation of the birth of Jesus in the Bethlehem stable,[65] the heart of the episode consists in God's revealing to the shepherds the good news that will bring such joy to them and to the whole people:

> *Today in the town of David a Saviour has been born to you;*
> *he is Christ the Lord.* (2:11)

This, I believe, is the central message or proclamation of the entire Infancy Narrative. This tiny child is the consummate expression of God's saving love; his life's purpose is to bring about our salvation. This announcement gives greater significance to the later statement that after eight days *they gave him the name Jesus, the name the angel had given him before his conception.* (2:12) It is significant that the first to hear the good news are shepherds, poor people on the margins.

This motif is taken up in the subsequent scene when Simeon comes to the Temple and receives the child in his arms. He blesses God for God's faithfulness in bringing his own and his nation's hopes to fulfilment, and he proclaims that he is happy to die, *for my eyes have seen the salvation which you have made ready* - a salvation which is not limited to Israel, but will extend to all the nations. (2:32) He is now ready to depart in peace and contentment.[66] The prophetess Anna, still alert and sensitive in her old age, praises God and speaks about the child *to all who looked forward to the deliverance of Jerusalem.* (2:38)

Another salient characteristic of Luke's presentation of God in the Infancy Narrative is the activity of the Spirit. At the beginning of the story, Gabriel informs Zechariah that the child to be born to the aged couple *even from his mother's womb will be filled with the Holy Spirit.* (1:15) In the case of Mary, she is told by the angel that *the Holy Spirit will come upon you, and the power of the Most High will cover you with its shadow.* (1:35) These images recall the description of God's presence at the dawn of creation; a new creation is now taking place. It is through the presence and power of the Spirit that she will conceive, and that her child will be called *Holy* and *Son of God.* Later, when she reaches the hill-country home of Zechariah and Elizabeth and greets her kinswoman, we are informed that *Elizabeth was filled with the Holy Spirit*, and she becomes aware of what is happening in Mary – her blessedness as the mother of the Lord. (1:41) After the birth of John the Baptist, and the debate about his name, Zechariah insists that he be called John, at which his power of speech returns, and he too *was filled with the Holy Spirit* and was led to prophecy in the words of the *Benedictus.*

Finally, when, forty days after his birth, Jesus is presented in the Temple, the presence of the Spirit is very much in evidence. Simeon is described as upright and devout; *and the Spirit rested upon him.* Through the Spirit, it has been revealed to him that he will not die before setting eyes on the Messiah. It is through the Spirit's prompting that he comes to the Temple that day. I believe that we are meant to understand that it is through the Spirit that he recognises the identity and significance of the child, as expressed in the terms of the canticle *Nunc Dimittis*:

a light of revelation for the gentiles
and glory for your people Israel. (2:32)

Though the Spirit is not specifically mentioned with regard to Anna, who comes into the scene at that point, her piety and prophetic gifts and her offering of praise are an indication of the Spirit's presence in her life.

Later, at the beginning of his ministry, when invited to read in the synagogue at Nazareth, Jesus chooses the text from Isaiah:

The Spirit of the Lord is upon me, because he has anointed me to bring good news to the poor. He has sent me to proclaim release to the captives and recovery of sight to the blind, to let the oppressed go free, to proclaim the year of the Lord's favour. (4:18-19)

With the eyes of everyone in the synagogue fixed on him, he tells them, *Today this scripture has been fulfilled in your hearing.* The Lukan stories which we shall examine in this book will illustrate how God's faithful and compassionate love breaks unexpectedly through the Spirit-empowered person of Jesus into the lives of certain individuals, *Little People,* bringing them forgiveness, salvation and new life.

## John

John begins his Gospel with an inspiring, rather poetic piece usually referred to as *The Prologue*, which Raymond Brown calls the pearl within the Gospel.[67] It is possibly an adaptation of an early Christian hymn based on reflection about Wisdom in the Old Testament. This could have originated in Johannine circles. It provides a kind of summary of salvation history. It furnishes us with a key with which to unlock the deepest meaning of the narrative which follows, introducing the central character, the plot and the main themes. It tells about the Word, the *Logos.*

### Background

This term *Logos* already had a long history in Greek thought, from the time of Heraclitus in the sixth century BC, who considered the *Logos* to be the principle of unity and order in the flux and change of the universe. Later, the Stoic philosophers considered the *Logos* to be the power which shaped and guided the world. It was, however, the Jewish background which seems to have had the determining influence on the Evangelist.

The biblical concept of the *word of God* (*dabar* in Hebrew) is extremely rich. This term (*dabar*) is used in two ways. Firstly, it has to do with understanding, enlightenment and revelation. In this sense God manifested his will for the people in the conduct of their lives, the ten *words*, the Law. Through the prophets God enlightened Israel about the events of its history. God's word was also a word of promise and of judgement. A word inevitably entails communication, and so something of God's mystery and identity came to be understood by the people of Israel. Secondly, the word of God is dynamic and creative; it directs the course of history; it is healing, sustaining and life-giving.

In the Old Testament presentation of Wisdom there are parallels for almost every detail of *The Prologue's* description of the Word.[68] Wisdom (in Greek *Sophia*) is said to come from the mouth of God and exists at the beginning before the world was created.[69] Wisdom remains with God, and has a role in creation.[70] Wisdom is light and life for human beings, and sets up her tent among them. By some, Wisdom is rejected.[71] The Wisdom literature identified Wisdom and the Law (*Torah*).[72] The concept of Wisdom has a profound influence on *The Prologue*, and on the Christology of the whole Gospel. Another influence on John may have come from rabbinical reflection on the Law, which was said to be light and life and the supreme example of God's love. Law (*Torah*) and the *word of God* are often interchangeable terms. It is even said to have been created before all things, and as having served as the pattern on which God created the universe.

### The Text

In the beginning was the Word, and the Word was with God, and the Word was God. He was in the beginning with God. (1:1-2)

*The Prologue* commences, like the book of Genesis, *in the beginning.* But this beginning is beyond the beginning, beyond our time and space categories in the realm of the utterly and unimaginably Other, *The Word was with God, and the Word was God. With* can denote presence with, or *turned towards* in dynamic communion. There is profound intimacy and clear distinction. The whole of the created universe came into being through the Word. The twin themes of life and light are introduced, and light's opposite, the darkness, and the inevitable conflict between these polarities. Creation through the Word of its nature entails communication and revelation:

All things came into being through him, and without him not one thing came into being. What has come into being in him was life, and the life was the light of all people. The light shines in the darkness, and the darkness did not overcome it. (1:3-5)

Light is an image for the presence and enlivening power of God, and darkness symbolizes ignorance, unbelief, and sin, which lead to death. In this way the role of the Word in the human situation is broached, as the Word in God becomes the light of the world, the source of a revelation which is life-giving. But where there is light, there is the possibility of darkness. The issue of our human response is introduced, as darkness vainly struggles to comprehend or overpower the light. Some scholars believe that reference is made here to a specific past event in which light and darkness clashed, the Genesis story of the Fall. Others take it as a general reference to the fact that darkness always attempts to extinguish the light, and that this has been a pattern throughout human history.[73] The light continues to shine, nevertheless, because of God's saving promise.

The movement of *The Prologue* accelerates and the texture changes with the rather abrupt introduction of a historical figure, *sent from God, whose name was John.* His mission in life is then outlined:

He came as a witness to testify to the light, so that all might believe through him. He himself was not the light, but he came to testify to the light. The true light, which enlightens everyone, was coming into the world. (1:7-9)

His principal role is to be a witness, to testify, to point to another. The genuine light, the world's revealer, stands at the threshold. Words look for a response. The phrase in *The Prologue* which speaks of light and darkness, and the fact that the darkness could not overcome the light, is the first suggestion of human response. This is rendered more explicit when we are informed that the world, created and sustained by the Word, did not recognise or welcome the light, and that his own people, Israel, did not accept him.[74] Others, however, responded positively, coming to accept him and to believe in his name. These, by God's gift, became children of God. The plot of the story is thus revealed, as in the course of the narrative which unfolds, human beings respond to the revelation Jesus brings either by accepting in faith, and are drawn into the life of God, or by remaining closed, thus opting for darkness and death.

That decisive coming of the authentic light of revelation is described in the memorable phrase which juxtaposes two incompatibles, *The Word became flesh* and *lived amongst us.* That Word enfleshed shares our human experience, our human story, and has a human name, Jesus. In the subsequent narrative of his ministry he is presented as the light of the world, the Revealer, and as the source of life, as the Evangelist carefully develops these *Prologue* motifs. The term *flesh* denotes humanity in its weakness, vulnerability and change; but, in John, it does not include the aspect of sinfulness which is found in Paul's writings.

The verb here translated as *lived* really means *pitched his tent.*[75] The tent or tabernacle played a significant role in the unfolding history and life of the people of Israel. Being initially a nomadic group, the tent was obviously a basic commodity, a survival guarantee. It signified home and family and security and belonging. The tent later came to have profound religious significance for the people too. In Exodus 25:8-9 Israel is told to make a tent or tabernacle so that God could dwell amongst his people, *The tabernacle became the site of God's localised presence on earth.* (Raymond E Brown)[76] And later, when Israel finally settled in Jerusalem, and life became more sedentary, the Temple which Solomon constructed took over this role and became the religious centre of Israel, the place of God's presence. This was true also of the Second Temple, which stood proudly, richly embellished by Herod, in Jesus' day. Now, it is Jesus who is the localisation of God's presence, the place where God dwells.

The Christian community behind this hymn and this Gospel narrative (*we*) claims to have seen God's glory, God's powerful presence, in Jesus, the revealer of God's enduring love. From now on the relationship between God and the *Logos*, with which *The Prologue* began, will be described in terms of a relationship between Father and Son. *The Prologue* provides the reader with the information which will serve as clarifying background for the narratives to be considered in this book, as Jesus, the incarnate Word of God, reaches out to bring the light of revelation and new life to those whom he encounters.

# Jesus

After his description of the Baptist, Mark brings Jesus on stage. He journeys from Nazareth in Galilee to the Judean Jordan area, and submits to John's baptism. After this episode comes Jesus' testing, or temptations. Finally, after the arrest of the Baptist, Jesus embarks on his *ministry/mission*, with his proclamation of the advent of the Kingdom, and the exhortation to repent and believe. The centrepiece is the baptism.[77]

## The Baptism

Mark describes the baptism of Jesus as follows:

> In those days Jesus came from Nazareth of Galilee and was baptised by John in the Jordan. And just as he was coming up out of the water, he saw the heavens torn apart and the Spirit descending like a dove on him. And a voice came from heaven, *You are my Son, the Beloved; with you I am well pleased.* (1:9-11)

The structure of the episode is straightforward: an introductory verse, followed by two phenomena, visual and auditory, as Jesus emerges from the water after his baptismal immersion. The actual baptism is stated, not described; John is the actor and Jesus the recipient. For the Evangelist, the baptism itself is not important; the emphasis is placed on the accompanying phenomena, where God is the actor and Jesus the recipient.[78]

The opening phrase, *It came to pass in those days,* a typically solemn biblical introduction with a strong eschatological flavour, links the narrative with what has just preceded, and so presents Jesus as the fulfilment of the expectation which the Baptist has aroused; the *coming one* has come.[79] Having been presented to us in the opening verse of the Gospel as the *Christ,* his origin in the obscure village of Nazareth in Galilee may seem something of a let-down.[80] Mark provides no information about Jesus' earlier life or background, nor about his age. Jesus joins the thronging crowds from Judea and Jerusalem, mentioned earlier, who flock to John for baptism. He expresses his solidarity with them.[81]

Nazareth was a small town located on a hillside about 1,300 feet above sea-level in Lower Galilee; it is not mentioned in the Hebrew Bible or the writings of the Jewish historian Josephus or early rabbinical literature. The Mediterranean lies twenty miles to the west, the Sea of Galilee fifteen to the east.[82] Given the lack of real roads between the villages of the area, it was rather isolated amid a beautiful landscape, though the north-south road from Jerusalem to Sepphoris ran fairly close to the town. The population was between 1,600 and 2,000.[83] Houses were scattered on the south sunniest slope, probably groups of single-roomed buildings around a central courtyard; there were probably no public buildings. There were vineyards and olive groves; wheat, barley and millet grew on the broad hillsides, and vegetables in the shadier areas.

Galilee was ruled by Herod Antipas, the son of Herod the Great, from 4BC to 39AD; technically, he was a tetrarch rather than a king. Unlike Judea, Galilee was beautiful, green and fertile. It is usually divided into three areas, *Upper Galilee*, which is over three thousand feet high, the source of the Jordan, and sparsely inhabited; *Lower Galilee*, an area of lower hills, including Tabor and Hermon, and the fertile plain of Jezreel, containing numerous villages (maybe as many as 200), *and the city of Sepphoris; the Lake Region*, which was densely populated, with a good fishing industry, and the important cities of Capernaum, Magdala and Tiberias. Herod rebuilt the city of Sepphoris, three miles north of Nazareth, and Tiberias on the western shore of the Lake, named after the emperor. This became the capital in 18AD.[84] Jesus' Nazareth provenance is mentioned again at the end of the story.[85]

The description of this episode as the *baptism* of Jesus is perhaps a misnomer, since the Evangelists in varying degrees seek to focus our attention on the accompanying phenomena. The baptism by immersion is quickly passed over.[86] The Baptist recedes and God takes over. *Immediately,*[87] as Jesus emerges from the water, moving away from John, the heavens are *torn open*. The common view at the time was of a three-decker universe. This piece of graphic imagery is a frequent symbol in late Jewish apocalyptic literature, and also in the Old Testament, as a way of indicating that God is about to communicate from above, to reveal himself to human beings below.[88] A new era is dawning. Isaiah 64:1 reads, *O that you would tear open the heavens and come down.* Here the prophet is referring to the moment of eschatological salvation when, after what seemed like a drought or absence of divine communication, God will finally and decisively intervene for the deliverance of God's people. The verb will be used later in Mark when the temple veil is torn from top to bottom at the death of Jesus. (15:38) In Mark, then, *God has ripped the heavens irrevocably apart at Jesus' baptism, never to shut them again. Through this gracious gash in the universe, he has poured forth his Spirit into the earthly realm.*[89] It is like an invisible curtain being pulled back, allowing us to stand in the presence of a different reality.[90]

Then the Holy Spirit gently glides down, *dove-like*, and rests upon Jesus. Several scholars believe that the point of comparison would seem to be the flight and gentle alighting of the dove, rather than the bird's objectified form (as clearly and typically in Luke). Most, however, prefer the adjectival interpretation: the Spirit (who cannot be seen) descends in the form of a dove, which Jesus can see. The dove is not important; it is the descent of the Spirit that matters. The image is probably intended to evoke the Genesis picture of God's creative Spirit hovering over the waters of chaos at the dawn of time, *in the beginning*, likened by the rabbis to a dove brooding over her young.[91] It suggests that God's creative Spirit is once more active in the world, an activity focused on the person of Jesus. Or it could also be a reference to Noah's dove at the time of the flood, a harbinger of peace, restoration after God's judgement, hope and salvation.[92] There is no precedent for Mark's linking a dove and the Spirit.[93] *Jesus Christ and Son of God, the Lord, and the Stronger One, who will dispense the Holy Spirit, has now been gifted with the Spirit.* (Francis J Moloney)[94] So he can baptise with the Spirit, as John the Baptist has indicated.

It appears that the Jews of Jesus' day believed that God's Spirit had long been inactive since the days of the prophets, and had withdrawn from Israel. They looked forward to a new manifestation of the Spirit's power sometime in the future when God would bestow the Spirit on the Messiah to inaugurate the time of salvation. For Mark, the descent of the Spirit at the Jordan denotes that this moment has arrived. This is an eschatological event. God anoints Jesus with the Spirit, empowering him for mission. He is the anointed one, the Messiah, the Christ. In Mark's version of the story it is Jesus alone who perceives this vision-like phenomenon.[95]

Then the second phenomenon occurs. From heaven *a voice* speaks to Jesus, and in Mark, to him alone; there is no hint that anyone else hears it, except the reader, *You are my Son, the Beloved; with you I am well pleased.* In the absence of prophets from God, the rabbis spoke of a *bat qol* sound, which denoted the echo of a voice heard in heaven, a substitute for the prophetic word of God. Here the voice is clear and direct. These words, restating the opening verse of the Gospel, indicate for us the immense significance which the Evangelist saw in the event. Note the emphasis on *you,* which clearly refers to Jesus, not the Baptist. There can perhaps be discerned here a distant echo of God's words to Abraham concerning his son Isaac, not his only son, but certainly uniquely beloved. Possibly there is an allusion to sacrifice, a subtle hint of Jesus' destiny.[96] The words are used again in the Transfiguration, and linked with Jesus' death and resurrection; they are echoed in the centurion's declaration at Calvary, and also hinted at in 12:1-11, when the *only son* is put to death. For Mark, sonship is linked to and revealed through crucifixion; he would have seen the connection between the baptism and the end of Jesus' life.[97]

A large consensus of commentators see in these words a fusion of two Old Testament texts, Psalm 2:7 and Isaiah 42:1. Jesus is addressed in words similar to those addressed by God in the coronation formula, *You are my son; today I have become your father*, which was applied to the new king at the moment of his anointing and coronation, when he was considered to become God's son in a special way. In this royal Psalm the words are adapted to the future messianic king.[98] These words and the symbolic anointing with the Spirit proclaim that this son of God is the Davidic Messiah. Israel as a nation was understood to be God's son, *Jesus is here revealed as the one man in whom that role of Israel's sonship is revealed.*[99] The adjective *agapētos* is used in the Septuagint, mainly to describe an only child. Taking *huios* and *agapētos* together, we could translate them as *my only son.*[100] The other source passage refers to the Servant of Yahweh, called and ordained by the Spirit's anointing to a saving mission, *Here is my servant whom I uphold, my chosen one in whom my soul delights. I have endowed him with my Spirit that he may bring true justice to the nations.* (Isa 42:1) Jesus is also the Servant. This text is also used in Matt 12:18, which confirms the view that the early storytellers portrayed Jesus as the royal Messiah, son of God, in accordance with Psalm 2, verse 7, and *Servant of Yahweh* in accordance with Isaiah 42, verse 1. This was a status and a function which they saw to have been inaugurated by Jesus' anointing by the Spirit at Jordan.[101] The beloved Son and the Servant of the Lord turn out to be one and the same.[102]

What is most important here is that it is God who addresses these words to Jesus. God is an actor in the story; and God clearly identifies for the reader who Jesus is; God reveals how he *thinks* about Jesus. At the outset of the Gospel, God affirms that this Jesus from Nazareth is the specially chosen and favoured one, the only Son, designated as the (Davidic) kingly Messiah, and anointed for mission by the Holy Spirit. If the Isaian text is linked with later servant passages, it could be that his task is radically interpreted in terms of the Servant of Yahweh; he is to fulfil his role according to a pattern of service and self-emptying.[103] This text contains a surplus of meaning, combining royal and servant motifs along with language from the tradition of the suffering just person.[104]

The evaluation of Jesus as Messiah, Son of God, with which Mark began the Gospel, is thus in conformity with God's own view of him. In the depths of his being, Jesus is in a unique relationship with God. *The descent of the Spirit, literally into Jesus, and the declaration of his divine sonship are the two features that define his unique identity. He could pray Abba, father, and he was the Spirit-endowed agent of the Kingdom.* (R Alan Culpepper)[105]

The plot of the whole gospel narrative revolves around how Jesus lives out this relationship and role, and whether people come to recognise his identity as Messiah, Son of God. In fact, as we shall see, those who witness Jesus' mighty works and hear his words do not conclude that he is God's Son. It is his death which reveals his divinity. The Gospel challenges us, the readers, about our response and understanding and acceptance of Jesus as Messiah, Son of God.

## Some Historical Considerations

That Jesus was baptised by John, in the Jordan, is a firm historical fact.[106] It was a reality which seems to have caused some embarrassment in the Early Church. For Jesus' submission to John's baptism could be interpreted as an indication of John's superiority.[107] Another problematic aspect is the open link between John's baptism and the people's turning away from sin, which has implications for the sinlessness of Jesus.[108] The clear impression is that Jesus associated himself with his people in their acknowledgement of their need for God, in their longing for renewal and greater faithfulness to the Covenant, and their desire to be prepared for the new age to come. This is what John's baptism was about. Jesus must have shared John's vision of Israel's current state and his hope for restoration.[109] For Israel, confession of sin did not entail a laundry list. It was an act of worship, and included thanksgiving, praise, the recalling of God's gracious deeds, admission of membership of a sinful people, the recalling of Israel's apostasies over the years, and the resolve to be different from their ancestors. A person was part of a history of sin because of membership of a sinful people. Confessions are often found in prayers uttered by individuals who had no part in apostasy but felt involved because of membership of the nation.[110]

The historicity of the phenomena which Mark describes as accompanying Jesus' baptism is another problematic issue. As the Gospel story unfolds, it becomes evident that Jesus experienced a close relationship with God, whom he referred to familiarly as *Abba*. God is clearly at the centre of his life. Jesus is taken up with God's closeness and gracious love. Jesus is likewise deeply committed to mission, to the proclaiming of the presence of God's kingly rule, and making this a reality. He is also convinced of the presence and the power of the Spirit working through him, enabling him to heal and confront evil.[111]

31

This made an impact on his disciples, and as they later remembered and recalled it, they linked it with the event with which his active ministry began,[112] using Old Testament texts to describe it. The story of Jesus' baptism thus came to be told in a way which brought out these distinctive features.

Many contemporary scholars believe that at the time of his baptism Jesus had a profound religious experience which changed his life, an experience of the Spirit not unlike the calling of the prophets.[113] Our information, however, is inadequate to clarify whether this experience was something unexpected, a new revelation about himself, or whether it *represented the end of a long development, of deepening appreciation of the divine fatherhood and his own filial responsibility, of growing insight into his mission and the world's need, of meditation on the meaning of the scriptures and their application to himself.*[114] His convictions concerning his relationship with God and his mission must have crystallised at some point. Tradition links it with the Jordan baptism. However, we do not know whether his baptism was the cause, the ritual celebration of a decision already made, or a step to a later decision.[115]

## The Temptation Scene

And the Spirit immediately drove him out into the wilderness. He was in the wilderness forty days, tempted by Satan; and he was with the wild beasts; and the angels waited on him. Now after John was arrested, Jesus came to Galilee, proclaiming the good news of God, and saying, *The time is fulfilled, and the kingdom of God has come near; repent, and believe in the good news.* (1:12-15)

The previous scene of the Markan narrative describes the baptism of Jesus, when he is anointed by the Spirit for his messianic mission, and hears the voice of God proclaiming him as *My Son, the beloved.* Jesus does not linger there by the Jordan; he embarks on his mission without delay. *Immediately* Jesus is *driven* into the wilderness by the Spirit. The verb is strong.[116] The purpose for this foray into the Judean desert is to engage Satan in conflict. This encounter and cosmic confrontation is central to the saving plan of God.[117]

In scripture the *wilderness* or *desert* has different connotations; it is a place of ambiguity. In some contexts it signifies a privileged place of encounter with God and a place of refuge. Elsewhere, the wilderness is envisaged as the haunt of demons, the theatre of temptation, the domain of evil.

Together, the baptism and the testing of Jesus embrace both aspects. So Jesus, under the Spirit's compelling influence, is moving into enemy territory. Some scholars forge a link between the desert and the story of the fall in Genesis. There, after their sin of disobedience, Adam and Eve are driven out from the peace and harmony of the paradise garden into a wilderness, where the land and the animals rebel against them.[118]

Mark's storyline is brief. The accounts of the episode in Matthew and Luke are much fuller and more elaborate. They provide dramatic content for the temptations, and link them more closely with the Old Testament, the testing of Israel during the forty years of desert wandering, and with the *Son of God* motif.[119] Mark simply states the fact, harsh and unadorned. Whilst mentioning the period of forty days, which links the experience with that of Moses on Sinai and of Elijah, as they prepare for mission, Mark does not mention that Jesus fasted during this period.[120] For Mark, Jesus is not preparing for mission, but, empowered by the Spirit, is already fully engaged. The verb *tempt* or *test* here points to *a contest of opposing forces.*[121]

Mark's most original detail is his comment about the presence of the *wild beasts*. Perhaps he intends to emphasise the awesomeness of the place and of Jesus' experience, since wild animals were not infrequently associated with the powers of evil. There is danger lurking, and loneliness and distance from human resources.[122] However, it could be that this detail holds the key to the whole narrative.[123] Instead of the hostility and fear in creation introduced through Satan's victory over Adam, the beasts can be understood as friendly to Jesus. The prophets of old dreamed that when the Messiah came, the wild animals would become tame, and live in harmony, and not be a threat to human beings, thus restoring the original order of God's creation as it was in the beginning, *they will not hurt or destroy on all my holy mountain.*[124] So, following on from the Baptist's preaching and baptising, this is a further sign that prophecy is being fulfilled, and the long awaited time of God's saving intervention, the new era, a fresh creation, is dawning. Mark does not specifically say that Jesus is victorious, but an initial victory is implied in the reversal of the effects of the fall.[125]

The Evangelist informs us that the *angels* minister to Jesus not just at the end of the forty day period of trial, as in Matthew and Luke, but throughout the whole time. Again there are links with the ancient story of Israel. Angels, the agents of God's providential care, help the people as they wander through the desert.[126] Elijah is served by angels during his desert experience.[127] There is a Jewish tradition that Adam and Eve were fed in the garden by angels. The angels, then, are expressions of God's presence, power and care for Jesus.[128]

Mark here provides us with the key to what is to happen in the course of the Gospel, for the mission of Jesus consists in his joining battle with the forces of evil as God's anointed messianic agent. Inspired by the words of Isaiah, Israel, over centuries, had longed for a further liberation from exile and captivity. The people were aware of their captivity and enslavement by the forces of evil, led by Satan. They viewed physical illness and suffering, psychological problems, and moral evil as brought about by demonic forces exerting control over their lives. In apocalyptic circles in Jesus' day, Isaiah's expectations of restoration, liberation and renewed Covenant relationship, were understood as pointing to God's intervention to bring release from the grip of the demonic. For Mark, in the ministry of Jesus the great cosmic conflict, the final battle between God and Satan is taking place. It will reach its climax in the passion. The vanquishing of Satan, the liberating from his stranglehold, evidenced later and perceived in Jesus' exorcisms and healings, signals the coming of this new liberation, the inbreak of the Kingdom of God, God's reigning in love.[129]

## The Opening of the Ministry

After the period in the wilderness, the story moves forward, as Jesus decisively embarks on his public mission. Mark writes:

> Now after John was arrested, Jesus came to Galilee, proclaiming the good news of God, and saying, *The time is fulfilled, and the kingdom of God has come near; repent, and believe in the good news.*
> (1:14-15)

The ministry of Jesus begins, and it is carried out, not in the Judean desert, but as an itinerant lay prophet in the country villages and by the lakeside of Galilee, and, at times, further afield.[130] Only at the end of his ministry, as Mark describes it, will he enter Jerusalem.[131]

Some scholars believe that Jesus was greatly impressed by the Baptist and his message, and for a time joined his circle as a follower and collaborator, perhaps without being a disciple in the strict sense of the word.[132] Jesus certainly spoke of John with great admiration.[133] Maybe there was a gradual separation of their ways, or perhaps John's arrest and imprisonment, which effectively put an end to his mission, served as a catalyst for Jesus to break out on his own. In the Fourth Gospel, Jesus and John exercise parallel ministries for a while, and Jesus too engages in baptising.[134] Mark is responsible for the clear demarcation of their ministries; for him, it is after John's arrest that Jesus takes centre stage. The verb *handed over* is later used of Jesus too.[135] Jesus developed his own characteristic style as a wandering preacher and healer; his language and life-style were gentler and less ascetic; his emphasis was different, focusing on the present and on God's mercy and nearness.

Preaching or proclaiming is a salient aspect of Jesus' mission. Here Mark specifies that he announces *the Good News from God,* and then he provides a succinct summary of his message, a kind of manifesto,[136] articulating the heart and essential significance of his whole ministry. Dramatically, Jesus claims that *The time is fulfilled.* The lengthy period of hoping and waiting for the liberating and decisive intervention of Israel's God is over.[137] A new phase of history is now beginning, *God's appointed moment of opportunity.*[138]

The kernel of this gladdening news is that *the Kingdom of God is close at hand,* God's reigning presence has arrived.[139] God is now drawing near to His people and His world in love and forgiveness and salvation, and is engaged in the overthrowing of the captivity imposed by Satan. The terminology signifies the dynamic exercise of God's sovereignty or dominion, rather than a static territorial area.[140] Throughout his ministry from now on, Jesus will proclaim and make present the kingly rule of God, and will enable people to experience it at first hand.[141] The kingdom was clearly Jesus' passion.[142]

At the same time, there are many sayings of Jesus which point to the future, a near future and an indeterminate future. And there is an unresolved tension between the present transforming reality (the *now*) of God's reigning, its imminence, and its eventual definitive completeness (the *not yet*), when the Son of Man returns. *Jesus shared the belief of his Jewish contemporaries that the fullness of God's kingdom is future, and yet, according to Mark and the other evangelists, Jesus saw in his own person and ministry the beginning or inauguration of God's reign. Whatever Jesus said or did was in the service of God's kingdom.* (John R Donahue & Daniel J Harrington)[143] The teaching of Jesus was remembered as being characterised by an emphasis on both present and future dimensions of the reigning presence of God.[144]

Central to Jesus' understanding of the Kingdom is the acceptance of the renewed relationship which God is freely offering here and now.[145]

With a clear sense of authority, Jesus summons his hearers to a twofold response, repentance and belief, conversion and confidence or trust. The term *metanoia* means a change of mind, a coming to one's senses, a turning away from sin and back to God, a reorientation of personality, a new way of thinking and valuing and living, a turning round in one's tracks and resuming the right path.[146] Such an about turn is not simply a personal issue. Jesus' call is for a national conversion, religious, social, and political, a returning to genuine loyalty to God at all levels. In this way, God's reign will be restored and more fully established, and evil in its varied forms and dimensions will be displaced and overcome.

Jesus was calling the people to trust, not in laws, Temple, land and ancestry, but in the good news that God was doing something new, to entrust themselves to what was beginning to happen. His words are also a call to trust in him, as the one appointed by God as the agent in offering and bringing about this change and liberation. Throughout the Gospel narrative faith or trust is demanded if the transforming power of the Kingdom is to be effective; it is the *essential component on the human side for the advent of the Kingdom*.[147] The proclamation of Jesus and his powerful works of healing and exorcism and the subjection of natural forces go hand in hand, loosening Satan's ruinous grip in the world.

When Jesus spoke about *the kingdom of God* in this manner, he was using a phrase which was not unfamiliar to his hearers. Admittedly, the phrase does not appear in the Hebrew Bible; it is found only in later writings. But the idea that *God rules* or *will rule*, that God is *king*, has deep roots in Israel's history, going back perhaps to the period of the early settlement in Canaan. It is one of Israel's basic affirmations.[148] God's lordship was considered as a present reality and as future also. Firstly, Yahweh reigns as powerful king over Israel in the here and now, and his reigning is experienced through his deeds, his activity, his interventions in her history, whereby God established Israel as his own people, as his kingdom and domain.[149] God's rule is eternal,[150] and God is present with his people especially in the Ark, the city of Jerusalem and in the Temple; this is expressed in the cultic life of the nation, particularly in the enthronement psalms, which acclaim that *God reigns*.[151] Gradually, the notion of God's kingship widened, and Israel came to view God as ruler of all the nations and of all creation.[152]

Secondly, Yahweh's kingship is referred to in terms of the future, as hope and expectation, yet to be fully accomplished, and the longing grows for the time when *The Lord God will rule* definitively.[153] This yearning is coloured by the disasters in Israel's history, by the failure of human kingship, and the oppressive regimes of her conquerors and foes. God's future rule comprises, therefore, a dual element: *salvation/liberation* and *judgement/ punishment*, both for Israel and for the nations.[154] The prophets dream of a time of peace, abundance, joy, prosperity – for Israel and the world. That day, the eschatological day, would surely come, when the Lord God will openly and decisively visit his people as King, manifesting his sovereignty to all.[155]

In the period immediately prior to the time of Jesus, this eschatological hope in some circles took a distinctly nationalistic turn, finding expression in terms of political liberation and the inauguration of a new state of Israel. In other circles emphasis was laid on the transcendence of God: the coming of the Kingdom would be accompanied with great signs and catastrophes; there was a strong stress on judgement in this strain. Among the Pharisees many thought that the Kingdom would be characterised by greater faithfulness in the observance of the Law.

Thus, the history of his people, and their writings and hopes, supplied Jesus with the language, the symbols and the story of God's kingly rule. But the phrase *kingdom of God* was not a dominant or central feature of the Judaism of his day, nor a necessary way for him to present his message. It was a conscious and creative decision on his part to make it the core of his proclamation and of his mission.[156]

Jesus' presentation of the Kingdom, then, is built on these foundations, and shares their richness and complexity. Two elements stand out strikingly. In the first place, Jesus proclaims that the time of waiting is over, that God is near now and is establishing the ardently longed-for, end-time Kingdom now in the present, and is doing so through him. His preaching, especially to the poor, and his mighty works, especially his exorcisms, and his table-fellowship are signs that the messianic joy and liberation have dawned.[157]

Secondly, although the element of judgement is contained in this teaching, especially with regard to those who reject God's rule, the salient, characteristic emphasis is placed on salvation. For Jesus, the lordship and sovereignty of God consists in the sovereignty of his love, his ruling in love; God is *Abba, Father*. The otherness of God, his power and transcendence are manifested in his sovereign freedom to love and to pardon. The coming of the Kingdom is primarily an encounter with the boundless and unmerited mercy of God, the *all inclusive, unconditional love of God, his unreserved acceptance and approval*.[158] The Kingdom is gratuitous gift.

Whilst sharing the preference of several authors for expressing Jesus' proclamation as *God's reigning presence* rather than as a territorial reality, I believe that it is important not to overlook the socio-political implications of the term *kingdom*.[159] The world in which Jesus lived, the world which he was addressing, consisted of a political and religious domination system.[160] The Roman *imperium* was usually described as *kingdom*. Rome exercised its rule in Judea through governors or prefects based in Caesarea Maritima, assigning to the priests and aristocracy of Jerusalem the task of managing the practical, day-to-day administration of the city and territory. The high priest owed his appointment to Rome; Caiaphas held office from 18-36AD, a suggestively lengthy period. The Temple again became the most important political and economic centre of the country, whilst maintaining its religious influence.[161]

But it was now also the centre of Jewish collaboration with Rome, responsible for the keeping of order and the paying of tribute. The resulting Jewish domination system under the hegemony of pagan Rome was oppressive and exploitative. The wealthy and landed elite minority prospered, whilst the condition of the peasants was becoming increasingly onerous. In Galilee, Herod was the Roman appointee; he ruled for 43 years. In addition to the Roman taxes, he had his own tax system, all the more necessary because of his rebuilding of Sepphoris and his construction of the city of Tiberias. It is clear that the tax burden on the peasants was overwhelming, up to a third or half of what a family was able to produce from its land. The spectre of debt was feared by all. Many peasants felt trapped, many lost their land, and so became day-workers or slaves, beggars or prostitutes. Times were very difficult.[162]

Although Jesus eschewed ideas of establishing a new nationalistic form of government, the implications of the alternative way or kingdom which he was proposing were far-reaching. The world which Jesus dreamed about was based on compassionate love, inclusion, and justice; it was a kingdom in which only God was sovereign. This was radically different from the Roman system, and also from the Temple-based religious system of Judaism.[163] *By his inclusivity, his transgressing of purity boundaries, his reimagining of sin and forgiveness, he was dismantling a kind of carefully structured religious world based on law and inaugurating a new way of relating to God with implications for a new way of relating to one another.* (Sandra M Schneiders)[164]

38

# Concluding Thoughts

The purpose of this chapter has been to set the scene for what follows, to open up the context within which the encounters between Jesus and the *Little People* occur. Most of the episodes which we will consider are to be found in the Gospel of Mark, which, as I observed in the Introduction, is generally thought to be the first Gospel to have been written. The reader is now aware of Mark's views on the identity and mission of Jesus. As Messiah and Son of God, Jesus proclaims the advent of God's reign, and makes it present through his exorcising and healing. As this takes place, the control of Satan is overcome; the demonic power-base recedes.

The passages chosen for consideration from the Gospel of Luke are good illustrations of the presence of the God of faithful love in and through the ministry of Jesus, the God who offers forgiveness, healing and salvation. Only one incident has been included from the Gospel of Matthew, though many of the Markan stories are also found there in abridged form. In Jesus, God is present as saviour and as the shepherd-leader of his people, bringing healing and wholeness. The extracts selected from John's Gospel show how Jesus, the incarnate Word, is both the revealer of God's love and the giver of life.

As readers, we now approach the various texts already knowing to some extent the salient aspects of the theological agenda of each Evangelist. This awareness will facilitate our understanding. At the same time, we doubtlessly feel caught up in the story of Jesus. We wish to see how Mark's Jesus, anointed by the Spirit in his baptism, and proclaimed God's beloved Son, will live out, in practice, this relationship and mission. We are interested in following up his shepherding role as presented in Matthew, and in exploring any sequel to the coming of the Magi. The God of Luke, faithful and compassionate, stirs our longing and hope in our poverty and need. The tent-pitching of John's incarnate Word opens up new possibilities for our humanity, new dimensions of our aliveness.

# Chapter Two – The Forgiven

orgiveness needed and sought, forgiveness received, forgiveness granted to others. Forgiveness is such a central feature of our human experience, an issue which touches us all, in our personal lives, in the family, in the parish or religious community, in the places where we work and minister, in the neighbourhood in which we live, and on the national and international stage as well. Forgiveness is also right at the heart of the story of Jesus. In this second chapter I would like to consider four of the *Little People* who experience God's forgiveness through Jesus: the paralysed man in Mark; in Luke, the woman in the house of Simon the Pharisee, and Zacchaeus; and in John, the woman taken in adultery. Each of these narratives is beautifully and skilfully crafted. Before we consider them in detail, however, it would be helpful, I feel, to examine briefly that significant aspect of Jesus' ministry usually referred to as his table fellowship; this offers a broader setting for the individual episodes.

## Jesus' Table-Fellowship

### Mark

Mark introduces this theme in a wider context of conflict, controversy and confrontation, aspects of human experience with which we are all familiar, and which were not foreign to the life of Jesus.[1] The people mainly responsible for the presence of this element in his ministry were the religious leaders. There are two sections of the Markan narrative in which the Evangelist has brought together, in concentrated form, episodes which feature controversy. The first is found early in the ministry and seems to be located in Capernaum; the second block of material is situated near the end of the story in the city of Jerusalem.[2] These two collections of conflict stories are obviously artificial constructions.[3] In reality, Jesus' whole ministry was punctuated with controversy. Mark suggests this by including other examples here and there.[4] The stories tend to illustrate the freedom and authority of Jesus, and the surprise and originality of the Kingdom which is breaking in through his words and actions. They also bring to the surface the blindness and obduracy of the Jewish religious leaders, their resistance which leads to hostility and rejection, a rejection which will culminate in the Passion.[5] This is another way in which the power of evil is present.[6]

The issue of table fellowship[7] occurs in connection with the call of Levi to discipleship, and its aftermath. It is the second conflict story of the first series:

Jesus went out again beside the lake; the whole crowd gathered around him, and he taught them. As he was walking along, he saw Levi son of Alphaeus sitting at the tax booth, and he said to him, *Follow me.* And he got up and followed him.

And as he sat at dinner in Levi's house, many tax-collectors and sinners were also sitting with Jesus and his disciples – for there were many who followed him. When the scribes of the Pharisees saw that he was eating with sinners and tax-collectors, they said to his disciples, *Why does he eat with tax-collectors and sinners?* When Jesus heard this, he said to them, *Those who are well have no need of a physician, but those who are sick; I have come to call not the righteous but sinners.* (2:13-17)

## *The Call*

The format used for the description of the call of Levi is similar to that used earlier for the call of Simon and Andrew, and then James and John, among the fisherfolk by the lakeside.[8] Jesus is once again by the lake, and is teaching the crowds who have gathered around him. He then sets off, *walking along.* In this Gospel Jesus seems always to be on the move, there is a restless urgency about him, as he seeks to fulfil his mission. As he walks he sees Levi, son of Alphaeus, at his daily work, *sitting at the tax booth.*[9] Jesus pronounces his authoritative summons *Follow me*; and Levi immediately jumps up and follows.[10] It is not explicitly stated that he leaves everything, though this is implied. Whereas the earlier disciples were self-employed fishermen and could have returned to their work; Levi, having resigned from Herod's tax administration, may not have been able to get his job back later, had he so wished.[11]

However, a new facet of the discipleship motif is introduced here. It consists in the kind of person Jesus calls. Levi is *sitting in the custom house.* The trade route, the *Via Maris,* from Damascus to the coast, passed that way; Capernaum was the closest town to the border between the territories of Herod and Philip. Because of his occupation, Levi is a man despised, a sinner in the popular estimation, outside the community of Judaism.[12] Technically, Levi was a customs officer in the service of Herod, a Jewish client king (or, more accurately, tetrarch) appointed by Rome.

41

He was not one of the publicans who were contractors and who bought the right to collect, and then farmed out the taxes. The *telōnai* of the Gospels were most likely minor employees of royal officials who collected taxes or tolls at customs booths for the transporting of goods.[13] They had a reputation for dishonesty and extortion; they also mixed with prostitutes and with non-Jews, and so were ritually impure.[14] In any society tax collectors are not popular, but in Jesus' day they would be understood as serving Herod, who was feared and hated in Galilee, and also as supporting the pagan Roman domination system centred in the Jerusalem Temple. They therefore contributed to the severe hardship endured by the peasants. Their profession made them religious and social outcasts. The freedom, originality and generosity of Jesus are startlingly evident, as he cuts through conventional barriers, and reaches out to those on the margins of religion, an outreach which upsets the religious elite. It was scandalous that he should include such a person in his circle.[15] It was a challenging gesture, which powerfully conveys a message about the nature of the Kingdom.

## The Meal

Some time later, Jesus shares a meal with *tax collectors and sinners,* those on the fringes of society and religion, and many other followers. By *sinners* Mark probably means not only the indifferent or irreligious, or ordinary people who weren't able to observe many of the laws, but genuinely disreputable folk, people of questionable morality, and people who lived outside the Law. There is no mention of their conversion, repentance, or offer to make restitution; the story connects with the previous narrative, the forgiveness of the paralysed man.[16] Jesus' approach is different from that of the Baptist. The ambiguous reference to *followers* suggests a wider group of disciples than the few explicitly called, a broader spectrum of followers which included irreligious people. The text is unclear as to whether the venue for the party is the house of Jesus or Levi; probably Mark intends the latter, as Jesus does not have a house of his own.[17] Presumably, Levi wishes to express his gratitude to Jesus, and introduce him to his friends. Such a banquet would also have been a public spectacle; passers-by could look in and also listen to the conversation.[18]

Jesus is criticised, probably on a later occasion, by some Pharisee scribes for dining in such company. The Pharisees, *separated ones*, were a lay movement, who were noted for their strict observance of the Law and its oral interpretations. Generally sincere and devout, they believed that, in obedience to God's will, they had to shun sinners so as not to be defiled. They would eat only in their own homes or with other Pharisees.[19] This is their first appearance in Mark's gospel; they will feature frequently, usually in conflict with Jesus about his actions or his way of interpreting the Law.[20] Some functioned as scribes, as in this case. In reply Jesus states:

> It is not the healthy who need the doctor, but the sick. I came to call not the upright, but sinners.

In the first sentence he is using a proverbial saying.[21] It is wrong for doctors to spend their time exclusively with the healthy. Their role demands that they attend to those who need their services. The mission of Jesus, his *having come*,[22] demands similar attention to sinners. *Upright* or *righteous* is to be taken as irony; those who believe themselves so, like these Pharisees, do not feel the need for Jesus and his message. It could also be that Jesus' declaration means *more than* instead of *rather than*; the righteous are not excluded.[23]

Perhaps there is more than simply a proverb here, for in the Old Testament, it was God who was considered to be the doctor, the physician. The presence of the Healer, the Physician, was a sign that the messianic era had dawned.[24] For sinners are the ones to whom in a particular way the offer of the gift of the Kingdom is made. This is Gladdening News indeed, that in Jesus the love and forgiveness of God seeks out and encounters those most in need, beyond all the barriers of status and class and occupation and education and religious practice and law-abiding observance. Such openness Jesus has practised in summoning Levi to be a follower. The words and profoundly original actions of Jesus are contrary to current views and expectations, and raise questions about the way the Old Testament was understood.[25] Forgiveness is not merely an external pronouncement; for Jesus it is a new relationship and a new community, the community of sinners who, like Levi, are followers of Jesus.[26] Forgiveness and table fellowship are a gift, not a reward. Inclusive table fellowship is an anticipated experience of the banquet of the Kingdom. *The call of Levi and the party at his house are not an individual case, but a paradigm of God's reconciling act.*

(M Eugene Boring)[27]

## The Significance of Table-Fellowship

In that culture to share table was a very significant gesture. It was a sign of acceptance, respect and trust, an offer of peace, fellowship and friendship. To share table indicated a being *at home* with others, a willingness to share life, an identification and oneness with them; it was an expression of solidarity. Jesus' action bridged the social and religious divide in a culture extremely conscious of status and class and prestige. It showed the sinners and outcasts that they mattered to him, that they had a value. It was a healing and liberating event. Since Jesus was looked upon as in some way a man of God, a prophet, his gesture of friendship communicated and experienced through table fellowship, would have been understood as an indication of God's acceptance and forgiveness. Through the welcome he extended, *he was declaring on his own authority that anyone who trusted in him and his kingdom-announcement was within the kingdom.*[28] This gesture is, I believe, the most powerful parable of the Kingdom; it proclaims the message and makes present the reality of God's nearness in saving love.

The great scripture scholar Joachim Jeremias writes that *the inclusion of sinners in the community of salvation, achieved in table fellowship, is the most meaningful expression of the message of the redeeming love of God.*[29] This symbolic gesture contains the whole Gospel, the Good News, in a nutshell. It says it all – that in Jesus, God is freely reaching out in saving love, wanting to share life with us.

## Luke

Of the three Synoptic writers, Luke gives greatest emphasis to the theme of Jesus' table fellowship. It has been suggested that in Luke's narrative Jesus is always going to a meal, present at a meal, or coming away from a meal! This may be a slight exaggeration, but it is certainly true that sharing meals with others seems to have been a key feature of his ministry. In the villages of Galilee, where hospitality was an essential aspect of life, it was quite natural that Jesus should frequently be invited to the table. Sometimes it would be an expression of gratitude, perhaps for his having healed someone, or an indication of respect; sometimes it would be an occasion for him to teach. In that culture to share table was a very significant gesture. It was above all an expression of social inclusion. An excellent example is found in the middle of this Gospel:

> Now all the tax collectors and sinners were coming near to listen to him. And the Pharisees and the scribes were grumbling and saying, *This fellow welcomes sinners and eats with them.* (15:1-2)

Though brief, this is a significant passage. The marginalised and religious outcasts in large numbers are drawing close to Jesus; Jesus is comfortable with people who would normally be excluded. Their purpose is to listen to him, which for Luke is an indication of an openness to conversion.[30] In the background are the religious elite, the *Pharisees and scribes*, who keep their distance to avoid contamination, and shun table fellowship with sinners. They *grumble* repeatedly and openly. Their criticism is focused not only on Jesus' eating and drinking with these people, as on earlier occasions,[31] but also on his welcoming them, his offering them hospitality. To host or entertain sinners was a more serious offence in their eyes than simply to eat with sinners informally or to accept invitations, which was itself scandalous enough.

As in the Markan episode considered above, Jesus responds to the criticism levelled against him for sharing table with *sinners*. However, he here explains his attitude and conduct in a different way, by recounting three parables. There are two short parables presented in parallel and carefully matched: the parables of the lost sheep and the lost coin. Then there is the longer and very familiar parable of the two lost sons, normally and misleadingly referred to as the parable of the prodigal son. In fact, I think that the usual emphasis on *lostness* in these parables is misplaced. In the Lukan context I prefer to see them as parables of seeking and finding that which is lost, a seeking which is demanding and costly, and a finding which calls for joyful celebration.

### Two Parables of Seeking and Finding
The twinned parables, which reflect Luke's typical interest in equal opportunities, with male and female protagonists, build on our human experience of losing things which are important to us, and taking great efforts to find them, and the joy, relief and satisfaction which rediscovering them brings. Jesus is saying that God is no less persistent in seeking nor less jubilant in finding. God sets a high value on the lost, and spares no effort to recover it. One aspect which I find fascinating is that Jesus chooses as pointers to the depths of the being of God, a shepherd and a woman. To tend sheep was a low-class occupation, a role avoided by religious people; it was one of the proscribed trades; the one carrying it out would be considered a sinner by the religious elite. Women in that cultural milieu suffered religious and social discrimination, and had very little value. Yet, a member of each of these groups is put forward by Jesus as an image of God. Jesus is here shocking his hearers, upsetting fixed mindsets. Another significant point is the fact that the sheep and the coin do nothing; the seeking and the finding are gifted. For Jesus the emphasis is not on conversion or repentance, but on God's gratuitous searching love.[32]

So Jesus is clearly stating that he bases his ministry on his understanding of the mind and heart of God. He takes his cue from that knowledge. His table fellowship is his way of articulating his mission. It is revelation of God and of God's purpose. The longer parable brings this out in a most beautiful and powerful manner.[33]

### The Parable of the Two Lost Sons

The father, the main character in the story, is probably a farmer or landowner, and quite well off. In the culture of Jesus, any transfer of the ownership of property usually took place after the father's death. There are some instances where a father divided his property as a gift before his death, despite the cautions against such a course of action found in the Book of Sirach 33:20-24. But it was unheard of for a son to ask for it.[34] The younger son's request is tantamount to wishing for his father's death, and is an extraordinary insult. In granting the request, the father demonstrates enormous love for his boy.

The young man must have made a further request to dispose of his share, which would have amounted to a third of the estate, and this request too was granted. Having quickly realised his not inconsiderable assets, he wastes no time in departing. He leaves home, rejecting all that it stands for. He is prepared to sever his relationship with his father, showing no regard for his feelings or future well-being. Leaving his brother does not seem to pose a problem; it appears that they are not particularly close. The elder brother apparently makes no attempt to mediate, to reconcile, as was expected in that culture. Without protesting,[35] he benefits from the transaction, since the father *divided the estate between them*. The closely knit village community would have been horrified at what had happened.

The young man sets off for the *diaspora*. This was not uncommon at the time, given the precarious nature of the Palestinian agrarian economy.[36] There he squandered his money on a life of pleasure and extravagance. The situation changes dramatically with the onset of famine, and, penniless and friendless, he is obliged to hire himself out to a Gentile landowner, who sends him to tend the pigs. As a Jew, he is thus totally alienated, the epitome of *lostness*. He is starving to death, unable to eat the carob pods supplied to the pigs. His hunger galvanises him into action. He makes a snap decision to return home, where his father's *hired men have all the food they want*. He is prepared to acknowledge that he has done wrong in

God's sight and has offended his father,[37] and there are signs of regret and remorse. His plan is to ask his father to take him on as a hired servant. This would enable him to maintain his independence and social respectability, living in the village. And he could use his income to fulfil the financial responsibilities to his father which he had selfishly abandoned. He seems to wish to return on his own terms, to do things his way.

The spotlight switches and focuses on the father. The key word in the whole parable, or the key phrase in translation, is, I believe, the verb which describes the father's response when he catches sight of the returning younger son in the distance:

So he set off and went to his father. But while he was still far off, his father saw him and was filled with compassion; he ran and put his arms around him and kissed him.

All that follows in the narrative springs from compassion.[38] The father runs to meet his son. Normally an elder would not run; it was socially unacceptable. But it enables him to meet the young man outside the village boundary and protect him from the inevitable hostility of the villagers, outraged by the whole saga. A remarkable reconciliation takes place. The father says nothing; there is no lecture or blame or criticism. The past is past. His actions express his profound paternal love, acceptance and welcome. He kisses him repeatedly in a firm embrace, a sign of forgiveness, a recognising that he is his son, and this is public, for all the villagers to see. None of them will cause him harassment now.

The son forgets the crippling hunger which prompted his decision to return, and cuts short his rehearsed speech, abandoning his plan of maintaining his independence as a hired servant. He comes to realise that what is at issue is a broken relationship, a relationship which he cannot heal. The possibility of that relationship being re-established can only come as a pure gift from his father. He perceives from his father's behaviour that such an offer is being made. The robe, signet ring, and shoes are symbols of this. The father's compassionate love brings about a change within him, and he graciously accepts the gift freely and generously offered, beyond his wildest dreams. The father sets in motion the arrangements for a great celebration to which the whole village community would be invited so as to participate in their rejoicing, and share in the restoration and reconciliation which has occurred.[39] The father sums up his view of things:

for this son of mine was dead and is alive again;
he was lost and is found!

To the lost-and-found language of the two shorter parables is added the image of death and resurrection. The son had cut himself off from the life of the family and his religion; now he is alive and restored once again.

The other son returns in the evening from the fields. He gets wind of the party, for there is music in the air. He plies one of the local children with questions. The youngster without guile informs him that his brother has returned home and that his father has killed the fatted calf to celebrate. The older brother reacts angrily and refuses to participate in the meal which has been prepared. He remains outside, refusing to join in the fun, and unwilling to fulfil his role as master of ceremonies. This is a public insult to his father. The father reacts by coming out of the house and pleading with him. He comes in search of his older son.[40] The latter's response reveals the extent of his alienation. There is no respect, no affection; he complains bitterly, betraying the attitude of a slave rather than a son. He is self-righteous about his impeccable obedience, disparagingly critical of his father's other son whom he refuses to acknowledge as his brother. Obviously, he is quite incapable of understanding and entering into his father's joy. From the father there is no outburst of anger, no criticism, no recall to duty. Rather, he reaches out with reconciling love and compassion, searching to bridge the gulf between them – *My son, you are with me always and all I have is yours.*

He affectionately acknowledges his ongoing presence in the home, and reassures him that his rights and inheritance are still secure and protected, and finally reminds him that it really is right to celebrate. He explains his joy in the terms used earlier – dead and alive, lost and found – but this time *your brother* replaces *my son*. It is an appeal for understanding, for reconciliation and acceptance, an appeal that he join them, the family, and the whole community in fellowship and festivity. The parable ends at this point, and we never learn the sequel.

The parable responds magnificently to the initial context. The sinners are sharing the banquet, found by the searching Jesus. The religious leaders stand critically aloof, refusing the invitation to accept the Good News and join the party. The table fellowship of Jesus is a celebration of seeking and finding. The three parables reflect the way in which Jesus understands his ministry, what he is about. At the same time these parables reveal a great deal about Jesus' understanding of God. Jesus operates in the way he does, shares table fellowship as he does, because he knows the compassionate heart of his Father, his all-inclusive, unconditional love, his unreserved acceptance and approval.[41] Table fellowship expresses it all.

## Conclusion

Through these parables Jesus reveals his understanding of the mind and heart of God, and it is this understanding which is the inspiration behind his table fellowship and his mission. Jesus wishes to enable people to experience the gift of God's inclusive compassion and forgiveness, which is his Kingdom. Jesus breaks through barriers, and seeks out the outsiders and lost ones in order to bring them into the circle of God's salvation. This key activity of Jesus provides the background and wider context for the four stories which we are about to examine, stories in which individual characters, *Little People*, rather than groups, experience God's acceptance and forgiveness through Jesus. These are small but significant dramas within the context of the Great Drama.

# The Paralysed Man

In the previous section of this chapter we noted that controversy and confrontation are aspects of human experience which Jesus was frequently obliged to face. In examining the call of Levi and its aftermath, under the heading of *Table Fellowship,* we met for the first time those who were mainly responsible for this aspect of Jesus' ministry.[42] From a structural viewpoint, that episode is the second story in the first block of controversies which the Evangelist has brought together. The conflict sequence is introduced, in fact, by the story of the healing of a paralysed man:

> When he returned to Capernaum after some days, it was reported that he was at home. So many gathered around that there was no longer room for them, not even in front of the door; and he was speaking the word to them. Then some people came, bringing to him a paralysed man, carried by four of them. And when they could not bring him to Jesus because of the crowd, they removed the roof above him; and after having dug through it, they let down the mat on which the paralytic lay. When Jesus saw their faith, he said to the paralytic, *Son, your sins are forgiven.* Now some of the scribes were sitting there, questioning in their hearts, *Why does this fellow speak in this way? It is blasphemy! Who can forgive sins but God alone?* At once Jesus perceived in his spirit that they were discussing these questions among themselves;

and he said to them, *Why do you raise such questions in your hearts? Which is easier, to say to the paralytic, 'Your sins are forgiven,' or to say, 'Stand up and take your mat and walk'? But so that you may know that the Son of Man has authority on earth to forgive sins* – he said to the paralytic *I say to you, stand up, take your mat and go to your home.* And he stood up, and immediately took the mat and went out before all of them; so that they were all amazed and glorified God, saying, *We have never seen anything like this!* (Mark 2:1-12)

In this story we find a controversy about forgiveness enclosed within the framework of a healing miracle. This results in a dramatic and compelling presentation of the nature of the Kingdom, which Jesus proclaims and makes present, and of the authority of Jesus.[43]

## The Setting

Jesus has returned to Capernaum after seeking refuge in the countryside because large numbers of people were flocking to him as a result of the cleansed leper broadcasting widely what had happened to him.[44] The original commotion and excitement amongst the people must have abated somewhat. The time indication is *some time later* or *after several days.* Jesus seems by now to have made Capernaum his home base. He is again in a house.[45] It is not specified whether the house belongs to Simon Peter or to someone else. The generally accepted view is that it is Peter's.[46]

Word of Jesus' presence gets round, crowds gather as before, spilling outside, so that *there was no room left, even in front of the door.* There is clearly something magnetic about Jesus' personality. Characteristically he is proclaiming his message to them, the gladdening news about the coming of God's kingly reign.[47] *Some people came bringing him a paralytic carried by four men.* Paralysis or lameness was a form of impurity in the Old Testament, and thought to be due to sin.[48] The four are deeply committed to their friend, determined to get him to Jesus, whatever the obstacles. Thinking laterally,[49] they make an opening in the roof over the place where Jesus was, when they have broken through, they lower the bed on which the paralysed man is lying.[50] The roof would probably have consisted of wooden crossbeams overlaid with a matting of branches and hardened mud. Access would have been by means of an outside stairway or ladder. Presumably they use ropes to lower the man down, but there must have been quite a bit of debris too. They show initiative and ingenuity, great affection and the willingness to take a risk and put themselves out on their friend's behalf. They also evince great faith in the power and compassion of Jesus. The word for bed used here indicates the pallet or mat of the poor.[51]

## Jesus

Jesus does not seem to be disturbed by the noise, the falling debris. the interruption. He recognises immediately the trust or faith of those bringing the man,[52] and presumably of the man himself. With authority and warm affection, he speaks the word of forgiveness, *My son, your sins are forgiven*, the prophetic announcement of the in-break of the Kingdom, God's reign in love, into the contorted frame of the paralytic's life, assuring him of the gift of God's unconditional, saving acceptance. The passive verb (*are forgiven*) indicates that it is by God's action that his sins are removed.[53] *Jesus' authoritative word communicates God's forgiveness.*[54] (Francis J Moloney) Mark understands it as a statement and claim made by Jesus on his own authority.[55] The idea of gratuitous forgiveness was outside the scope of the Law.[56] As in the previous incident in the narrative, in which Jesus heals the leper, he is doing something that the Law cannot do; he deals with the root of the problem. He ignores the established religious procedures in Judaism which linked forgiveness with the offering of sacrifice in the Temple.[57] His forgiveness is sheer gift.

This forgiving word is uttered within the context of an act of healing. The man is paralysed, a helpless cripple. His physical affliction entails further disabilities: he cannot live a normal family life; he cannot work and earn a living; nor can he take part in the political, social and religious life of the community to which he belongs. It is also a pointer to a more radical need and disability, his need for God, his sin, his poverty of being. In that culture, physical misfortune was often popularly considered to be the result of sin.[58] It is this poverty that Jesus comes to enrich and transform. When approached for a cure, it is to this more fundamental and urgent need that, with intuitive empathy, he turns his attention first.

## The Controversy

Some scribes, scholars and teachers of the Law of Moses, happen to be present (perhaps a little artificially; this may argue for the joining of two originally separate narratives).[59] They do not voice their objections, but are thinking harshly within themselves. Perhaps their criticism was made on a later occasion. From now on the relationship between Jesus and the scribes is hostile. *Such criticism certainly could have been made during the lifetime of Jesus and so be included in the story from the earliest days, but it would also doubtless be familiar both to Mark and to his readers from their own experience of arguments with Jewish opponents.*[60] (Morna D Hooker)

Inwardly they contemptuously or disrespectfully accuse Jesus (*this fellow*) of blasphemy for talking in this way, for only God can forgive sins. By New Testament times blasphemy was understood not only as cursing God, but as any violation of the power and majesty of God.[61] This is the charge on which Jesus will later be condemned.[62] Whether the scribes heard Jesus' use of the divine passive as a claim to be able to forgive sins or speak on God's behalf, to their way of thinking he was usurping a divine prerogative, for forgiveness is the prerogative of God.[63] The scribes see themselves as defending God's honour. Normally confession, change of heart and a sacrifice were required. Such forgiveness was hoped for at the end, in heaven. Jesus has made an authoritative declaration of forgiveness in his own name, and on earth in the present. The scribes' error is that they take Jesus as an ordinary man; they fail to see him as God's messianic agent bringing in the Kingdom; they do not recognise the power within him as of God.[64]

Jesus discerns their thoughts,[65] and asks why they are thinking in this way. Perhaps their faces gave them away; perhaps Jesus was aware that his words would jar with Jewish scholars; or perhaps Jesus had a special kind of prophetic insight into people's thoughts, also a divine prerogative.[66] He then challenges them by asking publicly whether it is easier to pronounce sins forgiven or to heal. From a theological standpoint it is easier to heal than to forgive, since forgiveness depends on God. But Jesus asks not which is easier to do, but which is easier to say, *You are forgiven*, or *Take up your pallet*. A word of forgiveness cannot be assessed; a word of healing can easily be tested and verified. Since the scribes think that Jesus has used empty words, he will now demonstrate that for him, as for God, to speak is to act.[67] The reader is aware from Mark's *Prologue* that God's prerogatives have been passed on to Jesus.

### The Healing

To guarantee the forgiveness of sins is difficult, but Jesus offers to demonstrate his power to forgive by performing the cure. This is the key sentence of the story. Jesus claims to have the divine prerogative, the authority to forgive *on earth*, and refers to himself as the *Son of Man*. In fact, it is as Son of Man that he exercises this authority. This title, which probably comes from Dan.7:14, where the *ancient of days* gives his authority to a Son of Man figure, indicates that, for Mark, Jesus acts as God's representative and with God's authority, not in his own name.[68]

Only later in the story will the full significance of Jesus' being *Son of Man* become clear; only then will the reader be made aware why this Son of Man has authority on earth.[69] It can hardly be doubted *that Jesus regarded the forgiveness of sins as a chief part of the good news he came to bring, or that the early community's own unprecedented claim to forgive sins was rooted in and a reflection of a similar claim by Jesus.* (James D G Dunn)[70]

The effect and effectiveness of Jesus' prophetic word of forgiveness are illustrated, then, by the ensuing physical cure:

> I order you: get up, pick up your stretcher, and go off home. And the man got up, and at once picked up his stretcher, and walked out in front of everyone.

The man too, shows faith in Jesus, for he does what Jesus tells him. The result is that he is immediately restored to bodily wholeness. The verb translated as *got up* is *egeirein, arise,* which will later be used of Jairus' daughter and Jesus' resurrection; *release from paralysis is a form of restoration of life.*[71] (John R Donahue & Daniel J Harrington) He can stand erect, bend and carry; he can hike, work in the fields, and saw wood; he can stand to his waist in the water and cast a net. His feelings of guilt, inadequacy, frustration, anger, failure, resentment, feelings which must have weighed heavily or torn him apart, are dissipated like the early morning mist on the lake. He is restored to his family and the life of the local community. A new day has dawned. All this reflects that deeper wholeness, new life and fellowship which is the full reality of the Kingdom. For *forgiveness and healing are not here two distinct acts, but are different aspects of one thing - the total restoration of the paralysed man.* (Morna D Hooker)[72] The one guarantees the other, because they belong together. *Healing is also the outward demonstration of wholeness which reflects the internal, redemptive effect of forgiveness. By healing and forgiving, Jesus both demonstrates his divine authority as the Son of God empowered by the Holy Spirit as agent of the kingdom, and carries out his mission to inaugurate the kingdom.* (R Alan Culpepper)[73] The visible physical healing is the proof of the more fundamental but hidden gift of forgiveness.[74] The choral response of the people, despite Jesus' previous miracles in the town, is one of astonishment. They are deeply impressed, and praise God, *We have never seen anything like this.* Doubtless, the man's four friends too were delighted and joined in the praise. The fact that the people give glory to God subtly counteracts the charge of blasphemy, for they acknowledge God's power and presence in Jesus.[75] The scribes will reappear in critical mode later.

# Reflection

This story, occurring early in Jesus' ministry as Mark presents it, is usually referred to as the healing of the paralysed man. The other *Little People* often get overlooked. Yet the quality of their friendship and concern for the poor sufferer is quite special. This is friendship at its best, its most beautiful. They go to extraordinary lengths to get the man to Jesus, showing strong determination, creative, practical imagination and ingenuity. It seems that nothing is too much trouble, so firm is their commitment. They also manifest a deep faith in Jesus, in his ability and willingness to help their friend and bring him healing. They take the risk of appearing quite foolish if Jesus fails to respond positively to their quest.

The faith of the paralysed man himself is not highlighted in the narrative. Yet, his willingness to go along with their plan, to suffer the additional pain and inconvenience of being carried along, taken up the staircase, and then lowered down into the house, suggests that he too hoped and trusted that all would not be in vain. When told by Jesus to pick up his mat, he responds immediately and does so.

Jesus seems unruffled by the sudden debris fall and unusual interruption, the turning of Simon's house into the inaugural drop-in centre. He takes it all in his stride. He was probably already impressed by the determination, lateral thinking, genuine care and concern of the man's friends, and their confidence in him. Jesus focuses his attention on the individual at his feet. He is sensitive to the whole person before him, aware of the different dimensions of his affliction and its effects. Perceiving the man's need for forgiveness and reconciliation, he freely offers this gift, with no demands or preconditions. Then he makes him whole, restoring him to family and friends, enabling him to rebuild his life again. This is what the Kingdom is about.

There is much in the story with which we are invited to identify. The friends of the man raise the issue of the quality of our friendships. Like them we are called to be open and aware of the needs of others, in our family or local community, or further afield. The man's friends challenge the level of our generosity and commitment, our creativity in responding. Our task, in compassion and care, is to bring the needy to Jesus, to enable them to encounter his healing, forgiving, life-giving love.

It isn't too difficult for us to identify with the paralysed man. While perhaps not being physically impaired, we are certainly not entirely whole within ourselves. We can be held back in our relationships with others, held bound by fear, a sense of inadequacy, or selfishness. Reaching out and involvement can be a challenge. We can be carrying around inner hurts, which fester and occasionally erupt. We need to be set free and made whole and become more fully alive. We are aware of our ongoing need for forgiveness, transformation, a new beginning.

## The Woman in Simon's House

Luke records several occasions in which Jesus is invited to dine with the religious elite, invitations which he graciously accepts. The first of these meals takes place in the house of a Pharisee by the name of Simon. It is preceded by the contextualising comment that Jesus had a reputation for being a friend of tax gatherers and sinners.[76] It is a wonderful story, *a literary gem*: (Kenneth E Bailey)[77]

One of the Pharisees asked Jesus to eat with him, and he went into the Pharisee's house and took his place at the table. And a woman in the city, who was a sinner, having learned that he was eating in the Pharisee's house, brought an alabaster jar of ointment. She stood behind him at his feet, weeping, and began to bathe his feet with her tears and to dry them with her hair. Then she continued kissing his feet and anointing them with the ointment. Now when the Pharisee who had invited him saw it, he said to himself, *If this man were a prophet, he would have known who and what kind of woman this is who is touching him — that she is a sinner.* Jesus spoke up and said to him, *Simon, I have something to say to you.* Teacher, he replied, *Speak. A certain creditor had two debtors; one owed five hundred denarii, and the other fifty. When they could not pay, he cancelled the debts for both of them. Now which of them will love him more?* Simon answered, *I suppose the one for whom he cancelled the greater debt.* And Jesus said to him, *You have judged rightly.*

Then turning toward the woman, he said to Simon, *Do you see this woman? I entered your house; you gave me no water for my feet, but she has bathed my feet with her tears and dried them with her hair. You gave me no kiss, but from the time I came in she has not stopped kissing my feet. You did not anoint my head with oil, but she has anointed my feet with ointment. Therefore, I tell you, her sins, which were many, have been forgiven; hence she has shown great love. But the one to whom little is forgiven, loves little.*

Then he said to her, *Your sins are forgiven.* But those who were at the table with him began to say among themselves, *Who is this who even forgives sins?* And he said to the woman, *Your faith has saved you; go in peace.* (7:36-50)

This story is found only in Luke. Mark and Matthew include a story in which an unnamed woman anoints the head of Jesus prior to his passion, while he is dining in Bethany at the house of Simon the Pharisee.[78] In John, while Jesus is at table with his friends after the raising of Lazarus to life, Mary of Bethany anoints his feet and wipes them with her hair.[79] It is generally agreed that Mark and John are describing the same incident, with some variations. Luke's story has no connection with the passion, has a clearly alternative focus, and is a different episode in the ministry of Jesus, though some cross-influence has probably occurred during the oral transmission.[80] As it stands, the story unfolds with great artistry in dramatic form, sweeping between the three central characters *with passion and power.* (Tom Wright)[81]

## Premise

To make sense of the story, it has to be assumed that the woman has already either had some indirect knowledge of Jesus and his message, which led her to repentance,[82] or has heard him proclaiming his message of God's love for sinners. Perhaps *she had seen and heard him from the fringe of the crowd, and that had been enough to soften the hardness of her heart and to set her back on the road to self-respect.* (George Bradford Caird)[83] Maybe there had been some direct contact between them previously. In some way she has been moved by his message, has believed, repented and now wishes to thank Jesus.[84] We are not told or provided with any further details.[85]

## Introduction

A Pharisee named Simon invites Jesus to dine with him, probably after the synagogue service on the Sabbath. Perhaps this invitation stems from his respect for Jesus as a rabbi, a prophet even; it could be that he even finds aspects of his teaching interesting and attractive.[86]

Jesus is open to the religious elite as well; they too need to hear his message. However, since Jesus' presentation of God's love for sinners was at variance with the normal Pharisee viewpoint, the invitation to the meal may have been an excuse to cross-examine, advise, correct or challenge him.[87] It was customary to extend the welcoming greeting of a kiss. When the guests had taken their places, olive oil and water were brought so that they could wash their hands and feet. The thanksgiving prayer would then be said. We learn later that the basic gestures of welcome and hospitality were not offered, an omission the other guests would have observed. This was a public insult, especially as Jesus was a teacher, as Simon himself acknowledges. Jesus would be well aware of this.[88]

Having left his sandals at the door on entering, Jesus reclines on a divan.[89] Normally the eldest or most senior guest would recline first, and then the others. Usually the door was left open, and sometimes beggars would come in to pick up the scraps, or admirers to relish the conversation.[90] No doubt the presence of Jesus would attract onlookers, genuinely interested or simply curious. On this occasion, the person who enters is a woman who has been living an immoral life in the town, a prostitute, who has come to hear that Jesus is at table in the Pharisee's house. Jesus later gives the impression that she was already there when he arrived, and therefore had seen the way in which he was publicly humiliated.[91] The reason for her presence is her desire to thank Jesus for setting her free.

## The Woman's Action

She brings with her an alabaster jar or flask of perfume. Her initial intention was probably to use the perfume to anoint his hands and head as a sign of gratitude.[92] Now her intention is also to compensate for the host's rudeness to him.[93] Her emotions get the better of her and she breaks down in floods of tears which wet Jesus' feet.[94] Without thinking, in an attempt to remedy the situation, she lets down her hair, which is quite unacceptable in public, to wipe his feet dry.[95] She repeatedly kisses his feet, a sign of reverence, and anoints them. In that context, and given that he was reclining, she could not anoint his face. By unloosing her hair she was making some form of an ultimate pledge of loyalty to him. With this dramatic act she also entered into Jesus' pain of rejection and public humiliation.[96] The onlookers would have expected Jesus to be as embarrassed and shocked as they were, and to have rejected her, but he calmly allows all this to happen and accepts her intimate gestures. It is Simon who is shocked, embarrassed and confused!

## The Dialogue

*Through all this*, writes Caird, *Jesus did not turn; for he had no need; all that he needed to know about the uninvited guest he could read in the mirror of Simon's shocked face, and all he needed to do for the woman he could do by accepting motionless the homage of her penitent love.*[97] What Jesus read in Simon's face was:

If this man were a real prophet, he would know who this woman is who is touching him, and what a bad character she is (7:39).

The words presuppose that prophets have extraordinary knowledge,[98] and imply that Jesus did not know, had he been aware, he would have withdrawn from contact with her, as Simon himself would have done. It is becoming apparent that Jesus cannot be a true prophet. He ought to have told the woman to follow the accepted procedures and go to the Temple and offer sacrifice in God's presence. In fact, however, Jesus shows that he does know who she is; she is a sinner, but a repentant and pardoned sinner. Her reputation had not changed, but she herself had.[99] Jesus knows what is going on in Simon's mind, so he turns to him, *I have something to say to you.*[100] Politely addressing Jesus as *Teacher,* Simon invites him to speak up.

## The Parable

Jesus responds by recounting a brief, straightforward parable in which a creditor has two debtors, one who owes him a little amount (50 denarii), the other a considerable sum (500 denarii), and, given that neither can repay him, unexpectedly he cancels both debts.[101] In Aramaic, the same word is used for debts and for sins. The Greek verb can be used both financially and theologically: to cancel and to forgive. Initially the creditor is assumed to be God; the debtors cannot pay God; and God freely and generously forgives them both. This is another beautiful description of God's mercy. For the reader there is also a sense in which the creditor then begins to look like Jesus, who forgives the woman and forgives Simon for his rudeness and insult. Through the parable Jesus shifts the focus of attention from the woman's sin to her response, her acceptance of the gift of forgiveness.[102]

## The Dialogue

Jesus then poses the question as to which of the two would respond with the greater love. Simon rightly supposes that it would be the one for whom the greater debt was freely cancelled. His reply is cautious and wary; maybe he anticipates what follows.[103] Jesus agrees with his verdict; love is the product of forgiveness.

## The Woman's Action

The woman has incurred the anger of Simon and his guests by her behaviour and by thwarting to some extent their plan. But Jesus defends her as he brings out the significance of her actions and the contrasting dispositions of his host. He invites Simon to look at her. He has, of course, observed her already with a negative, jaundiced, judgemental eye. Jesus is drawing him to see her in a different light as a person of quality.

Then, gently or accusingly, he points out to Simon his economical love, his lack of hospitality, his failure to do his duty as host.[104] In Simon's own home Jesus publicly lists his *oversights*. There was no foot bath, no kiss of friendship, no oil of respect. These, the woman has substituted abundantly, effusively, extravagantly, with great love and unrestrained, spontaneous affection, generosity and gratitude, which reveal the pardon she has come to acknowledge. The text is beautifully balanced. The woman *sees Jesus defending her, confirming her and in the process carving out a space for her in the community of his followers.* (Kenneth E Bailey)[105] But in the long-run there will be a price to pay for Jesus' defending her and criticising his host.

Jesus explicitly and publicly confirms God's forgiveness which she has already experienced.[106] There is some discussion amongst scholars as to whether the sense of the text is that the woman's manifestation of love towards Jesus brings her (or merits, earns) forgiveness, or that her love is a consequence of her having been already forgiven, though this has not been described in the story. The original Greek is open to both positions. Some of the early Fathers of the Church, like Augustine, Clement of Alexandria, Peter Chrysologus, took the former view, and this is adopted in the KJV and RSV versions. The latter position, in which the parable is integrated into the narrative, is the view of Ambrose, Origen and Cassian, and adopted by the JB, NRSV, NIV versions. This is the view which I have followed.[107] Jesus then finally speaks to the woman, something a rabbi should not do. His words are similarly unrabbinic, *Your sins have been forgiven.*[108] His confirming comment is reassuring, liberating and transforming.

## Conclusion

As those at table wonder who this man can be, who forgives sins, Jesus again addresses her, *Your faith has saved you; go in peace.* This is the first time in the account of the ministry that these two terms have been clearly joined.[109] The guests' question, focusing on the identity of Jesus,[110] is answered implicitly: precisely because Jesus is a prophet with divine authority, he receives and forgives sinners.[111] The woman has not uttered a word, but her actions in risking rejection and insult in entering the house, in expressing her gratitude, and in compassionately and daringly entering into Jesus' suffering, have manifested a deep and generous faith. Prior to this encounter, she must have shown trust in God despite her sinful past, and this facilitated the restoring of their relationship. As we saw when examining Luke's Infancy Narrative, Jesus comes to bring salvation and peace on earth.

## Reflection

This is a moving narrative of two-way love. The woman courageously breaks through the exclusion barrier, and shows so many signs of a love which is far from *economical*. There is a self-forgetfulness about her, a spontaneity and genuineness. She is deeply grateful. Jesus accepts her with great respect, allowing her to express her feelings, and even to touch him. He welcomes the service she renders, and allows her to remain close to him, refusing to send her away even though the cultural and religious expectations warrant it, and even though the atmosphere is pulsating with shock and disapproval. Her love and faith clash with the cold, self righteous, closed and withdrawn attitude of the male, religious elite present at the meal.

In contrast with Simon, who invites Jesus but violates the rules of hospitality, the woman, who is a member of the outcast poor, rejected by the religious elite as an untouchable, shows by her acts of hospitality that she does accept the prophet Jesus.[112] With a touch of genius, Luke's story highlights the contrast between these two very different people.[113] Jesus has made it clear that both law-keepers, the legal purists, and law-breakers are sinners and equally in need of forgiveness. That forgiveness is freely offered to both kinds. The woman has accepted the gift; her past now lies behind her, and she can move on into a new future. Simon's final response is unknown.[114]

Whether we have been forgiven much or little, God's forgiveness has frequently been offered us. Perhaps we sometimes take this gift for granted. Perhaps our sense of wonder and appreciation has become dull and muted. The story invites us to recapture the dream-like, scandalous magic of God's unfathomable compassion and forgiveness. Simon challenges us too, about genuine hospitality, about judging, and about openness to what is different and new. Jesus turns his religious world upside down, presenting a very different image of God, a new way of assessing and of relating. Maybe there is still a Simon lurking within us, and present in our Church.

# Zacchaeus

The next story which I'd like to consider is found only in Luke; this time the person concerned is given a name, a Jewish name, Zacchaeus. He is literally one of the *Little People* of the New Testament![115] The way in which the chapters of our Gospels have been arranged, since the time of Stephen Langton (1150-1228), Archbishop of Canterbury, is not always helpful. This story is now located at the beginning of chapter 19, but in the mind of the Evangelist it should be considered alongside the previous story, with which chapter 18 ends, the healing of the blind man. In Luke this man is not named, but in Mark he is called Bartimaeus.[116] The setting for both stories in Luke is Jericho. In Mark and Matthew, the healing of the blind man occurs as Jesus is leaving the city. Luke changes the stages of Jesus' journey, so that he encounters him as he enters it. This enables him to move easily into the subsequent story of Zacchaeus as Jesus makes to continue his journey. Taken together as a pair, the episodes speak of the salvation which comes through Jesus, picking up what we noticed in the Infancy Narrative; in this way the stories prepare for his arrival in Jerusalem as saviour.[117] The two stories offer us the opportunity to reflect on the way in which Jesus deals with someone who is oppressed, and with someone who is in a sense an oppressor.[118]

In its current location, the story of Zacchaeus is the final episode in Luke's journey narrative and the climax in Jesus' ministry to the outcast.[119] The text reads as follows:

> He entered Jericho and was passing through it. A man was there named Zacchaeus; he was a chief tax collector and was rich. He was trying to see who Jesus was, but on account of the crowd he could not, because he was short in stature. So he ran ahead and climbed a sycamore tree to see him, because he was going to pass that way. When Jesus came to the place, he looked up and said to him, *Zacchaeus, hurry and come down; for I must stay at your house today.* So he hurried down and was happy to welcome him. All who saw it began to grumble and said, *He has gone to be the guest of one who is a sinner.* Zacchaeus stood there and said to the Lord, *Look, half of my possessions, Lord, I will give to the poor; and if I have defrauded anyone of anything, I will pay back four times as much.* Then Jesus said to him, *Today salvation has come to this house, because he too is a son of Abraham. For the Son of Man came to seek out and to save the lost.* (19:1-10)

## Zacchaeus

The passage can be structured in the form of nine scenes.[120] Jesus has entered the city of Jericho, and is passing through en route for Jerusalem. It seems that he does not plan to stop there for the night.[121] The focus then switches to Zacchaeus, who is introduced as the *superintendent of taxes*, an unusual term, found nowhere else in Greek literature.[122] This could mean that he had responsibility for the collecting of the dues on goods passing into Judaea on the trade route from Peraea, and from further East. Possibly, he is a contractor in charge of the farming of taxes in a given area, or the senior agent in the taxation system.[123] He has evidently benefitted from the financial possibilities which such a post in a city like Jericho offered, for he is said to be extremely wealthy. Like Levi in a different town, he would have been very unpopular, hated and despised as a collaborator, and, from the religious viewpoint, considered unclean.[124] However, *he was eager to see what Jesus looked like,* having heard, no doubt, of Jesus' reputation in his treatment of people like him, and possibly aware that one of his disciples had been a member of his profession. His desire must have been more than mere Herodian curiosity.[125] We may speculate that it may have included a desire to escape from his self-imposed loneliness, the social ostracism which went with the job, to break free from a profession now burdening his conscience.[126] Given his social situation, he risks ridicule and violence from the crowd. So he runs on ahead, something which adults do not do in that culture, and climbs up a tree to get a view, since his smallness of stature precludes that possibility amidst the crowd. Rich and powerful people do not climb trees! This was an extravagant gesture, which illustrates the intensity of his desire.[127] Apparently, sycamore fig-trees have low branches, and are easy to climb; they have large, thick leaves, and thus provide good cover for someone wishing to hide. The regulations insisted that they should not grow within the city, so this tree would have been growing outside the city on the way to Jerusalem.[128]

## Jesus

The spotlight now focuses on Jesus. It is he who, in response to Zacchaeus' interest, seizes the initiative. Jesus is aware of his presence; he stops, looks up at him in the tree, and calls him by name. Perhaps he knew his name because of the insults being levelled against him by the crowd, who are relishing the opportunity afforded them. Jesus, to everyone's surprise, bursts through religious prejudice, and, presuming on his generosity, invites himself to a meal and lodging in his home, the house of a rich man, popularly regarded as a sinner:

> *Zacchaeus, be quick and come down,*
> *for I must stay at your house today.* (19:5)

Such a self-invitation is unusual. There is a note of urgency in Jesus' words; and the *must* draws what is happening into the ambit of God's saving plan.[129] Zacchaeus is delighted with the turn of events. This is more than he has ever envisaged. So he climbs down with alacrity and welcomes Jesus gladly. He is obviously touched by the graciousness of Jesus and his spontaneous offer of fellowship, and all that this implies. There is great joy in his offering hospitality.

By contrast, the bystanders, possibly including the disciples,[130] are scandalised by the fact that Jesus has chosen to be the guest of *a sinner*. They begin to murmur and voice their disapproval. Jesus seems to have incurred the hostility of the whole town.[131] For, to their way of thinking, to share this man's unclean table and home is to share his sin and emerge ritually defiled. Jesus frequently breaks through the barriers of religious prejudice with great freedom, and such freedom always creates a problem for others. Jesus does not lock people in their past; he can see beyond the present; he can see what is in the human heart; he has a vision of what is possible for the future.

## Zacchaeus

As far as Zacchaeus is concerned, this freedom *awakened to vibrant life impulses that had long lain dormant and revealed to him the man he was capable of becoming.* (George Bradford Caird)[132] In response to Jesus' graciousness, and also to exonerate him from the crowd's suspicion, and to deflect their anger, Zacchaeus stops,[133] and publicly declares that he turns his back decisively and without delay on his past:

*Here and now, sir, I give half my possessions to charity; and if I have defrauded anyone, I will repay him four times over.* (19:8)

Without any prompting from Jesus, Zacchaeus implicitly acknowledges his guilt, professing his intention to offer alms beyond the normally expected twenty per cent, and to pay restitution far in excess of the legal prescription.[134] In Judaism, repentance involved restoration. This is a clear illustration of conversion, that change of heart and ways which is the genuine response to Jesus.

He declares his intention to live a new life, and illustrates what this might entail.[135] The financial oppression of the Jericho community will now be relieved considerably.

## Jesus

Jesus, in his final words, acknowledges and affirms Zacchaeus and his attitude, as he addresses Zacchaeus and the crowd as well:

*Today salvation has come to this house - for this man too is a son of Abraham. The Son of Man has come to seek and save what is lost.* (19:10) Salvation has come to him that very day, *today*. It is not a thing of the future, a distant dream. It has come in the person of Jesus, who in an expression of costly love, has shifted to himself the crowd's opposition and hostility.[136] Zacchaeus accepts Jesus' love; he accepts being found and accepted so completely by Jesus. This is the true meaning of repentance. He is a man transformed. He is drawn into the Kingdom community.[137] Jesus proclaims him a genuine son of Abraham like any other Jew, an heir to Abraham's blessings. He is no longer an outsider, but is accepted in God's eyes. The final comment of Jesus sums up the scene, as it sums up his whole ministry. The language is that of the parables referred to earlier; it is the language and imagery of the Shepherd and of the compassionate father: *lost and found*.[138] Table fellowship, we have seen, is an initiative of searching, a seeking which saves and forgives, a reaching out to the *outcast*; it is an expression of the nature of Jesus' mission. Jesus did not leave Zacchaeus to waste away on the margins. He paused and reached out to him, and drew him into the circle of God's embracing love. This story concludes that part of Luke's travel narrative which has often been called *the Gospel of the Outcast*. (Joseph A Fitzmyer)[139]

An alternative view of Zacchaeus' dramatic declaration prefers to take the verbs literally as present rather than understand them as pointing to the future. It isn't that Zacchaeus has undergone a conversion; he does not ask for mercy or express sorrow as a sinner. Really, he is a decent fellow, but because of his job is unfairly branded otherwise.[140] In his words of defence he is not self-effacing, nor is he boastful.[141] He is describing the way in which he habitually behaves, his normal practice. This understanding of the text does not affect the final words of Jesus.

## Reflection

Understanding the Zacchaeus story in the traditional way, this unpopular citizen of Jericho, like the woman in the preceding narrative, experiences the transforming and liberating effect of Jesus' forgiveness. A social and religious outcast, he longs to see Jesus. Such a desire suggests that he wishes to be set free. He goes to great lengths in order to catch sight of Jesus, risking the antipathy of those around. On encountering the gracious acceptance of Jesus, he responds generously, an indication of a new beginning.

Jesus shows his typical awareness of what is happening around him. Probably the crowd's reaction to Zacchaeus alerts him to his presence in the tree and also his name. Jesus reacts to the situation by stopping, calling his name, and becomes himself a seeker by requesting hospitality in his home. It is a creative and sensitive move, acknowledging his own need, opening up for Zacchaeus the possibility of experiencing the presence of God's Kingdom. But it inevitably incurs the wrath of the onlookers, and their antagonism and critique. This, Jesus is obliged to absorb. His words are affirmation and defence of Zacchaeus, and challenge for the onlookers, inviting them to embrace a different way of understanding God and God's ways.

One of scripture's most beautiful themes highlights our yearning for God:[142]
> As a deer longs for flowing streams, so my soul longs for you, O God. My soul thirsts for God, for the living God. When shall I come and behold the face of God? (Ps 42:1-2)

Like Zacchaeus, deep in our hearts we wish to see Jesus, we desire to become more involved with him and more a part of what he stands for. This longing surfaces in different ways, at different times. And Jesus is aware of it. We trust that he will identify our tree and invite us down. Like the disciples and crowd, we can be adept at labelling people, using words and phrases which are dismissive, negative and hurtful. Such strategies stifle compassion, and often betray attitudes and prejudices which are destructive, which imprison us and blind us to the remarkable transformations which Jesus can make possible.

## A Woman Rescued

One of the most problematic extracts in the Fourth Gospel is the story usually referred to as *The Woman Taken in Adultery*. It is problematic not because of its content, but from a textual point of view. Based on early manuscript evidence and issues of vocabulary and style, it is a passage which scholars maintain was not part of the original Fourth Gospel, but a later insertion. It is to be found in some ancient manuscripts, but not in others. In some manuscripts the passage is found after John 7:36 or 21:25, or after Luke 21:38. However, the origins of the story are believed to be rooted in authentic early tradition, possibly in Johannine circles, though it does have a rather Lucan flavour. Bruce Metzger comments that the account has all the earmarks of historical veracity, and is obviously a piece of oral tradition which circulated in certain parts of the Western Church.[143]

After circulating as oral tradition, scribes began to add it to the Gospel text. Its earlier omission could be due to the fact that the story violated deeply-rooted cultural attitudes.[144] *There is nothing in the story itself or its language that would forbid us to think of it as an early story concerning Jesus. Its succinct expression of the mercy of Jesus is as delicate as anything in Luke; its portrayal of Jesus as the serene judge has all the majesty that we would expect of John.* (Raymond E Brown)[145] It is easy to understand, however, why some Christian scribes and community members did not wish it to be lost, for it is a valuable witness to the person and style of Jesus:

> Early in the morning Jesus came again to the temple. All the people came to him and he sat down and began to teach them. The scribes and the Pharisees brought a woman who had been caught in adultery; and making her stand before all of them, they said to him, *Teacher, this woman was caught in the very act of committing adultery. Now in the law, Moses commanded us to stone such women. Now what do you say?* They said this to test him, so that they might have some charge to bring against him. Jesus bent down and wrote with his finger on the ground. When they kept on questioning him, he straightened up and said to them, *Let anyone among you who is without sin be the first to throw a stone at her.* And once again he bent down and wrote on the ground. When they heard it, they went away, one by one, beginning with the elders; and Jesus was left alone with the woman standing before him. Jesus straightened up and said to her, *Woman, where are they? Has no one condemned you?* She said, *No one, sir.* And Jesus said, *Neither do I condemn you. Go your way, and from now on do not sin again.* (8:2-11)

I think this is a wonderful story.[146] In the present context in John, Jesus is in Jerusalem for the celebration of the feast of Tabernacles (*Succoth*). On the last day of the week-long feast, the climax, he has offered to provide living water for all who thirst, using language reminiscent of God's word in Isaiah.[147] To this there was a mixed reaction. Some of his hearers were impressed; others had problems with his Galilean origin. The religious leaders had sent the temple police to arrest him, but they returned empty handed, commenting that *No man ever spoke like this man.* Their masters were far from pleased, speaking disparagingly about the crowd, who are ignorant of the Law and are therefore cursed, and then dismissing out of hand Nicodemus' plea for fairness.[148]

## The Situation

After spending the night on the Mount of Olives, Jesus courageously returns to the Temple in the early morning. In the Temple precincts the people come to him, and he sits down as rabbis were wont to do, and begins to teach them. The religious leaders, referred to as the *scribes and Pharisees*, which is unusual in John, interrupt Jesus, bringing before him a woman caught in a sexually compromising situation with someone not her husband, and they make her stand before him in public view. They have probably arrested her the previous evening. The offending male seems to have managed to slip away. The religious leaders seek to use the situation as a way of entrapping and publically discrediting Jesus; they have formulated an astute *game plan*. They show no real interest or concern for the woman in her shame and distress. She is a pawn in their power-play, not a person. The Temple courtyard enclosure was overshadowed by a military fort constructed by Herod the Great. Everything takes place under the observation of the Roman garrison.[149]

The issue is stated in clear terms. She has been caught in adultery, about that there is no question. According to the Law of Moses, adultery is a capital offence.[150] She should be executed by stoning. The religious leaders ask Jesus for his view. It seems a no-win situation. If Jesus urges her release, he will stand accused of rejecting the great law-giver, and failing to uphold the Mosaic Law and tradition. To their way of thinking, this would clearly show everyone present that he cannot possibly be from God. It could also be interpreted as an acceptance of the Roman decision to deny the Jews, and especially their religious leaders, the right to put people to death, thus manifesting his allegiance to Rome rather than to Judaism and God.[151]

If, on the other hand, he advocates that she be stoned to death, he will appear as lacking in compassion, contradicting much of his teaching and his normal way of acting. He will also be revealing that his image of God coincides with theirs, a God who is harsh and unrelenting. He will be in open breach of the Roman regulation. They seem to have effectively cornered him: choose Moses and be arrested; choose Rome and be discredited.

## Jesus

Jesus is aware of the trap and the hidden agenda. He declines to become involved in discussion and argument about the validity of the Law, the legitimacy of capital punishment, the authority of the religious leadership, the power of Rome, the nature of God and issues connected with sexual ethics. He doesn't ask about the man involved, or seek to question the witnesses.[152] He simply kneels on the ground and doodles in the dust. That day, the eighth day of the feast, was kept as a Sabbath. The rabbis considered writing to be work, and therefore forbidden, if a permanent mark was made. Jesus' reaction is very clever. Writing in the dust was permissible, for it would soon be erased. He shows his awareness of the legal scene.

His action is quite brilliant; it completely wrong-foots his adversaries, turning the tables on them. When insistently pressed for an answer, he stands upright and reveals his decision, which releases the woman from lynch-law justice. The first stone is to be thrown by someone who is without sin. The ball is back in their court. Jesus kneels again and recommences his doodling in the dust. He has gently forced those present to focus on themselves and their own lives, rather than on the woman. He has found a way of enabling everyone to acknowledge their own guilt, and abandon their judgemental attitude. Fixing his gaze on the ground, he spares their embarrassment, as the crowd melts away, the oldest first, in accordance with tradition.

Jesus is now alone with the woman, who stands there waiting. So far she has not spoken a word. As St Augustine succinctly puts it, *Relicti sunt duo: misera et misericordia; two are left, the unfortunate woman and mercy personified.* Jesus, with his questions, *Where are they? Has no one condemned you?* establishes a relationship with her. He does not reject her because she has violated the sexual code of his people. She is a person again, with an identity and a dignity. He addresses her with gentleness, respect, understanding and compassion. She replies with quiet reverence, and no doubt with profound relief, *No one, sir.*

He is also true to the reality of the situation. He does not condone what she has done; he names it as sin. She is not an innocent victim. Nevertheless, he has rescued her from the death which threatened her. He assures her that he joins the others in not condemning her. She is free to leave. But he offers her the possibility of conversion, a fresh start, encouraging her to change her self-destructive way of life, *Go away and sin no more.* His acceptance and compassion make this transformation possible. Jesus has shifted the hostility of the Pharisees from her to himself. Beating them on their own patch, in order to save her life, will create greater problems for him. *Jesus demonstrates the life-changing power of costly love.* (Kenneth E Bailey)[153]

Jesus has followed the understanding of justice proclaimed by Isaiah in the Servant song, *A bruised reed he will not break, and a dimly burning wick he will not quench* (42:3). He lives out a core meaning of the cross, offering the woman a costly demonstration of unexpected love.

## Reflection

The scribes and Pharisees who appear in the story are not strangers to us. Frequently we encounter people who are manipulative, insincere, self-satisfied, legalistic, negative, judgemental, destructive. There are folk who seem to relish the possibility of stone-throwing, some who are quite adept at the sport. This is our world, our Church. Our media flourishes on it all. We may recognize some of these tendencies in our own hearts and lives too. Jesus' words give us cause to stop in our tracks, to think and take stock. In Matthew he refers with amusement to our human aptitude for noticing a speck in the eye of our neighbour, and failing to observe a log in our own. (Matthew 7:1-5) The *metanoia* and conversion to which we are repeatedly invited must touch us here. Jesus doesn't ask us to deny that others, like ourselves, make mistakes. He does deny us the right to judge them, to gossip about them, to destroy their name and character, to throw stones. Maybe before launching into negativity we should pause more frequently and spend a little time doodling in the dust; we should ponder a while and welcome a fresh perspective on people, ourselves and on life in general.

The text invites us to imagine ourselves in the woman's place, standing before Jesus. We are aware that he knows our story, knows our shadow side, knows what drains our life-energy, knows the areas in which we are only half alive, knows what holds us bound. Our fragility and sinfulness are open before him. We can gaze at him as he kneels before us, writing in the sand, the one who has come to take away our sin, to remove our darkness, to set us free, to bring us life, phrases used elsewhere in John's Gospel. And he straightens up, looks us in the eye, and, addressing us by name, says, *I don't condemn you. Go your way, you are forgiven. From now on, sin no more*. The possibility of a new future opens before us too. Perhaps we share her relief, her surprise, and her wonder.

Jesus also challenges our understanding of God. He communicates a God who is compassionate and forgiving, a God who doesn't believe in oppression, condemnation, coercion, vengeance or exclusion. It was hard for the religious leaders of his day to accept such a God, for such a God was alien to their mind-set, challenged their structures and threatened their power-base.

As Christians we too can find it difficult to entrust ourselves to the God of Jesus, to believe in such extravagant, inclusive and freely bestowed love. Deep down we also realise that acceptance of such a God makes demands on our own way of relating to others, as individuals and as Church institution. The stance and style of Jesus are profoundly prophetic.

## Concluding Thoughts

The Jesus whom we have encountered in this chapter is so attractive and inspiring. There is a remarkable freedom about him, and a deep compassion. He communicates a sense of wholeness and integrity and personal truth.

His surprising choice of Levi as a member of his close circle shows great originality. He knows his own mind; he is clear about his values and priorities. This he shows again in his table fellowship. He is open to the outcast and the marginalised; he is comfortable in their presence and company. *The Prologue* of John rightly claims that the Word *pitched his tent in our midst.* The way in which he expresses his acceptance, openness and genuine concern for people whose lives are sinful, his refusal to ignore them, is remarkable. His conduct induces raised eyebrows, provokes surprise, criticism and hostility. He allows a local prostitute to touch him and wash his feet with her tears at a formal meal in the home of a respected Pharisee. He takes the initiative in going to dine and stay in the house of a despised and wealthy tax-man, a sinner; and he incurs criticism and hostility for it. He rescues an adulteress and restores her dignity, respectability and freedom. His whole approach is utterly un-rabbinic, and quite revolutionary, counter-cultural.

Despite the criticism and hostility, he is true to himself, to his vision of his mission in life, and to his understanding of what God is like. This level of genuineness and truth, leading to such freedom and courage, is very rare. It is also profoundly prophetic, revealing a compassionate and forgiving God, making such a God present to people on the fringes, drawing them into the ambit of God's love. No wonder Jesus could speak about *Good News.* As prophetic, his style is dangerously challenging, for it suggests an alternative set of values, a different mindset, a new world.

Another aspect of the Jesus portrayed in these stories is his calm adaptability, his capacity to cope with the unexpected, to take things in his stride. When confronted with a hole appearing in the roof, bits of debris cascading around him, and the sight of a man being lowered down into his presence, he doesn't fuss. He seems fascinated by the creative thinking and deep faith of the man's friends. When the woman bursts into the male company around the Sabbath dinner table and creates a scene and provokes an atmosphere of disapproval, he quietly sits there, accepts her closeness and loving attention, refuses to react and dismiss her. When unexpectedly cornered by the religious leaders and faced with flagrant adultery, he calmly assesses the situation, and doodling in the dust, he gently finds a brilliant way to solve the dilemma. He seems able to deflect hostility directed to others and absorb it in himself, and move on.

At the same time Jesus does try to help those who criticise him and assess him harshly to understand what he is about, and why he chooses to live and relate as he does. He isn't a soft touch. The three Lukan parables are so clear and profound, but also very challenging. His explanation to Simon is straight, but also gentle and open-ended. He leaves him, and his friends too, with something to think about, and an indication of how to change.

The Reign of God is about wholeness, physical, spiritual, social. It is about compassionate acceptance and hospitality, the breaking down of barriers and prejudices. It is about transformation, and moving into newness of life. In these stories, Jesus takes our breath away.

The variety of *Little People* whom Jesus encounters in these stories is rich and interesting. The people who bring the paralysed man to Jesus exhibit friendship at its best, determined, creative, and generous. Their profound faith in the power and willingness of Jesus to heal the man spurs them on to risky lengths.

The woman who braves the male gathering in Simon's house expresses appreciation and gratitude for the forgiveness she has experienced, and shows generous love towards Jesus. Zacchaeus is an outcast who longs to see Jesus, and goes to unusual lengths to do so. When Jesus offers him an opening, he grasps the opportunity with joy and enthusiasm, welcoming him into his home, and seeking to protect him from the hostility of the crowd. The guilty woman experiences her dignity restored and the opportunity of a different future. Jesus' encounter with these people is a profound life-transforming experience. Their role in the story is to highlight the possibilities for change and growth which the advent of God's Kingdom offers.

As Christians, in attempting to articulate what God has offered us through the life, death and resurrection of Jesus, we have traditionally used ideas like redemption, justification, salvation, and whole theologies have emerged in explanation. An alternative approach, found in the New Testament, only in the writings of Paul, is the term *reconciliation*. In a beautiful and profound extract in his second letter to the community in Corinth, he writes:

> So if anyone is in Christ, there is a new creation: everything old has passed away; see, everything has become new! All this is from God, who reconciled us to himself through Christ, and has given us the ministry of reconciliation; that is, in Christ, God was reconciling the world to himself, not counting their trespasses against them, and entrusting the message of reconciliation to us. So we are ambassadors for Christ, since God is making his appeal through us; we entreat you on behalf of Christ, be reconciled to God. (2 Cor 5:17-20)

There is an exciting emphasis on newness and transformation; a new creation has taken place. This is clearly the initiative, the work, the gift of God, freely bestowed. In parallel phrases Paul proclaims that God has reached out to *reconcile us to himself through Christ;* that *in Christ God was reconciling the world to himself.* The Gospel stories on which we have been reflecting illustrate this in action, as Jesus encounters the *Little People*, ignoring their *trespasses,* creating their lives afresh, drawing them into the circle of God's love. Centuries later, we too have been embraced by God's reconciling in and through Christ Jesus. Reconciliation, forgiveness; this is the heart of the Gospel. There is another set of parallel phrases in Paul's text, this time focusing on mission, the ongoing responsibility of the reconciled to proclaim what God has done and what God is offering, *God has given us the ministry of reconciliation*, and *entrusting to us the message of reconciliation.* Like Paul, as baptised individuals and as Church communities, we are *ambassadors for Christ,* proclaiming and working for reconciliation.

At different levels of society in our world today, forgiveness and reconciliation do not come easily. Families, communities, countries are deeply fractured because people are unwilling or unable to reach out in forgiveness. This can lead to an escalation in bad-feeling, mistrust, retaliation and even violence. Forgiveness is not a soft option, a sign of weakness; it is difficult and demanding. But it is the only way forward if healing and change and resolution are to take place. As disciples of Jesus, his *ambassadors,* we are called to find ways of enabling forgiveness to occur, and of carrying forward in this way the *new creation.* As in the case of Jesus, this will be a costly option, but it is an indication that we are caught up in God's seeking the world's reconciliation.

# Chapter Three – The Gentiles

Not all of the Gospel's *Little People* are Jewish, even though the ministry of Jesus was directed primarily to his own nation. In Mark, Jesus encounters a demoniac, and later a deaf-mute, in an area called the Decapolis, a predominantly Gentile territory. He also journeys north west to Tyre, where he is approached by a Syrophoenician woman, seeking a cure for her daughter. On Calvary, it is a Gentile who professes faith in Jesus as Son of God.[1] Matthew and Luke narrate an additional story in which Jesus is approached by a Gentile centurion in Capernaum. In the course of his ministry Jesus also has contact with people from Samaria. Samaritans were despised by the Jews, and considered to be as bad as Gentiles.[2] It is fascinating that despite the hostility shown by the inhabitants of a Samaritan village who refuse to welcome Jesus because he is en route for Jerusalem, Jesus makes a Samaritan the hero of one of his most famous parables.[3] In this chapter we shall meet four of these Gentile *Little People*: Legion, the Syrophoenician woman, the deaf-mute, and the Capernaum centurion. The first three of these figures were particularly significant for Mark and his Church, for their experience of Jesus' power and generosity illustrates his openness to the Gentile world, and validates their presence in the Christian community. The same would be true of Matthew's centurion.

## Legion

### Context

The story of the Gerasene demoniac is part of a sequence of episodes intended by Mark to illustrate Jesus' authority and his domination of Satan in a wide spectrum of life situations. Jesus has controlled with a word the raging of the sea, calming the violent storm which suddenly erupted on the lake, and terrified the disciples, including the seasoned fishermen. Now, the Legion incident demonstrates his overwhelming power over raging demons, as again by a mere word he is victorious over a very severe form of multiple devil possession.[4] He even goes on to purify the whole land of devils. If Jesus can thus deal with an army of spirits, it is clear that Satan's kingdom is finally being destroyed.[5] An important aspect of this narrative is the fact that Jesus' mission of healing and liberation now reaches Gentile territory. Having confronted demonic evil in a Jewish context, particularly in the Capernaum synagogue early in his ministry, he now faces it in the Gentile world.[6] The episode reveals the identity of Jesus and the nature of his mission: he is God's instrument in the vanquishing of Satan.

The Decapolis was a group or federation of ten cities situated, in the main, east of the Jordan. The population was mixed, but mainly Gentile.[7] It was part of the sophisticated Hellenistic world, strongly Greek in culture and religion, and quite wealthy.[8] The people had a certain degree of independence, and were under the protection of the Roman Governor of Syria. The storyline is as follows:

They came to the other side of the lake, to the country of the Gerasenes. And when he had stepped out of the boat, immediately a man out of the tombs with an unclean spirit met him. He lived among the tombs; and no one could restrain him any more, even with a chain; for he had often been restrained with shackles and chains, but the chains he wrenched apart, and the shackles he broke in pieces; and no one had the strength to subdue him. Night and day among the tombs and on the mountains he was always howling and bruising himself with stones. When he saw Jesus from a distance, he ran and bowed down before him; and he shouted at the top of his voice, *What have you to do with me, Jesus, Son of the Most High God? I adjure you by God, do not torment me.* For he had said to him, *Come out of the man, you unclean spirit!* Then Jesus asked him, *What is your name?* He replied, *My name is Legion; for we are many.* He begged him earnestly not to send them out of the country. Now there on the hillside a great herd of swine was feeding; and the unclean spirits begged him, *Send us into the swine; let us enter them.* So he gave them permission. And the unclean spirits came out and entered the swine; and the herd, numbering about two thousand, rushed down the steep bank into the lake, and were drowned in the lake. The swineherds ran off and told it in the city and in the country. Then people came to see what it was that had happened. They came to Jesus and saw the demoniac sitting there, clothed and in his right mind, the very man who had had the legion; and they were afraid. Those who had seen what had happened to the demoniac and to the swine reported it. Then they began to beg Jesus to leave their neighbourhood. As he was getting into the boat, the man who had been possessed by demons begged him that he might be with him. But Jesus refused, and said to him, *Go home to your friends, and tell them how much the Lord has done for you, and what mercy he has shown you.* And he went away and began to proclaim in the Decapolis how much Jesus had done for him; and everyone was amazed. (5:1-20)

Some aspects of the narrative are somewhat bizarre and disconcerting.[9] It is *by far the most elaborate and enigmatic gospel miracle story.* (John R Donahue & Daniel J Harrington)[10] the only true exorcism story connected to a pagan city. A widely-held scholarly view suggests that a simple exorcism narrative became more developed as the tradition evolved; the insertion of the legendary swine episode may have taken place before Mark; it now furthers his theological purpose and becomes the focus of the story.[11] The storyline follows the normal exorcism pattern: Jesus meets the possessed; the demons utter an exclamation, and identify Jesus; there is an expulsion formula, and, finally, a complete transformation. There is, however, no command for silence in this story, because the demons are silenced by being engulfed in the sea.[12] The structure which I shall follow illustrates the care with which the Evangelist has crafted the episode:[13]

| | |
|---|---|
| 1-5 | Introduction. The man's approach to Jesus |
| 6-10 | Jesus' Encounter with the Demoniac |
| 11-14a | The Swine Incident |
| 14b-17 | Jesus and the Townsfolk |
| 18-20 | Conclusion: The man approaches Jesus |

## Introduction (1-5)

After the calming of the storm, Jesus and the disciples complete their boat journey to the other side of the lake. We are not informed why they headed for this destination. They reach the territory of the Gerasenes, a predominantly pagan or Gentile area. There are textual variants because the place is difficult to locate: alternatives include Gergesenes and Gadarenes. The town of Gerasa is situated over 30 miles south east of the lake, and so does not fit the story as it stands, but the textual evidence favours this reading; the original story probably took place inland, and not by the lake.[14] Gadara is on a hill some five or six miles from the lake, but with no steep cliffs. It is the presence of the pigs in the narrative, a later development, which creates the geographical problem.[15] Mark clearly thought that the place was near the lake; his geographical knowledge often leaves much to be desired.

*Immediately* upon arrival Jesus is confronted by a man *with an unclean spirit*, who sees him from afar and comes out from the tombs towards him. The gravity of the man's situation is amply and vividly brought out.

He is living in social isolation amidst the tombs, which are probably caves cut into the mountainside.[16] In the popular mind demons were thought to inhabit tombs and cemeteries. For Jews graveyards were considered to be places of uncleanness and ritual contamination.[17] No one can secure the man even with a chain; he snaps the chains and breaks the fetters. The phrase *no one had the strength to control him* is significant, for he now encounters the *mightier one*, who can subdue the *strong one*.[18] Night and day, among the tombs and in the mountains, he would howl and gash himself with stones, perhaps in an attempt at self-destruction.[19] The mad outcast is a fearsome sight! He is a profoundly disturbed individual, a human wreck.

### Jesus' Encounter with the Demoniac (6-10)

On catching sight of Jesus from a distance, the man runs up and falls at his feet. The Greek verb can mean to *worship*;[20] but its basic meaning is to kneel in respect and supplication; it can also indicate submission. In response to Jesus' command to leave the man, which is mentioned a little later in the story, the demon loudly shrieks:

What do you want with me, Jesus, Son of the Most High God?
In God's name do not torture me.

These words echo the exorcism in the Capernaum synagogue.[21] With supernatural or preternatural insight he recognises something of Jesus' identity, authority and superior power. For Mark, demons belong to the realm of the supernatural, and have access to truths which other characters in the narrative lack. The demoniac resists the presence of Jesus on his turf. The kingdom of God here confronts the kingdom of evil.[22] The demon attempts to appease Jesus, to control and render him powerless by the use of his name.[23] The form of address, *Son of the Most High God*, is found in the Old Testament on the lips of non-Israelites, and is therefore not inappropriate for a Gentile.[24] His reaction is violent, protesting at Jesus' invasion of his patch. He adjures Jesus, ironically in God's name, not to torment him. In doing so he implicitly recognises that with the coming of Jesus, the eschatological event has begun.[25] An expected concomitant of this event was God's punishing Satan and his minions. So the demon begs to be spared this anticipated punishment and sues for terms, tacitly acknowledging defeat.[26] Alternatively, this can be interpreted simply as a request to be spared the agony of an exorcism; the victim prefers to be destroyed rather than released.[27]

Jesus turns the tables and demands to be given his name. He gets an immediate response, which illustrates his power, *My name is Legion, for we are many.* The name is interesting. The Roman term could have been known in the area; the man could have seen a legion on the march, or even been treated badly by soldiers. In the Decapolis the Romans would probably not have been viewed negatively. For Mark, the detail brings out Jesus' power, as he vanquishes a whole host of demons, a very large number.[28] At an earlier stage of transmission these words may have been a boast whereby the man unwittingly discloses his name, or an attempt at evasion. It has been suggested that the original Aramaic means *soldier,* for *we are many and resemble one another like soldiers.* The translator used *legion,* which led to the interpretation that he was possessed by a whole regiment.

The demon takes the initiative again and pleads for terms, asking not to be sent out of the district. In popular belief, demons were associated with particular buildings or localities and usually did not wish to be dislocated. They would often ask favours or concessions of an exorcist in return for leaving. The word used here can mean region or space. The demons wish to remain in the area so as to bring destruction to other human beings.[29] It is clear that Jesus is recognised as being superior. In fact, his presence will purify simultaneously both the man and the district.

## The Swine Incident (11-14a)

The perplexing section about the swine is usually taken in scholarly circles as a later pre-Markan addition to the Legion story, a secondary accretion, easily detachable.[30] It is a folk tale, perhaps deriving from a Jewish exorcism in a pagan land. It is historically improbable; herds are rarely so numerous; they tend to scatter rather than stampede, and pigs can swim![31] It is not Jesus' way to indulge in the spectacular, or perform destructive miracles which injure people, such as the owners of the animals. The story continues the theme of cleansing. The unclean spirits (plural), now less defiant, beg to be allowed to go into the unclean pigs feeding on the mountainside in the care of swineherds. The animals like the demons are to the Jewish mind unclean. Jesus gives them leave to do so; this is the equivalent to the usual exorcism command.[32] The herd, about 2000 in number, charges down the cliff into the lake; they are all drowned.

Wherever the story originated, for Mark it is significant and is integral to the whole narrative. Firstly, it provides clear confirmation of the exorcism.

Secondly, it was commonly thought that demons vented their spite by doing damage as they left; so, if great harm was done, it would show the number, size, and power of the evil spirits. Thirdly, on Jesus' first visit to a Gentile land he banishes uncleanness, purifying both the man and the land. Both demons and swine are destroyed.[33] The expulsion is a great victory for Jesus over the empire of Satan. Satan's kingdom is clearly crumbling, his house is being plundered. Jesus in cleansing the land prepares the way for the Christian mission.[34] At this, the herdsmen run off and tell in the city and surrounding countryside the story of what has occurred. They serve as witnesses.

## Jesus and the Townsfolk (14b-17)

Naturally, the local people, filled with curiosity, come to investigate for themselves. They see the possessed man completely transformed and restored to well-being; he is properly dressed, and of normal mind again. The language deliberately aims to counterbalance the earlier description of his condition. He can now be restored to family and community. The effectiveness of Jesus' word is verified.[35] Initially, the people's reaction is curiosity, and then, not joy but awe and fear. Their response parallels that of the disciples on the lake in the previous story. The witnesses report what has happened to the man and to the pigs. The identity of these *witnesses* is not clear; maybe the disciples, not mentioned so far in the story, are intended. In the end the people implore Jesus to leave the neighbourhood, not because they are angry at the loss of the pigs, but because they are uncomfortable and apprehensive about Jesus' more than human power and its possible implications.[36] There is irony in their request that Jesus, like the demons, should leave their land. Fear leads to rejection of the presence of the Kingdom.[37]

## Conclusion: The man approaches Jesus (18-20)

The narrative concludes with a further encounter between the man and Jesus. As Jesus is on the point of embarking, Legion begs to be allowed to stay with Jesus as a disciple; the language of the earlier call story (*be with*) is used.[38] Jesus does not accede to this request. It is always he who takes the initiative and makes such significant choices. Besides, the man is a Gentile, and Jesus' mission is mainly to the Jews. However, he does have a special mission and role for him, and issues a further authoritative word:

> Go home to your people and tell them all that the Lord in his mercy has done for you.

In telling him to *Go home*, Jesus is restoring him to normal life and to his family and people. *Lord* here on Jesus' lips probably refers to God's activity and mercy. The man is commissioned to proclaim this, because for Mark it is important that the cures and the message go together; cures have to be seen in the context of the message about the Kingdom. Jesus has not preached in this Gentile area, so the man will now fulfil that role.[39]

The man accepts the unique responsibility bestowed on him, and goes around the whole Decapolis proclaiming what Jesus has done for him, which is not exactly what he was told to announce! The technical Christian verb for the proclamation of the Good News is used here; for Mark, the later mission of the Church to Gentiles is reflected. The parallel usage of *Lord* and *Jesus* underlines the fact that in the activity of Jesus is to be seen the activity and power of God.[40] *It is the authority of God which lies behind what Jesus has done for him.* (Francis J Moloney)[41] People are amazed at his proclamation, but no conversions are mentioned.[42] For the first time the Good News penetrates Gentile territory, and *the door has been opened to faith.* (Francis J Moloney)[43] The people's reaction to the man's words is no longer fear, but amazement.

## Reflection

In this story Legion can serve as a symbol of our human lostness. He is an isolated individual, a prisoner, excluded, self-destructive, fearsome to others, dehumanised, overcome by the power of evil. Admittedly, he can be considered a rather extreme and terrifying case. Nonetheless, we may identify aspects of his condition in our own lives, and we may long for wholeness and liberation. We may recognise traits of his experience in the lives of others whom we know. We sometimes encounter situations of severe physical or mental incapacitation, situations crying out for liberation and restoration, situations which are difficult to handle.

Legion is obviously deeply grateful to Jesus for the healing and new freedom which he has experienced. He is powerfully drawn to him, and wishes to *be with* him as a disciple, to *have a part* with Jesus in his project.[44] Jesus offers him this opportunity, but in a different way from what he has in mind. This alternative challenge he readily accepts, and engages in mission to his own people in the Decapolis region, the first apostle to the Gentiles. His ministry actually extends beyond that limited geographical area, for, decades later, the Gentile members of the Markan Church find comfort and inspiration in his story and his response. We too can find inspiration in

Legion, and in his desire to *be with* Jesus, to have Jesus at the centre of our lives. We can also join him in his enthusiasm to share with others what he has experienced through Jesus, and to draw them into the Kingdom.

In the story, Jesus shows courage in calmly confronting this profoundly disturbed individual. He is not put off by the man's appearance or wild behaviour. He treats him as an individual, a person in great distress and need. He asks his name, as he reaches out to him in his desperate isolation.[45] Once again he is ignoring religious taboos, this time those linked with Gentiles and with graveyards. For the first time he is venturing into Gentile territory, and although it is clearly not yet integral to his mission, he is open to the opportunity to engage and conquer evil, bringing freedom and wholeness there also. It is paradoxical that in the end the local people invite him to leave their territory. Shortly, it will be the people of his own native place who reject him too.[46] Rejection is a constant factor of his prophetic ministry. People find it difficult to recognise his identity, and to realise what is happening through his presence. This process will culminate on Calvary, where, through his loving surrender in isolation and intense pain, Jesus opens up the possibility of genuine liberation, wholeness and new life for all people.

## The Syrophoenician Woman

Our next Gentile story concerns a woman of Syrophoenician origin,[47] who approaches Jesus seeking a cure for her daughter, who is possessed by an unclean spirit. It is an episode which provides us with one of the most powerful and moving expressions of poverty of spirit to be found in the New Testament. Mark's version reads as follows:

> From there he set out and went away to the region of Tyre. He entered a house and did not want anyone to know he was there. Yet he could not escape notice, but a woman whose little daughter had an unclean spirit immediately heard about him, and she came and bowed down at his feet. Now the woman was a Gentile, of Syrophoenician origin. She begged him to cast the demon out of her daughter. He said to her, *Let the children be fed first, for it is not fair to take the children's food and throw it to the dogs.* But she answered him, *Sir, even the dogs under the table eat the children's crumbs.* Then he said to her, *For saying that, you may go – the demon has left your daughter.* So she went home, found the child lying on the bed, and the demon gone. (7:24-30)

This story and the one which we shall be considering next in this chapter form part of an interesting wider structural framework. The sequence of events in the overall Markan narrative consists of five episodes. It begins with the feeding of the 5000, followed by a lake crossing. There follows a controversy between Jesus and his opponents about cleanliness and the old traditions. Finally, there are the two stories of the Syrophoenician woman, in which there is a reference to bread, and the healing of a deaf mute. This structure is then immediately paralleled in the subsequent literary block. This time 4000 are fed; there is a brief lake crossing, a controversy (the demand for a sign), a reference to loaves of bread, and a healing, this time of a blind man.[48]

For the sake of convenience we shall discuss the stories of the Syrophoenician woman and the deaf-mute separately. However, in Mark's mind they belong together, for he places them clearly and explicitly in a geographical setting which is Gentile territory.[49] The pattern of the story is similar to that which we will meet in the later episode of the cure of the centurion's son. Theologically, it is particularly significant for the Evangelist that the miracles occur on behalf of Gentiles. Mark is keen to illustrate how Jesus sets about breaking down the traditional barrier which separates Jew and Gentile.[50]

## The Setting
The last place explicitly referred to was Gennesaret, where Jesus and the disciples moored the boat after crossing the lake, and the villages and towns in the vicinity. This crossing took place after Jesus provided food for the crowd of 5000, an episode in which there is a strong emphasis on the Jewishness of the situation. Some Pharisees and Jerusalem scribes then engage Jesus in debate about the fact that the disciples do not observe the traditions concerning ritual washing. Jesus explains to the crowds that people are defiled not by what enters them, but by what comes out from within. Later he gives further explanations to his disciples, encouraging them to break free of this closed system. At this point the Evangelist indicates a change of scene, for from there Jesus moved away from Israel and *set out and went away to the region of Tyre*.[51] This is clearly Gentile territory, though there were many Jewish inhabitants there too. Tyre was an ancient Phoenician cosmopolitan city, mentioned in the Old Testament.[52] It still flourished as an important urban seaport, and its territory bordered on Upper Galilee; the inhabitants were not friendly towards the Jewish minority; they were an economically dominant and oppressive group.[53]

No explanation for the journey is provided, and it is not stated that the disciples accompanied him.[54] Possibly Jesus wanted to leave Galilee because it was under Herod's jurisdiction, or maybe this was just another way of getting away from the Jewish crowd.[55]

Jesus enters a house, a typically Markan feature. Clearly he is seeking some privacy. However, his presence cannot go unnoticed; anonymity is difficult to come by. A local woman gets to hear that he is in the vicinity and searches him out.[56] She enters the house and falls respectfully at his feet as a suppliant.[57] The verb used (*prospiptein*) means to place oneself at the mercy of another. Her reason for approaching Jesus is her concern for her little daughter, who has an unclean spirit. She trusts his ability to remedy her condition. The narrator points out unequivocally the theologically crucial fact that, being of Syrophoenician origin, the woman is a Gentile; her culture is Greek. As the first Gentile to make such a request, she introduces an air of suspense into the narrative's unfolding.[58]

## The Dialogue
The woman begs Jesus to cast the demon out of her daughter. Her pleading is an expression of her motherly concern for her daughter and an admission of the hopelessness of her situation. It is also an expression of her trust in his power and his willingness to help her. The response of Jesus is surprising and something of a puzzle:

> Let the children be fed first; for it is not fair to take the children's bread and throw it to the dogs.

Jesus' words seem rather harsh, shocking, insulting even, a put-down, and at odds with what would be expected after the previous controversy, and with Jesus' normal mode of acting.[59] His reply clearly suggests that he understands his mission as confined to the people of Israel, who saw themselves as God's privileged sons and daughters. His vocation is not to spread the Gospel to the Gentile world, but to tell the Jewish people that their long-awaited deliverance is at hand. The use of the word *first* suggests that when this is accomplished it would be time for the Gentiles. For the moment it is important that he doesn't lose his primary focus.[60] Despite the difficulties which have arisen in his ministry, Israel remains the privileged recipient of his gift of bread. However, Israel has in fact been fed in the lakeside banquet, and the amount of leftovers was considerable.[61]

Dogs were considered to be unclean scavengers, and were usually regarded negatively by the Jews. The term *dog* was a common traditional Jewish term of contempt for Gentiles. Some view the exchange as teasing banter,[62] or consider the diminutive form, puppy or little housedog, as humorous or as softening the harshness. Some understand the saying as parabolic: Jesus draws a picture of a home scene in which children take priority over the dogs.[63] Others understand the words of Jesus as a challenge to the woman to justify her request. The gospel of the Kingdom has not been proclaimed to the Gentiles. Jesus' miracles are closely linked with his preaching, since they are a sign and an expression of the breaking in of the Kingdom, and can occur only where there is faith. The woman's request seems to fall outside this context; she is perhaps taking advantage of the opportunity provided by the presence of the miracle-worker.[64] The woman is undeterred, and replies:

*Sir, even the dogs under the table eat the children's scraps.*

*Sir* is the normal polite form of Gentile address; it is not used elsewhere in Mark in this way. Probably Mark sees a deeper significance in it here, as it also means *Lord*, and expresses insight into his identity.[65] The woman seems to take no offence; she accepts what Jesus says; she accepts the analogy and its implications, acknowledging that Israel has priority in God's saving plan. She, like the household pets of her culture,[66] is content to feed on the crumbs from the Jewish table. She recognises that she has no rights, no claims to assistance; that she cannot merit a cure, is utterly empty-handed, totally dependent; but she still trusts that he will do what she asks. It is not only a question of persistence fuelled by her need and her deep concern for her daughter. Nor is it simply that her womanly intuition senses from the look in his eyes or the tone of his voice that he is a man of immense compassion. Her reply, adapting Jesus' metaphor to her own need, also indicates some glimmering of understanding concerning the Kingdom, the recognition *that the children are already being fed, and that, in spite of their recognised priority, there is hope for her now.*[67] She is convinced that it is from Jesus, the Jewish Messiah, that salvation is to be obtained.[68] She moves into a context of faith, perceiving the presence of God's power in Jesus. This he recognises, (doubtless along with the exquisite quality of her repartee!) and grants her request, assuring her that when she reaches home again, she will find her daughter restored. The miracle is worked at a distance, which is unusual in the case of an exorcism:

*For saying that, you may go; the demon has left your daughter.*

Though the woman's faith is not explicitly mentioned, the cure is linked to the same kind of faith response which is characteristic of the other miracles described earlier in the narrative.[69] The healing power of the Kingdom is available for Gentiles too.[70]

## The Sequel

The woman takes Jesus at his word, and returns to her home, where she finds her daughter lying on her bed, liberated from her affliction. She is a woman of remarkable faith. The concluding expression of wonder, which is a typical element in stories of healing, is not found here, perhaps because she went home alone.[71] In the overall context, her faith stands in stark contrast to the legalism and self-righteousness of the Jewish religious leaders, which is illustrated in the section of the gospel leading up to this incident, a section in which Jesus has challenged and upturned some fundamental Jewish tenets.

In this story Jesus has reached out to a Gentile. But it would be inexact to speak of a programmatic mission of Jesus to the Gentiles as a body. This incident, along with a few others, are a departure from Jesus' plans, intentions and normal practice. They are exceptions and special cases, and something of an anomaly. They are, however, intimations of what will come later.[72] In keeping with Jewish tradition, Jesus thought of God as choosing Israel. Like the prophets before him, he understood his mission as directed to Israel. It would be for the renewed and obedient Israel to undertake the mission to the nations.[73] This is the wider perspective envisaged for the Servant by Isaiah.[74] The distinction between Jew and Gentile and their relative places in the order of salvation remain in force. There is, however, a refreshing freedom and flexibility about Jesus. Rigidity is foreign to his make-up. The woman's response to the presence of Jesus foreshadows the future offer of salvation to the Gentiles, and their coming to faith in him.[75] Perhaps the fact that the cure has been performed at a distance is to be understood as symbolic of the salvation which comes to the Gentiles, hitherto far away.[76]

## Reflection

One significant factor of the story is the crossing of boundaries. Jesus crosses into fairly hostile Gentile territory. The woman crosses the religious and gender barriers, and the social barrier between itinerant preacher and landed property owner.

She crosses the divide between stereotypical male dominance and female submissiveness, between woman and unknown male in a private place. *Jesus' harsh reply would be expected in a first-century androcentric culture; what would be shocking are the courageous reply of the woman and Jesus' ultimate capitulation.* (John R Donahue & Daniel J Harrington)[77]

This woman comes to Jesus as a mother pleading for the healing of her daughter. Like Jairus earlier, she is desperate. Her maternal love and concern are obvious, leading her to disregard accepted boundaries. Her persistence is striking, as are her perception and her quick-witted repartee. Fundamentally, as Jesus finally acknowledges, she is a woman of remarkable faith.

Jesus has gone to Tyre seeking privacy. He is located, and his plan is thwarted. Initially, he seems reluctant to accede to the woman's importunate request. In the end he changes his mind. His fundamental openness and flexibility win through. He is uncomfortable with rigidity and fixed boundaries.

The story gives us a glimpse into the struggle which took place in the Early Church in coming to terms with the inclusion of Gentiles; firstly in the Christian community, and then at the Eucharistic table. This was a struggle with which Mark and his community were not unfamiliar. The woman articulates the Gentile perspective in this divisive area.[78] Mark's readers would see this episode as the tip of the iceberg, and as the initial penetration of Jewish exclusivism, the crumbling of the barrier of separation.[79] Barriers are transcended, and must continue to be transcended. *If Jesus yielded to the cry of faith while the division between Jew and Gentile still stood, how much more should the Christian Church go out to the Gentiles.*[80]

In our Church today there are perhaps boundaries of a different kind which need to be transcended. The initial reluctance of Jesus was later reversed. This should be a cause for optimism, an invitation to persistence, and a challenge to rigidity. His example directs us towards openness, and the overcoming of prejudice and preconceptions.

## The Deaf-Mute

The episode of the Syrophoenician woman is followed immediately by this story of the healing of a man who is a deaf mute.[81] Although there is mention elsewhere of Jesus curing the dumb, there is no other narrative of such activity in the Gospels:[82]

> Then he returned from the region of Tyre, and went by way of Sidon towards the Sea of Galilee, in the region of the Decapolis. They brought to him a deaf man who had an impediment in his speech; and they begged him to lay his hand on him. He took him aside in private, away from the crowd, and put his fingers into his ears, and he spat and touched his tongue.

Then looking up to heaven, he sighed and said to him, *Ephphatha*, that is, *Be opened*. And immediately his ears were opened, his tongue was released, and he spoke plainly. Then Jesus ordered them to tell no one; but the more he ordered them, the more zealously they proclaimed it. They were astounded beyond measure, saying, *He has done everything well; he even makes the deaf to hear and the mute to speak.* (7:31-37)

This narrative is a perfect example of the miracle story form: the problem is identified; a request is made; Jesus responds by word, touch, gesture; the cure takes place; the miracle is greeted by wonder. The story is very similar to a later incident in which Jesus cures a blind man.[83]

## The Setting

After his sojourn in the region of Tyre, the length of which remains unknown, Jesus heads back towards the Sea of Galilee via Sidon to the north, at least a day's journey, and moving eastwards and then south, he eventually reaches the area of Decapolis. This is the territory in which he earlier encountered the Gerasene demoniac. The itinerary is rather circuitous and confusing, giving the impression that Mark's knowledge of the geography of Palestine was rather vague and imprecise.[84] On the other hand, Jesus may have deliberately chosen such a route, about a hundred miles, in order to be alone and have space for reflection and prayer.[85] Anyway, Mark's principal interest is not geographical but theological. His agenda is to continue the theme of Jesus' interaction with the Gentile world.[86] The area on the eastern shore of the lake, as we have seen, was predominantly Gentile. That is the context for what is about to take place; even if Mark does not explicitly state that the man concerned was a Gentile, that is the implication.

On his last visit to the region, the people asked Jesus to leave. Jesus commissioned Legion, the man whom he had restored to wholeness, to proclaim there the mercy which God had shown him. Legion, in fact, actually told the inhabitants how much Jesus had done for him!

Now, on this later occasion, some of the local folk take the initiative and approach Jesus, bringing to him a man in need of healing, a deaf mute.[87] The Greek word used here to describe the man's speech impediment is unusual. It means to be able to make noises, but not speak clearly and coherently. In the New Testament it is found only here, and in the Old Testament in the passage of Isaiah which reads:

> Then the eyes of the blind shall be opened, and the ears of the deaf unstopped; then the lame shall leap like a deer, and tongue of the speechless sing for joy. (Isa 35:5-6)

Mark probably had this text in mind, indicating as it does the Jewish hope of the Messiah's healing activity. Deafness does create problems with speech. Communication for the man is extremely difficult, and this leads to isolation and loneliness, especially in a culture where the majority of people were unable to read. The people bringing the man to Jesus, who are not identified, ask him to lay his hand on him. In this way they request a healing for their friend, and they express their faith in Jesus' ability and willingness.[88]

## The Response of Jesus

Jesus takes the man aside away from the crowd, walking along at his side; he does not intend to make a public show of power.[89] He then puts his fingers into the man's ears, spits and touches his tongue with the spittle.[90] This procedure is unusual for Jesus, though not uncommon in Greek and Hebrew descriptions of healing techniques; saliva was thought to have healing properties. But this is the only way in which Jesus can communicate with the man, establishing a relationship, and possibly eliciting his faith. His actions indicate that he is going to open his ears and enable him to speak properly.

Jesus then looks up to heaven, the source of his power. He sighs aloud, probably in prayer,[91] but also in deep feeling for the sufferer whose state is contrary to God's will and an indication of Satan's power. Then he speaks to the man, saying *Ephphatha,* which the narrator translates as *Be opened.*[92] The word of Jesus has immediate effect. The man's ears are opened and his tongue released; he is able to speak plainly and intelligibly. Some commentators suggest that the fetter-shattering word and the subsequent comment that *his tongue was released* indicate an exorcism, and suggest that Mark may have considered the man as having been bound by Satan and now reclaimed by Jesus as part of the ongoing conquest of evil and the presence of the Kingdom.[93]

## The Conclusion

Jesus then addresses the onlookers in a strongly worded injunction to tell no one about what has taken place. He wishes to avoid admiration and excitement; he does not do the spectacular. Paradoxically, too much talk about him could be dangerous. Naturally, they find this an impossible imposition, and proclaim the cure with enthusiasm. Their astonishment is unbounded, as, not unlike a Greek chorus, they comment, *He has done everything well; he even makes the deaf to hear and the mute to speak.* This is the first public recognition of Jesus, and it occurs in a Gentile context. The words are an allusion to the Isaian passage to which I referred earlier, a passage which was understood messianically in pre-Christian times.[94] Those who here recognise the possibility that Jesus is the fulfilment of this prophecy, and that the age of messianic salvation has arrived, are Gentiles. Some commentators add that this salvation has arrived also for the Gentiles, who, once deaf and mute in regard to God, can now hear his word and speak in His praise, thus becoming heirs to the eschatological promise to Israel.[95] The phrase *he has done all things well* may also be an echo of the Genesis creation story; Jesus is involved in a new creation.[96]

The officially recognised disciples of Jesus have not featured in the story of the Syrophoenician woman nor in this story. When last involved in the narrative they were criticised as being *without understanding.*[97] There is a contrast between them and the faith of the woman and the Gentiles of Decapolis. The Gentile theme will continue in the next episode of Mark's narrative, the second multiplication of loaves and fishes.

## The Secret

The injunction to secrecy in this story is part of a pattern in Mark's Gospel. Scholars refer to this motif as the *messianic secret.* Historically, Jesus may well have discouraged his followers and the crowds from interpreting his miracles as an indication of his possible messianic status. This would be to misunderstand who he was. He also felt uncomfortable with many of the current messianic expectations. His view of his mission failed to coincide with popular hopes. Such assertions were also politically dangerous. This could be the origin of the literary and theological feature which Mark develops, especially in the first half of the Gospel. After Caesarea Philippi (8:27-30), commands to secrecy finish. For Mark, the true nature of Jesus' Messiahship, revealed after Peter's profession at Caesarea Philippi, will not be fully understood until Jesus' death and resurrection. The commands to silence direct the reader to the conclusion of the story.[98]

## Reflection

Here we have another incident in which not only the power of Jesus but also his kindness and compassion for the suffering are shown, even if the recipients are not Jewish. There is a sensitivity about him, as he leads the man away from the crowds into privacy, and in his manner of indicating to him what is about to happen. And the man is a Gentile. There is hope for the Gentiles too. The man himself seems to just go along with what Jesus does. It is the man's friends, who, like the friends of the paralytic in the earlier story, bring him to Jesus, who show great concern for him. They also manifest trust in the power and the compassion of Jesus, even towards non-Jews like themselves.

I suppose that for us the issue may have to do with our deafness. For some it may indeed be physical deafness, which can make communication difficult, and cause us to feel isolated. My experience of living in community has given me some insight into the suffering which deafness entails, and the problems it can cause. But I think all of us can at times be deaf. In families and communities we have probably met individuals who don't hear what we want them to hear, yet who manage to hear what we would prefer them not to hear! Selective hearing, we call it. But we are all a bit like that. We don't always listen to the voice of God, God's word; it can sometimes pass us by. The challenging, demanding phrases of scripture we regularly overlook. We can be deaf to the needs of others in our immediate vicinity, and to pleas from far away. If we don't hear their cries, their problems, we feel we don't need to respond. Sometimes it may be a subconscious survival technique.

The ability to hear is a wonderful gift of God, as we hear birdsong, music, the voice of friends, the uncorking of a bottle of wine, the sound of silence. Linked with hearing is the art of listening, listening with non-judgemental empathy, creating a space of genuine hospitality, offering acceptance and freedom. Christian listening is an art; it demands an inner poverty, an ability to empty oneself, so as to be open to the other. We need to be able to listen to what is said and what remains unspoken, and to listen to the feelings beneath the words and to the silence. We need to have learned how to respond sensitively and appropriately. The gift of hearing is therefore a responsibility too.

At times we can be dumb, as well. We can fail to say the encouraging and helpful word, or express our thanks and appreciation. We can neglect to affirm and be positive. We can hesitate to volunteer and become involved. We can also be slow to share our views, or to speak our truth when it is necessary. At times we opt to be dumb, rather than proclaim our Christian values in certain situations, and make it obvious that we are disciples of Jesus. We don't always proclaim clearly our love and praise of our God. So we too stand in need of Jesus' compassionate outreach and healing touch.

# The Centurion

A story about Jesus healing a centurion's servant occurs early in the Gospels of Matthew and Luke. In Luke's version the centurion sends some of the village elders to intercede with Jesus, whereas in Matthew it is the centurion himself who personally approaches him.[99] It is this encounter which we shall consider in this section of the chapter. The episode is found in the block of material which is situated between the Sermon on the Mount and the missionary discourse. Here Matthew picks up the Markan narrative, but thoroughly reorders and streamlines his material, and inserts two episodes not included there. After his ministry of the word in the great sermon, Jesus, the messianic teacher, now exercises a messianic ministry of healing. In both words and works, Jesus shows great authority.[100] There are ten miracles (or more, if the general healings recorded after the cure of Simon's mother-in-law are taken into consideration), but nine stories, grouped in threes.[101] The encounter between Jesus and the centurion is located between the cure of the leper and the healing of Simon's mother-in-law;[102] all three individuals were disadvantaged and on the margins of the Jewish community:

> When he entered Capernaum, a centurion came to him, appealing to him and saying, *Lord, my servant is lying at home paralysed, in terrible distress.* And he said to him, *I will come and cure him.* The centurion answered, *Lord, I am not worthy to have you come under my roof; but only speak the word, and my servant will be healed. For I also am a man under authority, with soldiers under me; and I say to one, "Go", and he goes, and to another, "Come", and he comes, and to my slave, "Do this", and the slave does it.* When Jesus heard him, he was amazed and said to those who followed him, *Truly I tell you, in no one in Israel have I found such faith. I tell you, many will come from east and west and will eat with Abraham and Isaac and Jacob in the kingdom of heaven, while the heirs of the kingdom will be thrown into the outer darkness, where there will be weeping and gnashing of teeth.* And to the centurion Jesus said, *Go; let it be done for you according to your faith.* And the servant was healed in that hour. (8:5-13)

## The Man's Approach

The setting is the frontier town of Capernaum, which Jesus seems to have made his base. On arriving back there, Jesus is met by a centurion from the military garrison manned by soldiers in the service of Herod Antipas.[103]

He probably hails from Syria, and is a Gentile. Aware of Jesus' reputation, and addressing Jesus as *Lord,* he outlines his problem and concern, explaining that his servant is lying paralysed at home in considerable distress.[104] The response of Jesus to this approach can be taken in two ways. Usually, it is understood as a statement, *I will come and cure him.* Jesus responds immediately, even expressing his willingness to come to the centurion's house in order to bring the servant healing and relief. He is prepared to have dealings with a Gentile and even enter his home, thus incurring ritual uncleanness and some local displeasure.[105] The centurion is clearly dismayed by this unexpected offer which exceeds his original request, and, again addressing Jesus as *Lord,* acknowledges his unworthiness to welcome him under his roof. He recognises the authority of Jesus, going on to voice his conviction that a word of Jesus without making the short journey will be sufficient to effect a cure. For, in his position and with his army experience, he knows what authority is all about, and is well acquainted with the power of a word of command. If he can command with a word, all the more so can Jesus.[106]

An alternative view understands Jesus' words as a question, constituting an initial hesitation or rebuff, as in the episode of the Syrophoenician woman. In effect Jesus, surprised at the request, is asking *Am I supposed to come and heal him*? – This is in a Gentile house, thus breaking the rules on purity. Scholars who are of this mind maintain that such reluctance is consistent with Jesus' later response to the woman. The centurion is aware of his unworthiness; he is not expecting a personal visit to his house; he is conversant with Jewish rules about ritual cleanness; he respects Jesus' authority, which renders such a visit unnecessary; he offers Jesus an alternative course of action.[107]

## The Response of Jesus

On hearing this reply, Jesus is amazed, and observes to those with him that he has not found insight and faith of such quality among the people of Israel. This is the only occasion when Matthew uses this term of Jesus.[108] The man has shown some awareness of Jesus' closeness to God. He has also sensed that as a Gentile he is not entirely excluded from Jesus' care. Jesus then authoritatively makes a telling statement.[109] Looking ahead into the future, and echoing the vision of the prophets of old, he claims that there will be many Gentiles, people from east and west, who will come to share the messianic banquet of the heavenly kingdom with the great patriarchs Abraham, Isaac and Jacob, whilst their true natural heirs will be cast out.[110] The centurion, like the earlier magi, is the forerunner of these.

In the opening verse of his Gospel, Matthew has presented Jesus as Son of Abraham; Abraham is the father of the Jewish people, but also the one in whom all the nations of the world would be blessed. In 4:15, as Jesus inaugurates his ministry, making his home by the lake in Capernaum, Isaiah's reference to *Galilee of the nations* is recalled. Later in the narrative Matthew quotes Isaiah concerning the Spirit-filled Servant who will *proclaim justice to the Gentiles...And in his name the Gentiles will hope.*[111] In his final discourse Jesus predicts the preaching of the gospel to all the nations.[112] Finally, the focusing of his ministry on the Jews, *the lost sheep of the house of Israel,* as expressed in his dialogue with the Syrophoenician woman, is superseded after his death and resurrection.[113] Back in Galilee the Risen Lord gathers his disciples, scattered by the striking down of the sheep. He makes to them his final statement, *All authority in heaven and on earth has been given to me. Go therefore and make disciples of all nations...*[114] With the dawning of the new age, the blessings of the Kingdom are made available to all.

Jesus' words concerning the future also constitute a severe warning or threat for his Jewish hearers, who are in danger of missing the opportunity to embrace their destiny. A warning is also sounded for Matthew's Church in a different and later context; the community must not be complacent; they must continue vigorously to believe.[115] The story concludes with Jesus telling the centurion to return home with the assurance that in accordance with his faith, his request will be granted. In fact, the servant is healed, and healed at a distance. The power or authority of Jesus' word is evident; but the emphasis in the story is probably more on the centurion's faith than on the miracle.[116] *Although Jesus has come only for the lost sheep of Israel, the restriction is overcome when he meets genuine belief. Faith conquers the separation between Jew and Gentile.* (W D Davies & Dale Allison)[117] Perhaps the healing at a distance is intended to reflect the restriction of Jesus' ministry to Israel; maybe it is a spatial metaphor symbolising the historical fact that Gentile participation in the blessings of the Gospel is separated in time from the earthly ministry of Jesus.[118]

## Reflection

Following the traditional interpretation of the story, Jesus is clearly a man of authority. He is probably surprised at being approached for a cure by a Gentile. Unusual as this is, and contrary to the normal thrust of his ministry, he responds with great openness, even volunteering to go to the centurion's home in order to cure his servant. Clearly, such a visit was not part of the petitioner's scenario.

Jesus is prepared to incur ritual defilement in order to effect the healing, and is also open to incur criticism and hostility from the townsfolk for his trouble. There is a remarkable freedom and openness about him. He publically expresses his amazement at the man's extraordinary faith. Adopting the other interpretation of the story, Jesus manifests his flexibility, his openness to change his attitude when faced with strong faith. He generously acknowledges in public the faith he has encountered.

It is the centurion's faith which stands out from the narrative. He clearly believes in the power of Jesus to heal his servant; he trusts that his Gentile background will not prove an insurmountable obstacle. He is aware of his poverty and emptiness. He shows humility in readily acknowledging his unworthiness to have Jesus under his roof. For him a word from Jesus is enough.

In commenting so favourably on the Gentile's faith, Jesus puts him forward as an exemplar. This is the case not only for the Jews of the town in which the encounter took place; it is true for us today. There is something engaging and attractive about the man's humble awareness that he has no rights, and cannot demand a cure for his servant. Such poverty of spirit must be a characteristic which we share when we approach Jesus in our need. The man's words have been included in the new form of our Eucharistic celebration. They sum up the dispositions which are appropriate for our welcoming of the Lord into our hearts.

## Concluding Thoughts

The context for each of these episodes is Gentile territory. Jesus is crossing boundaries, which entails the incurring of defilement. Even if his mission is not directed to Gentiles, he is not rigidly exclusive; when approached by people in need, he reaches out to them. He courageously faces up to the deeply disturbed individual among the tombs. When Legion seeks to stay with him, he graciously finds a way of enabling him to serve and to share mission.

Having travelled to Tyre seeking peace and privacy, he is interrupted by the importunate woman who seeks healing for her daughter. His initial reluctance melts away in the face of her persevering faith. Jesus can be flexible and change his mind. When some people bring to him a deaf-mute, and ask him to touch him, Jesus immediately manifests his openness, even though those concerned are Gentiles. He shows sensitivity and gentle care in the responsive way in which he treats the man. Approached by a Gentile centurion in Capernaum, he does not back off; rather, he immediately shows his willingness to go to his house in order to attend to the servant. He is not slow to acknowledge publicly the faith of the man.

It is interesting that the Gentile context provides stirring examples of faith. Apart from Legion, the other *Little People* come to Jesus seeking healing for another: a possessed daughter, a deaf and dumb friend, a seriously ill son or servant. As Gentiles they are at a disadvantage. The woman and the centurion acknowledge their awareness of this and their inner poverty. All of them believe that Jesus can bring healing and wholeness, and they take the risk of trusting that he will respond favourably to their pleading. They are not disappointed. The response of Legion to his liberation from evil is quite beautiful, as he wishes to *be with* him as a disciple. As a Gentile, this would be premature, so he accepts the alternative which Jesus offers, and goes off to share with his people the Good News which he has experienced.

Many years ago, when still a teenager, I received a copy of Ronald Knox's new translation of the New Testament. It was something of a revelation to me. I still recall being deeply impressed by my first-ever reading of the letter to the Ephesians. That sense of wonder lingers still. The author[119] brings out so forcefully the transformation which has taken place. We, Gentiles, were *without Christ, strangers to the covenants of promise, having no hope and without God in the world.* The God *who is rich in mercy* changed all that through His love and immeasurable kindness by a free gift in Christ Jesus. The gulf and hostility between Jew and Gentile has been removed through the death of Jesus, so that now, through him, *both of us have access to the Father.* So we are no longer *strangers and aliens,* we are *citizens with the saints and members of the household of God.* Jesus' words during the encounter with the centurion have indeed come true.

I don't normally consider myself a Gentile! I've grown accustomed to being a Christian. But I know I run the risk of taking it for granted and losing sight of the wonder of it all. These episodes are powerful reminders of the incredible richness and surprise of God's wide-ranging saving love.

# Chapter Four – The Women

## Gospel Women

A striking characteristic of the story of Jesus is the number of women who feature amongst the *Little People*. After a section of his Gospel in which he has described the raising of the widow's son, and the forgiveness extended to the sinful woman, Luke writes:

> Soon afterwards he went on through cities and villages, proclaiming and bringing the good news of the kingdom of God. The twelve were with him, as well as some women who had been cured of evil spirits and infirmities: Mary, called Magdalene, from whom seven demons had gone out, and Joanna, the wife of Herod's steward Chuza, and Susanna, and many others, who provided for them out of their own resources. (Luke 8:1-3)

The society in which Jesus grew up and in which he carried out his mission was extremely patriarchal. It really was a man's world. Women were considered inferior to men; their role was to serve men and bear children, preferably males. They had no autonomy, and were considered a man's property. While they had influence within the family, and a major role in the home, they had no role in public life, no place in wider society. Stereotypically, they were sources of temptation, sources also of ritual defilement. In the Temple and possibly the synagogue they were separated from men; they were not required to recite the *Shema* prayer or attend pilgrimages.[1] They formed a segment of the marginalised in that society. In the small towns of Galilee customs were less strict; women left their houses more freely, worked in the fields with men and boys, and did not always cover their faces with a veil.[2]

The above Lukan extract is therefore very significant. It is clear that Jesus has views and an approach which are widely different from the normal understanding of a woman's place and role in contemporary society. There is an originality, a radicality and freedom about him. He welcomes them, talks with them, brings them healing, accepts them amongst his followers. Women accompany him and the inner group of the Twelve as they pass through the Galilean villages and towns, proclaiming the Reign of God, and making that reign present. In fact, the women's presence with Jesus is a sign of that new world which is breaking in. Religious teachers at that time did not welcome female disciples.[3] Grateful for what Jesus has done for them, these women provide for him and his band out of their own resources, which suggests that some of them are people of means.[4] Perhaps they also at times offered hospitality in their homes.[5] Some of them were married like Joanna, some may have been widows or repudiated wives, and some were single women like Magdalen.[6] Later in the story, they will play a significant role in connection with Jesus' death and resurrection, and their presence will spill over into the beginnings of the Church, as along with the mother and brothers of Jesus and the Twelve, they await the coming of the Spirit.[7]

In the course of Mark's narrative we meet Simon's mother-in-law, the woman afflicted with a haemorrhage, the daughter of Jairus, the Syrophoenician woman, the widow at the Temple, the woman who anoints Jesus, and the group of women present on Calvary and at the tomb. In addition, Luke mentions the woman who is forgiven, the widow of Nain, the crippled woman, and the two sisters, Martha and Mary; in the passion narrative there are also the sympathetic women of Jerusalem. Women have a role in some of Jesus' parables in Luke: the widow searching for her lost coin, the importunate widow, and the woman mixing dough. John includes the story of the Samaritan woman, the woman taken in adultery, and the two sisters of Lazarus. Mary of Magdala plays a significant part in John's presentation of the resurrection of Jesus. In all the Gospels there is mention of the mother of Jesus.

The stories of some of these women are found in the chapters on forgiveness, Gentiles, and the Passion and Resurrection. In this chapter I propose to reflect on the Markan stories of Simon's mother-in-law, the daughter of Jairus and the woman with the haemorrhage, the poor widow in the Temple, and the woman who anoints Jesus. I shall then include the two Lukan stories of the widow of Nain, Martha and Mary, and John's Samaritan woman.

## Simon Peter's Mother-in-Law

The first woman to play a part in Mark's Gospel is the mother-in-law of Simon Peter. The episode is brief, but quite detailed.[8] It occurs immediately after Jesus has made a striking impression in the local synagogue by his authoritative teaching style and powerful exorcising. Having just brought healing and release to a man, he now does the same for a woman.[9] Later that evening he cures many afflicted people who are brought to him:

As soon as they left the synagogue, they entered the house of Simon and Andrew, with James and John. Now Simon's mother-in-law was in bed with a fever, and they told him about her at once. He came and took her by the hand and lifted her up. Then the fever left her, and she began to serve them. (1:29-31)

## The Situation

On leaving the synagogue, Jesus and the four disciples, whom he has previously called by the lakeside, go to the house of Simon and Andrew, just a few yards away.[10] This was to become the home base of Jesus.[11] It is still the Sabbath. Some commentators observe that the story has the feel of eye-witness testimony. The names of James and John, included here, are omitted in the parallel passage of the other Synoptic Gospels.

Simon's mother-in-law is sick with fever. The symptom is taken for the illness, which could be malaria, which was endemic at the time.[12] It is clearly a situation of need. The pattern of the story is that of the classical healing narrative: problem, request, healing touch or word, miracle, acclamation by onlookers or demonstration that a cure has taken place. This is the only Gospel reference to Peter being a married man. In writing to the Corinthians, Paul refers to his having a wife, who accompanied him on missionary journeys.[13] The disciples tell Jesus about Simon's mother-in-law; it isn't clear whether this was an implied request for a cure, or simply an explanation of the difficulty of providing hospitality.[14] Given that Jesus has so far not performed any healing miracles, the latter seems more likely.

## The Response of Jesus

In responding immediately, Jesus doesn't speak a word but he *took hold of her hand, and raised her to her feet.* Such physical contact is characteristic of Jesus' healing actions; he is a Spirit-endowed person whose presence confers wholeness.[15] Effortlessly and without any special technique or show, Jesus brings healing. The phrase *the fever left her* suggests to some scholars that the incident is to be understood implicitly as an exorcism, as in the Lukan parallel: the demon of fever left her. According to the popular mentality of the time, physical illness is no less a mark of the rule of Satan than overt demonic possession.[16] Viewed from a different perspective, the incident is a prophetic sign, proclaiming and making present the Reign of God.

The action of Jesus in taking the woman's hand would have been considered reprehensible in that culture. No respected religious leader would have done so. Since she was ill, there may also have been the possibility of incurring ritual impurity.[17] It is fascinating that so early in his ministry Jesus quietly makes clear his priorities, refusing to permit a cultural taboo to deter him from reaching out to someone in need.[18] This is the first instance of a challenging and radical approach to such issues which will be a characteristic feature of his ministry. The use of the verb *raise* is not without significance. It will recur in later healing narratives, like the raising of Jairus' daughter and the lifting up of the epileptic boy. It carries a symbolic element, and hints at resurrection.[19]

## The Response of the Woman

The response of Simon's mother-in-law, on being restored to wholeness and vitality, is to reach out immediately in hospitality and provide a meal for her guests. Even though it is still the Sabbath, she begins to serve them at table. *As Jesus put his power at her service, she promptly repays the compliment by putting her renewed self at the service of Jesus and his disciples.* (Denis McBride)[20] By allowing himself to be served by a woman, Jesus was again contravening convention.[21]

In the opening stages of his narrative Mark already introduces a key theme of his Gospel message, namely, discipleship understood in terms of service. This ideal she embodies intuitively. Later in the Gospel narrative, after Jesus has predicted his passion for the second time, the disciples on the journey argue amongst themselves as to which of them is the greatest. Jesus states, *Whoever wants to be first must be last of all and servant of all.* And he takes a child in his arms as an illustration.[22] Shortly afterwards, two of the disciples who now benefit from Simon's mother-in-law's cuisine will raise the issue again by seeking positions of power and superiority. This leads Jesus to emphasise that those seeking to be great in his eyes must put themselves at the service of others, for he himself came *not to be served but to serve.*[23] Simon's mother-in-law is the first of many women who, as we shall see later, respond to Jesus' kindness by placing themselves at his service. The Gospel narrative is, in fact, bracketed by references to this phenomenon.[24]

## Reflection

As we ponder this story we can rejoice at the transforming presence of the Kingdom. God's reign conquers evil, and brings healing and new life. It also entails a reordering of priorities, putting people, especially needy people, at the centre. For Jesus this includes a reassessment and reappraisal of the value and role of women. At times in his ministry this leads to a radical departure from the norm, the overturning of dearly held views, attitudes and practices. As the prophet of compassion, Jesus blazes a new trail.[25] The authority evinced in his teaching and exorcising is evident also in his freedom of attitude and style.

The woman in the story is a paradigm of discipleship, for service is at the heart of the following of Jesus. It is so because of the style of Jesus himself, his servant way of living his messianic sonship. The way of Jesus prophetically turns upside down the way in which as human beings we tend to think and operate. He introduces a new value system, an alternative world-view. Servanthood is a major characteristic of the kingdom.[26]

# The Jairus Sequence

## Context

After a section of his Gospel in which he assembles a number of Jesus' parables, emphasising Jesus' ministry of teaching and preaching, Mark moves on to highlight the power and authority of Jesus in action. He links together a series of Jesus' miracles or *mighty deeds*. Firstly, as Jesus and his disciples head across the lake, a violent storm breaks, and Jesus is called upon to restore calm. On reaching the other side he encounters a man who is experiencing an appalling case of demon possession, and Jesus performs a spectacular exorcism.[27] The inhabitants of the area ask Jesus to leave, so he crosses the lake again and returns to home territory. Here he raises to life the daughter of a synagogue leader named Jairus, and heals a woman suffering from a haemorrhage. These two episodes belong together,[28] for they are linked structurally by the Markan literary device of framing or sandwiching, whereby one story is used as an interlude within the other, allowing the first part to develop.[29] The delaying tactic heightens the tension of the drama. Both stories are concerned with the themes of faith and life. Each is to be understood and interpreted in the light of the other. *The flavour of the outer story adds zest to the inner one; the taste of the inner one is meant in turn to permeate the outer.* (Tom Wright)[30]

In both incidents women benefit from the kindness and power of Jesus, and are given life. The interwoven story is perhaps Mark's masterpiece in terms of narrative art:[31]

> When Jesus had crossed again in the boat to the other side, a great crowd gathered round him; and he was by the lake. Then one of the leaders of the synagogue named Jairus came and,

when he saw him, fell at his feet and begged him repeatedly, *My little daughter is at the point of death. Come and lay your hands on her, so that she may be made well, and live.* So he went with him.

And a large crowd followed him and pressed in on him. Now there was a woman who had been suffering from haemorrhages for twelve years. She had endured much under many physicians, and had spent all that she had; and she was no better, but rather grew worse. She had heard about Jesus, and came up behind him in the crowd and touched his cloak, for she said, *If I but touch his clothes, I will be made well.* Immediately her haemorrhage stopped; and she felt in her body that she was healed of her disease. Immediately aware that power had gone forth from him, Jesus turned about in the crowd and said, *Who touched my clothes?* And his disciples said to him, *You see the crowd pressing in on you; how can you say, "Who touched me?"* He looked all round to see who had done it. But the woman, knowing what had happened to her, came in fear and trembling, fell down before him, and told him the whole truth. He said to her, *Daughter, your faith has made you well; go in peace, and be healed of your disease.*

While he was still speaking, some people came from the leader's house to say, *Your daughter is dead. Why trouble the teacher any further?* But overhearing what they said, Jesus said to the leader of the synagogue, *Do not fear, only believe.* He allowed no one to follow him except Peter, James, and John, the brother of James. When they came to the house of the leader of the synagogue, he saw a commotion, people weeping and wailing loudly. When he had entered, he said to them, *Why do you make a commotion and weep? The child is not dead but sleeping.* And they laughed at him. Then he put them all outside, and took the child's father and mother and those who were with him, and went in where the child was. He took her by the hand and said to her, *Talitha cum,* which means, *Little girl, get up!* And immediately the girl got up and began to walk about (she was twelve years of age).

At this they were overcome with amazement. He strictly ordered them that no one should know this, and told them to give her something to eat. (5:21-43)

## Jairus approaches Jesus

Having departed at the people's insistence from the Decapolis, Jesus returns to the other side of the lake, the western shore, back in a Jewish setting.

He is confronted with a large crowd of people, who are more positively inclined. The president of the local synagogue approaches him; he is not a rabbi or scribe. The exact structure of synagogue governance varied from place to place, depending on the size of the village or town.[32] The official's role probably entailed presiding over the conduct of synagogue worship, arranging the services, assigning readers, appointing preachers, preserving order, and maintaining the building. Mark sees him as a high-standing member of the local Jewish establishment, and provides his name, Jairus.[33]

In a manner hardly appropriate for one of his standing, but which betrays the depth of his distress, he casts aside his dignity and throws himself at Jesus' feet, his desperate concern and faith wordlessly expressed in his bodily posture. All else has failed. He then puts his genuine belief in Jesus' healing power, authority and closeness to God into words, as he repeatedly pleads:

> My little daughter is at death's door. I beg you to come and lay
> your hands on her so that her life may be saved.

The wording is significant. The term for daughter is affectionate.[34] Jairus asks Jesus to lay hands on her. This was normal in contemporary descriptions of healing, and also a frequent feature of Jesus' own healing ministry. The text speaks of the child's being *saved* (rescued from the power of death) and *living*. This language can be interpreted at two levels, and a Christian reader would sense a deeper level of meaning: being saved and experiencing eternal life.[35] Without saying a word, Jesus accedes to his request, and sets off, accompanying Jairus to his home.

## The Cure of the Woman with the Haemorrhage

As they walk along, Jesus is approached by a woman who has been suffering from haemorrhages for twelve years, a sensitive private concern of uncontrolled or chronic menstrual bleeding. This is the only Gospel story dealing with gynaecological problems.[36] The contrast between the woman and Jairus is striking.[37] She seems to have done the rounds of the medical profession to no avail, and this has drained her financial resources. Perhaps originally she was a woman of some financial means, who is now becoming severely impoverished.[38] It is clear that her situation is quite hopeless and is even deteriorating; there is nowhere else to turn. Her distress is compounded by the fact that her ailment was considered to render her constantly ritually unclean, and liable to communicate this to anyone with whom she has contact. Thus she is an outcast from society, unable to play an active role in the community of Israel.[39] In contrast with Jairus, she is outside the chosen people of God, a rejected one.[40] Because of her condition she may have been divorced or dismissed by her husband.[41] Having become aware of Jesus' reputation,[42] she comes up through the crowd from behind, probably because of her ritual uncleanness rather than from shyness or modesty. Breaching the purity barrier with courage she approaches Jesus and touches his cloak, convinced that this would suffice for a cure. In doing so, given her condition and the blood taboo, she runs the risk of considerable disapproval, exposing a holy man to ritual uncleanness. It was unusual for a woman to plead her own cause. She obviously has faith in Jesus, faith of a kind, faith that he can make a difference, faith tinged perhaps with a little superstition. She believes that because he is a holy man, his healing power can freely flow at a mere touch, without him being aware of it. Such views were not uncommon at the time; clothing was considered an extension of personality. She is proved right and is cured, delivered from her torment, on the spot.[43]

She is not, however, allowed to melt back into the crowd. One of the aspects of this incident which appeals to me very strongly is the way in which Jesus moves from anonymity to personal encounter. Jesus is aware that someone has touched him, and that *power had gone out of him*. He can distinguish between healing touch and ordinary touch. He knows that God has acted through him.[44] Jesus openly asks who has touched him. His question is greeted rather disrespectfully and insensitively by the disciples, who are locked into common sense, and consider his question absurd, given the press of the crowd. Jesus ignores them and persists in his attempt to meet the woman personally, looking around at the crowd.

The woman is filled with awe and reverential fear because of what has happened to her. *Fear and trembling* means holy awe; she recognises that she has been touched by the power and presence of the Kingdom.[45] She comes forward, falls at his feet, and *told him the whole truth*. Jesus can now relate to her personally, and he speaks to her with great warmth and respect and affection:

> My daughter, your faith has restored you to health;
> go in peace and be free of your complaint.

His words confirm her cure and affirm what she has done. She is addressed as *daughter*, and brought back into the chosen people of God, and into the new family of the Kingdom.

A relationship is established. Her faith is acknowledged; it was sufficient to enable her to take the risk involved in reaching out to him. Her first coming to Jesus brought healing; her second coming the assurance of salvation.[46] Jesus' words deflect somewhat the magical tone of the story by stressing her faith as the source of healing.[47] The Greek word is again *save,* implying that along with the physical and social cure, her restoration to normal life, comes the offer, the gift of salvation. *Peace,* a standard biblical dismissal, is more than freedom from embarrassment and anxiety. It connotes the wholeness and completeness of life which derives from being drawn into relationship with the Lord. *Be free* is better translated as, *Remain healed, Continue to be well,* since for this woman a new life is beginning. The sensitive beauty of the story masks the offence which Jesus' contact with her would have caused others.

## The Raising of Jairus' Daughter

While Jesus is speaking with the woman, the focus switches to Jairus and his daughter. Having successfully pleaded with Jesus that he accompany him the short distance to his home, Jairus is suddenly confronted with a message that his daughter has in fact died, with the rider that there is no point in troubling the Master further. It is now too late for him to do anything. All hope has been lost. Common sense must prevail. Jesus overhears the news. The Greek verb can mean both overhear and ignore.[48] Jesus certainly overhears, but does not ignore what has been communicated, rather, he encourages Jairus to do so. For he urges and invites him, *Do not be afraid; keep on believing.* An even greater degree of faith than that shown previously is now demanded. Despite all the odds and the pressure, Jairus summons up the faith to respond. Along with the girl's parents, Jesus allows only Peter, James and John to accompany him, as will later be the case at the Transfiguration, on the Mount of Olives, and in Gethsemane.[49] The three seem to form an inner circle, and are associated with Jesus at important revelatory moments.[50]

On their reaching the house, Jesus observes the commotion, the un-restrained weeping of the people there, probably the official professional mourners along with members of the household.

There were well-established rituals for beginning the grieving process, which made it possible for family members to give vent to their feelings without restraint or embarrassment.[51] Jesus enters the house and asks what all the fuss is about, for:

The child is not dead but asleep.

Jesus is taking a well-known euphemism and twisting it. The difference between death and sleep is its permanence. Jesus is not using the euphemism as a pointer to eschatological hope and last day resurrection. Jesus, who hasn't yet seen the child, knows that he is about to raise her from the permanence of death immediately. So *death is declared mere sleep not because of a cagey medical diagnosis or a comforting euphemism or a general eschatological hope but because Jesus wills in this particular case to make death as impermanent as sleep by raising the girl to life.* (John P Meier)[52]

The onlookers, aware that the child is well and truly dead, burst into laughter. This is the only miracle story in the Gospels where Jesus is made the direct object of such scornful ridicule. He personally excludes the crowd to avoid a public spectacle. His forceful physical action (a *bouncer* style!) is also unique in the Gospels. Jesus then takes Jairus and his wife and his three disciples into the room in which the girl is lying. They are present as witnesses, not helpers.[53] Without a prayer or special technique, but with great tenderness, Jesus takes her by the hand, and calls her back to life, *Talitha kum!* which is translated as *Little girl, I tell you to arise. Talitha* has affectionate overtones, and indicates smallness and youth.[54] Aramaic words are used in only two miracle stories in Mark.[55] Aramaic was the original language of the tradition, and its retention shows their importance.[56]

The child arises at once and begins to walk around, her activity confirming what has happened. Jesus has raised her to life, and he restores her to her mother and father, later suggesting that she be given something to eat – a deeply human touch (perhaps her parents are frozen with astonishment), but also an indication that she is real, and not a ghost. The reader is informed of her age; she is twelve years old. The reaction of the parents is described in unusually graphic language,[57] indicating that they are utterly astounded, ecstatic, which is hardly surprising, given the exceptional nature of what has occurred! Jesus then gives them strict orders not to let anyone know about it. This seems rather odd in the circumstances, as neighbours and parents know that she was dead; it is an injunction impossible to fulfil.[58] Jesus' point is that the emphasis should not be on the wonderful, but on the power and authority of God, present in his word. Also, such actions, taken in conjunction with his proclamation of the Kingdom, would pose a threat both to Herod and the religious leadership.[59] It is to his death and resurrection, through which he responds to God's saving design, that the commands to silence point forward.[60]

## Additional Thoughts

The reader notes Jesus' use of the term *arise*, in addition to *save* and *live*. For early Christians *sleep* was a euphemism for death, but indicated a death from which the believer would be raised.[61] The child's restoration to life is a symbol of Christian resurrection.[62] For those who have faith, Jesus can transform death into life and salvation. Salvation and faith are major themes in both stories.[63] The terms *made well* and *save* are familiar to the vocabulary of the Christian reader. Jairus and the woman show amazing faith in the midst of unbelief and common sense.

I mentioned earlier that the stories of the raising of Jairus' daughter and the cure of the woman with the haemorrhage are linked or paired. Besides the strong faith theme, one element which is common is the detail that the child is twelve years old, and the woman's affliction has been troubling her for twelve years, debarring her medically and socially from childbearing.[64] Whilst some believe this is coincidental,[65] others do not, *The girl of twelve years of age – now marriageable – gets up and walks. She rises to womanhood. The young woman, who now begins to pour forth her life in menstruation, and the older woman who experiences menstruation as a pathological condition, are both restored. They are **given** new life.* (Francis J Moloney)[66] The older woman was probably prevented by her medical condition and social state from the possibility of having a child.[67] Now both are rescued from death and rendered capable of birthing new life. They can *go and live in Shalom, in the well-being and happiness of God's reigning presence, which has touched their lives in Jesus of Nazareth.* (Elisabeth S Fiorenza)[68]

One element of Jesus' compassion is his reaching out to touch, an element which would have shocked the religious elite. He touches the physically and religiously unclean leper. He takes the hand of Simon's mother-in-law, as we have seen; later he allows himself to be anointed by another woman. He is touched by the woman with vaginal bleeding; in fact, the word *touch* occurs three times in the episode, and is clearly a key concept.[69]

He takes the hand of Jairus' daughter and raises her from her bed; she is dead (and so unclean), and is also of marriageable age, and so the gesture could be understood as ambiguous. It was unheard of for a respected rabbi to take a woman's hand or touch her or be touched by her, especially in public, and the gesture was open to misinterpretation. Jesus shows remarkable freedom, as he breaks through cultural, social and religious barriers and ritual taboos to be close to those in need and bring them wholeness and life. In both miracles Jesus is in contact with the unclean; his touch brings healing, wholeness and life.[70]

## Reflection

In the last chapter we encountered a mother who came to Jesus seeking healing for her daughter, a centurion for his servant, a group of people for their friend. In the passage we have just been considering it is an anguished father who approaches him. In his concern and need, Jairus ignores issues of status, and places his trust in the power and kindness of Jesus. His faith is subsequently put to a severe test, when news is brought that his daughter has died. He responds to Jesus' recommendation to continue believing, and experiences the joy of seeing her restored to life and to the family. The faith of the woman takes a different path, as she wrestles with her affliction and with the social and religious stigma attached to it. There is determination and conviction about her, as in her hopelessness and trust, she takes the risk of touching Jesus, and is brought to wholeness. Both Jairus and the unnamed woman are presented as models of faith.

Two aspects of the person of Jesus are brought out, besides his remarkable healing power, which overcomes evil and introduces the Reigning of God. Firstly, he relates to people so sensitively and appropriately. His initial response to Jairus' quest is positive and immediate. Without hesitation he sets off with him to his home. Aware that someone has been healed through contact with him, he seeks to establish a relationship. There is compassion in the way he addresses the woman, and warmth, as he acknowledges her faith, and welcomes her into new life. Despite the ridicule of the locals, he reassures the dead girl's parents by his confidence and determination, as he accompanies them into the house. Again, there is warmth and affection in his manner and voice as he raises the girl to life and restores her to them, even suggesting, doubtless with a smile, that they should give her something to eat.

Secondly, as in the previous narrative, there is a freedom about him as he disregards convention and religious taboos. He is not concerned with public opinion, nor put off by the disparaging comment of his disciples, or the ridicule of the crowd. His attention is focused on people in need; his priority is to enable them to experience the presence of the Reign of his loving and compassionate Father.

# The Widow at the Temple

### The Context

At this stage in Mark's narrative Jesus has finally reached Jerusalem, and has solemnly entered the city.[71] After spending the night in Bethany, he returns to the city the following morning. On entering the Temple he drives out those buying and selling, overturning the tables of the money-changers. The chief priests and scribes are deeply angered by this, and wish to kill him, but are afraid *because the whole crowd was spellbound by his teaching.* Jesus leaves the city for the night along with his disciples. The following day he retraces his journey to the Temple. Mark then brings together a series of controversy episodes.[72] The chief priests, scribes and elders question his authority for operating as he does. Jesus recounts the parable of the wicked tenants, which the leaders recognise is directed against them. They would have had him arrested, were it not for their fear of the crowds. The Pharisees and Herodians are sent to trap him with their question about paying taxes to Rome.[73] The Sadducees aren't far behind with an intriguing case-study about resurrection. A favourably disposed scribe moves in, seeking Jesus' opinion about the greatest commandment.[74] Jesus then continues teaching the people, and turns his criticism on some of the scribes:[75]

> As he taught, he said, *Beware of the scribes, who like to walk around in long robes, and to be greeted with respect in the market-places, and to have the best seats in the synagogues and places of honour at banquets! They devour widows' houses and for the sake of appearance say long prayers. They will receive the greater condemnation.* (12:38-40)

As well as being capable of dealing with administrative documents, the scribes were the interpreters of the Law. Some were both lawyers and theologians.[76] Some belonged to the priestly classes, others were Pharisees. They enjoyed considerable power, prestige and influence. Mark tends to present them generally in a bad light. Jesus' main criticism concerns the hypocrisy of their ostentatious religiosity,[77] their self-promotion, their insincerity in prayer, and their tendency to prey on the social and financial vulnerability of widows. It has been suggested that the accusation is directed particularly against trustees or guardians appointed to look after estates, who claimed generous expenses, but then misused their position; their long prayers were an attempt to persuade possible clients to entrust them with their property.[78] The reference to widows leads into the brief story about the widow in the Temple, which closes the series of controversies:[79]

> He sat down opposite the treasury, and watched the crowd putting money into the treasury. Many rich people put in large sums. A poor widow came and put in two small copper coins, which are worth a penny. Then he called his disciples and said to them, *Truly I tell you, this poor widow has put in more than all those*

*who are contributing to the treasury. For all of them have contributed out of their abundance; but she out of her poverty has put in everything she had, all she had to live on.* (Mark 12:41-44)

## The Widow's Action

Jesus is seated opposite the treasury of the Temple, observing what is happening there.[80] The Temple also served as a national bank, accepting savings as well as donations.[81] People are coming along and putting money into the coffers for the upkeep of the Temple. Thirteen trumpet-shaped baskets stood in the court of the women for this purpose. Apparently, many rich people are making large contributions, some with an element of self-promotion akin to that of the scribes.[82] A widow arrives on the scene. Widows in Israel had no inheritance rights, and had to depend on their children or on charity; their well-being was referred by the Torah to the community.[83] The woman places into the receptacle two small copper coins, the smallest in circulation in Palestine. In financial terms the amount is insignificant; it runs to one sixty-fourth of a labourer's daily wage.

## Jesus' Comment

Jesus sees things differently. He assumes the role of teacher, as, seated, he summons his disciples and solemnly points out that in reality she has contributed more than all the others.[84] As with the scribes earlier, appearances can be deceptive. For the other contributors are people with plenty of money, and it is from such abundance that they have made their offering. The widow, on the other hand, has very little, next to nothing in fact, and yet she has given everything that she has.

She had two coins, and could have kept one of them for herself. The Greek phrase carries two meanings. The normal meaning indicates that she has given to God her whole livelihood, everything she has to live on. It can also be understood as *given up her life*.[85] So central is God in her life, so unconditional is her service.

In the context, the poor, unobtrusive widow stands in contrast not only with the rich, but also with the scribes in the earlier section. As the ministry of Jesus comes to a close, we here find a person who, in giving everything, shares his mindset and values. Her response recalls the initial calling of the disciples, who left everything in order to follow Jesus.[86] Later, Jesus has challenged them to be willing to lose their life, to accept to live in humble service and self-giving.[87] Jesus holds up this poor widow to his disciples as an example and model. She surrenders herself completely to God;

she places her security and trust in God's providential care. The story *sums up what has gone before in the Gospel and makes a superb transition to the story of how Jesus 'gave everything' for us all.* (Nineham)[88]

An alternative approach to this episode suggests the possibility that the widow is portrayed by Mark as a victim of the Temple system and its religious exploitation. Jesus' words express his disapproval, and amount to a lament. Jesus does not agree with the Temple system; his recent symbolic exclusion of the merchants and money lenders, and the cursing of the unproductive fig-tree are indications of this. His critique of the religious leadership in the parable of the tenants, and his criticism of the scribes are further indications. The widow's situation of poverty is a critique of the religious system. Her goodness and generosity are manipulated by institutionalised religion; she has been taught and conditioned to generous giving, and this Jesus deplores.[89] Her action illustrates the way in which religious authorities, especially the Temple administration, prey upon the piety of the vulnerable in order to exact tribute from them which is far beyond what they can afford. *She wastes her life in supporting a religious system that is doomed.* (Denis McBride)[90] She is the final witness in the case against the Temple.[91] This unjust situation paves the way for Jesus' later prophecy concerning the coming destruction of the Temple in all its extravagant magnificence.

Whilst the prophetic denunciation view remains a possibility, the wider context seems to support the more traditional exemplar interpretation. This is suggested by the fact that Jesus adopts a teaching posture and role, calls the disciples to him, and uses the authoritative *Amen* to introduce his comment to the disciples.[92] The focus of the woman's action is not on the giving of money to the Temple, but on the giving of her livelihood and life to God. In a wider context, the story of her generosity needs to be understood in conjunction with the generosity of the wealthier woman who is soon to anoint Jesus in the house of Simon the leper. The self-emptying of both women point to the passion of Jesus and the gift of his life.[93]

## Reflection

The widow in this episode illustrates a different aspect of discipleship. Her utter self-forgetfulness and generosity is a reminder of the fundamental nature of the following of Jesus, a willingness to give not less than everything. God is at the centre of her life. Quietly and unobtrusively she abandons herself to God's providential care.

Jesus is always attentive to what is happening around him, sensitive too to what is going on in people's hearts and minds. In this episode he doesn't miss the widow's goodness, and brings her action and her generosity to the attention of the disciples. He has different criteria when it comes to judging the worth of an individual. Perhaps he was also sensitive to the tragedy of the situation, her destitution because of a perverted religious system, so alien to the mind and heart of God.

# The Woman who anoints Jesus

## The Context

The final week of Jesus' life continues to unfold. After the episode of the generous widow, Jesus, prompted by the comment of one of his disciples, who enthusiastically expresses his admiration for the Jerusalem Temple, foretells its destruction:

> Do you see these great buildings? Not one stone will be left here upon another; all will be thrown down. (13:4)

When the group reaches the Mount of Olives, four of his disciples, Peter, James, John and Andrew, ask him to tell them when all this will take place. Jesus uses this question as the cue for his final discourse about the end and the need to be alert. The story then moves on, as Mark provides another clear time indication, *It was two days before the Passover and the festival of Unleavened Bread,* the most solemn of the feasts. Two original feasts, the Passover, which entailed the sacrifice of a lamb among a pastoral people, and Unleavened Bread, a barley harvest festival among sedentary farmers, had over the years been amalgamated and historicised to remember the Exodus event. Families celebrated a festal meal with a lamb, unleavened bread and herbs. Key elements from the dramatic journey through the wilderness were recalled: the crossing of the Reed Sea, the manna and quails, the thirst and supply of water, the Sinai covenant and gift of the Law, the birth of the nation of Israel as God's chosen people. Obviously, a key figure in all this was the person of Moses.[94] The feast of Passover provides the backdrop for the rest of Jesus' life, and suggests the significance of his death.[95]

The religious leaders, here specified as *the chief priests and the scribes,* are bent on Jesus' destruction.[96] They want to find a stealthy way of arresting him, so as to be able to put him to death. For the time being their plans are thwarted by his popularity amongst the people. An attempt to take him into custody would, they feel, lead to an unwelcome riot. Their considered decision is to postpone action until after the festival.[97]

This atmosphere of darkness, hostility, hatred and secrecy is the setting for another fascinating story in which a woman plays a key role. The story is to be understood in tandem with the description of the widow's generosity in the Temple treasury. The next episode in Mark's narrative describes the move of Judas to instigate the process of betraying Jesus, which seems to persuade the leaders to alter their plan, anticipating his arrest and death. The Evangelist skilfully highlights the woman's generous action by framing it between conspiracy and betrayal.[98] If Mark is counting in the Jewish way, it would seem that the incident takes place on the day which extends from Tuesday evening sunset to Wednesday sunset.[99] Mark's version reads as follows:[100]

> While he was at Bethany in the house of Simon the leper, as he sat at the table, a woman came with an alabaster jar of very costly ointment of nard, and she broke open the jar and poured the ointment on his head. But some were there who said to one another in anger, *Why was the ointment wasted in this way? For this ointment could have been sold for more than three hundred denarii, and the money given to the poor.* And they scolded her. But Jesus said, *Let her alone; why do you trouble her? She has performed a good service for me. For you always have the poor with you, and you can show kindness to them whenever you wish; but you will not always have me. She has done what she could; she has anointed my body beforehand for its burial. Truly I tell you, wherever the good news is proclaimed in the whole world, what she has done will be told in remembrance of her.* (14:3-9)

## The Action

It would seem that Jesus is staying during this time with a man named Simon in Bethany, a village on the other side of the Mount of Olives. Perhaps this man was cured of leprosy earlier by Jesus, and had become a friend, or even a disciple.[101] Maybe he was known to the early community. Jesus continues his habit of mixing with those on the margins. He is reclining at table with his host, which suggests a formal late afternoon meal,[102] when this unnamed woman enters, boldly flouting convention. She brings with her an alabaster jar, which would be globular in shape and without handles.[103] It contains oil of nard, a rare perfume imported from India, and very expensive. Without speaking a word, in a significant gesture she breaks the flask open; it will not be used again.[104] Then she pours the ointment over Jesus' head. No reason for her action is indicated. Presumably, it is an expression of her devotion, reverence and love.

There is an extravagance about her gesture; she pours out all the contents of the flask; she keeps nothing back; her gift is total. There are echoes of the earlier unconditional generosity of the widow.

Some of those present, presumably disciples,[105] grumble together. They consider such extravagance, using oil of nard rather than the usual olive or vegetable oil, a waste, and ask one another why the woman has done this. They estimate the value of the ointment at *three hundred denarii*, the equivalent of about a year's salary for a labourer. A better alternative would have been to sell it, they opine, and to give the proceeds to the poor. It was customary at Passover time to make donations to the poor. They strongly remonstrate with the woman, reproaching her; some translate the Greek as *loudly berated her*. They are insensitive to the significance of her gesture.

## The Words of Jesus

Jesus, with gracious humanity,[106] springs to her defence, telling her critics to leave her alone, *Why do you place burdens on her?* Positively and with approval, he describes what she has done for him as a *beautiful work*, an action which is appropriate and good.[107] He points out the ongoing presence of the poor in society.[108] Poverty, and the greed and injustice which spawn it, is a constant feature of human experience.

It offers a permanent opportunity for kindness and actions to alleviate it. However, his time amongst them is now very limited.[109] This is a privileged moment.[110] Whereas they are in danger of missing its significance, the woman's perception and sensitivity are accurate.

Jesus accepts her anointing, for *she has done what she could.* He then proceeds to provide an interpretation of her action which gives it a significance which she did not originally intend. He links it with his coming death. It serves as a prophetic gesture; it is an anticipated honouring of his body as if he were already dead.[111] Later in Mark's narrative, after his death Jesus is buried in a hurried manner. The motive for the women's visiting the tomb early in the morning after the Sabbath day, is to remedy the situation and anoint his body.

Jesus solemnly makes a final comment or promise to the effect that wherever in the world the Good News is proclaimed, her action in anointing him will be remembered, even though her name remains unknown. Some suggest that this verse is a later addition to the story, recognising what had in fact happened during the early decades of the Church's story.[112] This incident had quickly become an integral feature of the account of Jesus' death. In fact, the woman is a model of Christian discipleship. Like the widow in the earlier story, she gave to Jesus everything she could. *In pouring her gift over his head, she has in one action anointed him Messiah, proclaimed his death and resurrection and made an act of total commitment to him as Lord.* (Morna D Hooker)[113]

Mark probably saw another dimension to the woman's action. He understood her action of pouring the perfume over Jesus' head as the anointing of Jesus as messianic king prior to his death. Since the heads of kings and priests were solemnly anointed, the woman's action evokes royal and hence messianic overtones. It is a proclamation of his messiahship, the true nature of which is closely linked, throughout the Gospel, with his passion and death, and finally revealed by it.[114] *The fact that the ritual was performed by a woman rather than a priest was one more anomaly in a story that was already anomalous from beginning to end.* (Morna D Hooker)[115] His kingship is a theme which, now introduced, will be developed as the passion story evolves.[116] *For those who know the end of the story then, the woman's action epitomises Jesus' death and resurrection, proclaims his status as king, and challenges others to share her devotion to him.*

(Morna D Hooker)[117]

## Reflection

In this story, proclaimed once more, and in its Johannine parallel, it is the woman's generosity which captures and holds our attention. There is a spontaneity, a recklessness and self-forgetfulness about her devotion to Jesus. She doesn't count the cost; she holds nothing back, using up the contents of the alabaster jar completely. The jar is broken. The Fourth Evangelist presents the woman as a friend of Jesus, whose brother he has raised from death. Mark provides no information about her background or possible reasons why she treats Jesus in this way.

This unnamed woman models the core value of discipleship: generous self-giving. She challenges us about the quality of our response to Jesus. I'm sure that all of us have come across some generous people, people who willingly give their time and energy, their talents and giftedness, their kindness and love, in the service of others. As disciples of Jesus we do try to be generous, at least sometimes. Looking back over my life, I'm aware that I haven't emptied the jar. I've been economical in responding to Jesus.

This isn't usually a deliberate, conscious decision, rather a subconscious and instinctive urge to self-protection, wishing to hold on to my life and not to lose it, a human problem Jesus himself highlighted.[118]

In the story, the woman's attitude and action clearly contrast with the stance of the disciples who are negative, critical and quite aggressive, probably revealing some prejudice too. This is a typical Markan scenario in which the disciples miss the point, and the *Little People* get it right. I suspect that we are acquainted with such negativity; we have perhaps become aware of that tendency within ourselves on occasion.

As in the story examined earlier in the chapter on forgiveness, the reaction of Jesus is fascinating. He copes effortlessly with rather overwhelming affection and unconventional attention. He graciously accepts the woman's generosity and act of service. Faced with the impassioned outcry of the disciples, he intervenes with firmness, bidding them to leave her alone. He defends her action, describing it as a beautiful thing. *She has done what she could* is an interesting phrase. Jesus recognises the love and devotion of which her action is an expression. Such love cannot be suppressed; but the phrase betrays a fundamental attitude, an attitude of acceptance, appreciation and affirmation, a positive and encouraging way of viewing and assessing what happens and of judging people's gifts and efforts. Jesus finds a way of justifying what she has done, by providing an interpretation which immortalises the woman. He links her anointing of his body with his coming death, a death which will be the expression of his own generous self-giving for our salvation.

# The Widow of Nain

One of the outstanding traits of Luke's Gospel, as we have seen, is his emphasis on the mercy of God made real in the person and ministry of Jesus. It comes as a surprise, therefore, that the quality of compassion is attributed explicitly to Jesus on only one occasion. It is found in Luke's moving description of the raising to life of the widow's son at Nain, an episode not recounted by the other evangelists. Nain, which is not mentioned elsewhere in the Bible, was a small town some six miles south-east of Nazareth and twenty five from Capernuam, where in Luke's narrative Jesus has just healed the centurion's servant, who was seriously ill.[119] These two incidents are followed in the overall narrative by the Baptist's question as to whether Jesus is the one who is to come; they provide part of the evidence which Jesus can draw upon in his reply:[120]

115

Soon afterwards he went to a town called Nain, and his disciples and a large crowd went with him. As he approached the gate of the town, a man who had died was being carried out. He was his mother's only son, and she was a widow; and with her was a large crowd from the town. When the Lord saw her, he had compassion for her and said to her, *Do not weep.* Then he came forward and touched the bier, and the bearers stood still. And he said, *Young man, I say to you, rise!* The dead man sat up and began to speak, and Jesus gave him to his mother. Fear seized all of them; and they glorified God, saying, *A great prophet has risen among us!* and *God has looked favourably on his people!* This word about him spread throughout Judea and all the surrounding country. (7:11-17)

## The Setting

Jesus goes to the town accompanied by his entourage and a large crowd. As they approach the gate they meet a funeral procession moving out to the place of interment, probably a cave on the hillside.[121] It was the custom for burials to take place outside town and as soon as possible after death. Our attention is focussed on the sad plight of the woman: she has lost her husband and is therefore a widow, and now her only son, the support and hope of her life, has also died. She is therefore alone, without economic support, and very vulnerable. A life of hardship, loneliness and poverty beckons.[122] The woman is accompanied by a large crowd of mourners, for it was considered meritorious to attend funerals and share in the grieving. Besides, a death in a small town touches everyone. Mourning was greater for an only child. The professional mourners would also be noisily present.[123]

## The Action of Jesus

No request is made of Jesus to intervene; the initiative is entirely his. *He moves first, because he is first moved:*[124]

When the Lord saw her, he had compassion for her, and he said: *Do not weep.*

Jesus, described here as *the Lord,* is deeply concerned and is *moved to compassion* for the woman.[125] Firstly, he tells her that she need weep no more. In showing such care for the woman, Jesus once again crosses the boundaries of religious propriety and custom.[126] He then ignores the risk of incurring ritual defilement by approaching and touching the bier on which the corpse lay in a linen shroud. The bearers halt, and Jesus, with a word clearly audible to the crowd, raises the man to life again, *Young man, I say to you, get up!* The man sits up and begins to speak again. Then, showing his deep concern for the woman, Jesus *gave him back to his mother*.[127] Jesus' action in restoring life to the deceased young man, is clearly remarkable, but it is subsumed into his care for the grieving mother.[128] In the story there is no mention of the woman's faith, or that of the onlookers. The focus is entirely on Jesus' compassion.

## The Reaction of the Crowd

The witnesses to what has occurred are numerous. Their initial reaction is one of fear and awe. Jesus has done what only God can do. Then they burst into praise of God, chorus-like, recognising that *a great prophet has arisen among us*, and concluding with words which closely echo the words of Zechariah's *Benedictus, God has shown his care for his people*.[129] The compassion of Jesus, his deep concern for human suffering, reveals the presence amongst them of God's saving mercy. Jesus is for the first time publicly and explicitly recognised as a prophet who serves God's people. *His ministry extends not only to the poor, the imprisoned, the blind, and the downtrodden, but even to those in the grip of death*.[130] The story is another example of Jesus' care and concern for those in society who are poor and needy; once again, issues to do with the law of uncleanness yield to the more important law of mercy.[131]

## Reflection

The woman in this story has no active role. She represents the many bereaved and vulnerable in our world, people whose lives are in shreds, whose futures look grim. In her emptiness she can only receive. Her poverty is a catalyst. In her need she moves Jesus to compassion, a compassion which transforms her life. Yet she is a valuable reminder to us of our own inner poverty, our poverty of being. Awareness of our poverty, our areas of inadequacy and need, can open us to the healing and life-giving presence of Jesus. It is when we find ourselves in situations of loss that we can be found by him, loss of health (of sight, hearing, mobility); loss of independence; loss of friends and family; loss of position or job; loss of confidence. In our lives there are many death experiences which we have to embrace and work through. Jesus comes as the compassionate one who will be supportively with us, sustaining us in our struggle. He can also open up new possibilities, transforming death into life.

Concerning Jesus, Denis McBride writes: *Luke presents us with a very touching image of Jesus in this passage. Jesus is the one who takes the initiative, who speaks first, who notices suffering and desolation, and who does not bypass them along the road. Jesus is not afraid of getting his hands dirty, of being regarded as unclean, in his movement of compassion. When he meets suffering at the crossroads, he does not take the route of least resistance and flee from the face of pain. He transforms it by his touch and by his word. He brings happiness to life.*[132]

# Martha and Mary

One of the best known Lukan narratives, still capable of stimulating quite heated group discussions, describes the visit of Jesus to the home of Martha and Mary. The encounter is located early in Luke's journey narrative, the dynamic framework which he uses as the context for a great deal of his special material. *When the days drew near for him to be taken up, he set his face to go to Jerusalem.*[133] The episode is found only in Luke; presumably it stems from his special source:

> Now as they went on their way, he entered a certain village, where a woman named Martha welcomed him into her home. She had a sister named Mary, who sat at the Lord's feet and listened to what he was saying. But Martha was distracted by her many tasks; so she came to him and asked, *Lord, do you not care that my sister has left me to do all the work by myself? Tell her then to help me.* But the Lord answered her, *Martha, Martha, you are worried and distracted by many things; there is need of only one thing. Mary has chosen the better part, which will not be taken away from her.* (10:38-42)

## The Context

In Luke's mind the story of the two sisters, Martha and Mary, is to be taken in tandem with the parable of the Good Samaritan, which precedes it in the text. Taken together, they illustrate the two aspects of the one commandment of love which the lawyer has articulated in reply to Jesus' question:[134]

> You shall love the Lord your God with all your heart, and with all your soul, and with all your strength, and with all your mind; and your neighbour as yourself. (10:27)

The story is also an instance of Luke's tendency to juxtapose two narratives in which a woman and a man are in turn the principal protagonist.[135] He is a forerunner in the call for equal opportunities! In the much loved parable, the contrast is drawn between the Samaritan and the two Jewish wayfarers who have close connections with the Temple. Here, it is the sisters who are contrasted. The two sisters appear in the Fourth Gospel in connection with the raising of their brother Lazarus from death. Their home is in the village of Bethany, situated just outside Jerusalem. Such a location does not fit Luke's scheme.

## The Story

As Jesus proceeds on his journey to Jerusalem, he reaches an unnamed village. He is in need of hospitality, and a lady named Martha makes him welcome in her home. Luke does not indicate whether Jesus arrives at the door by chance or by design; I suspect that the latter is implied. Martha appears to be the head of the household,[136] and immediately gets involved unselfishly in busily preparing a rather elaborate meal. Mary, her sister, *seated herself at the Lord's feet and stayed there listening to his words.* She adopts the normal posture of a disciple, and is clearly keen to listen to what Jesus has to say and, student-like, to learn from him. She acknowledges his authority, and is attentive to his word, a key motif for this Evangelist. Jesus, far from shrinking from this, as most rabbis would have done, encourages her interest. This is another example of his freedom with regard to social and religious convention in his treatment of women, and of his advancing their status. They too are allowed to listen and learn, and are deemed capable of doing so.

It soon emerges that Martha has a problem. The pressure of hospitality, as she understands it, prevents her from listening, which she doubtless would have appreciated and enjoyed. She is *distracted by all the serving.* The verb means to be pulled or dragged about.[137] There is just too much to do. She probably feels rather peeved that she has been left to do everything herself, and maybe thinks her sister is being a little selfish. Perhaps she is somewhat disappointed that Jesus does not seem to notice her frustration, so she attempts to enlist his support. She assumes a slightly confrontational attitude. One might detect a touch of resentment in her voice, a tone of accusation against her sister, *Tell her to come and lend a hand.* Martha really ought not to have asked her guest to become involved in a family dispute.

# The Response of Jesus

As is generally the case in the Gospel narrative, Jesus resists the pressure to intervene.[138] He is not unsympathetic to her plight and her problem, and her feelings of annoyance; but he insists on priorities. There is great affection in his voice as with a gentle reproach he indicates the real issue:

*Martha, Martha, you are fretting and fussing about so many things.*

The first verb means to be anxious, to be unduly concerned. Anxiety usually has a negative connotation in scripture, implying a lack of trust in the presence and power of God; it can inhibit the growth of the word.[139] The second verb means to be troubled, distracted, even to create an uproar.[140] Martha, then, is far too troubled and anxious; she is exaggeratedly concerned. She is losing the right perspective. It is not really necessary to *go over the top*, to prepare such an elaborate *cordon bleu* menu. Perhaps she could cut back a little, and then she would also have time to listen. What Jesus needs is not a generous table but a listening ear.[141]

There are two aspects to discipleship: there is service and kindness and practical living; and there is listening to Jesus, hearing the word of the Lord. As Caird puts it so well: Martha *has not yet learned that unselfishness, service, and even sacrifice can be spoiled by self-concern and self-pity, that good works which are not self-forgetful can become a misery to the doer and a tyranny to others.*[142] Jesus continues:

*Mary has chosen the good portion,*
*which shall not be taken away from her.*

After the story of the Samaritan's generous response to a traveller's need, which Jesus proclaims should be a permanent way of living, his comment here comes as a surprise. It has also proved something of a problem for subsequent readers, as the manuscript variations testify. The good or better part, portion, course or dish (a little wordplay is evident here), the thing which is most essential, the right choice, is to make space for Jesus, and to listen to his word. Besides, the one thing necessary for hospitality is attention to the guest, and if the guest is a prophet, the appropriate way to express welcome is to listen to his message. This is what he would wish for.[143] Listening is service too. In the scale of values, it is listening to the word which has priority. Jesus defends Mary; she has made the correct choice.

# Reflection

*To love God with whole heart and mind and the neighbour as one's self demands both compassionate and effective entry into the world of the neighbour as well as undistracted attentiveness to the word of the Lord. Far from exalting one mode of discipleship above the other, the two narratives say that one cannot authentically exist without the other.*[144] For Luke it is important both to hear and to do.[145]

The two *Little People* of this narrative invite us to examine the priorities in our lives. Most of us take ministry and mission seriously, and try genuinely to reach out to others in care and compassion. But there are times when we become aware that we are becoming too busy, and such overactivity induces tension and stress into our lives. Symptoms of workaholism, incipient or verging on the chronic, become evident. The quality of our service begins to deteriorate, and relationships become a little fraught. We are losing perspective and focus. *Frenetic service, even service of the Lord, can be a deceptive distraction from what the Lord really wants.*[146] We realise that somehow we are neglecting to make time to reflect prayerfully on the Lord's word.[147] Such reflection centres our lives on Jesus. It is Jesus who is our inspiration, whose life enlivens our vision, reveals true values, informs our style of serving. Without regular times of prayer in which we listen to God's love, our apostolic ventures can become jobs or careers rather than ministries, and we run the risk of building our own kingdoms rather than that of Jesus. Values other than those of the Gospel can influence our decisions and actions. Selfishness, individualism and pragmatism and the seeking of success, instead of the Spirit, can determine the outcome of our discernment.

The Jesus of this story is not unwilling to be served, but is conscious of a message which he desires to share, and this clarifies his priorities. His normal affection and care are again evident, but he is gently assertive. He makes his point in unambiguous terms. His friends come to know his mind and priorities; they know where he stands. It is a point which he probably needs to make with us repeatedly. The balanced integration of reflection and action is an ongoing challenge. His manner of dealing with this situation can serve as an example for us too in other situations which we frequently face. He addresses the issue with sensitivity and with clarity.

# The Samaritan Woman

The Gospel of John provides some wonderful narratives.[148] Perhaps the most fascinating is the story of Jesus' encounter with the Samaritan woman.[149] This episode is situated in a block of material which runs from Cana to Cana, from the story of the wedding feast and Jesus' first sign,[150] the changing of water into wine, to the story of his healing the royal official's son.[151] The Evangelist uses this structure as a framework within which to present, in a variety of contexts, key aspects of the identity and the role or mission of Jesus, and to illustrate different responses which he receives. In the dialogue between Jesus and the Samaritan woman the twin themes of water and Spirit, which formed part of Jesus' discussion with Nicodemus earlier in the narrative, are again raised.

Now when Jesus learned that the Pharisees had heard, *Jesus is making and baptising more disciples than John* – although it was not Jesus himself but his disciples who baptised – he left Judea and started back to Galilee. But he had to go through Samaria. So he came to a Samaritan city called Sychar, near the plot of ground that Jacob had given to his son Joseph. Jacob's well was there, and Jesus, tired out by his journey, was sitting by the well. It was about noon:

> A Samaritan woman came to draw water, and Jesus said to her, *Give me a drink.* (His disciples had gone to the city to buy food.) The Samaritan woman said to him, *How is it that you, a Jew, ask a drink of me, a woman of Samaria?* (Jews do not share things in common with Samaritans.) Jesus answered her, *If you knew the gift of God, and who it is that is saying to you, "Give me a drink", you would have asked him, and he would have given you living water.* The woman said to him, *Sir, you have no bucket, and the well is deep. Where do you get that living water? Are you greater than our ancestor Jacob, who gave us the well, and with his sons and his flocks drank from it?* Jesus said to her, *Everyone who drinks of this water will be thirsty again, but those who drink of the water that I will give them will never be thirsty. The water that I will give will become in them a spring of water gushing up to eternal life.* The woman said to him, *Sir, give me this water, so that I may never be thirsty or have to keep coming here to draw water.*
>
> Jesus said to her, *Go, call your husband, and come back.* The woman answered him, *I have no husband.* Jesus said to her, *You are right in saying, "I have no husband"; for you have had five husbands, and the one you have now is not your husband. What you*

*have said is true!* The woman said to him, *Sir, I see that you are a prophet. Our ancestors worshipped on this mountain, but you say that the place where people must worship is in Jerusalem.* Jesus said to her, *Woman, believe me, the hour is coming when you will worship the Father neither on this mountain nor in Jerusalem. You worship what you do not know; we worship what we know, for salvation is from the Jews. But the hour is coming, and is now here, when the true worshippers will worship the Father in spirit and truth, for the Father seeks such as these to worship him. God is spirit, and those who worship him must worship in spirit and truth.* The woman said to him, *I know that Messiah is coming* (who is called *Christ*). *When he comes, he will proclaim all things to us.* Jesus said to her, *I am he, the one who is speaking to you.*

Just then his disciples came. They were astonished that he was speaking with a woman, but no one said, *What do you want?* or, *Why are you speaking with her?* Then the woman left her water-jar and went back to the city. She said to the people, *Come and see a man who told me everything I have ever done! He cannot be the Messiah, can he?* They left the city and were on their way to him. Meanwhile the disciples were urging him, *Rabbi, eat something.* But he said to them, *I have food to eat that you do not know about.* So the disciples said to one another, *Surely no one has brought him something to eat?* Jesus said to them, *My food is to do the will of him who sent me and to complete his work. Do you not say, "Four months more, then comes the harvest"? But I tell you, look around you, and see how the fields are ripe for harvesting. The reaper is already receiving wages and is gathering fruit for eternal life, so that sower and reaper may rejoice together. For here the saying holds true, "One sows and another reaps." I sent you to reap that for which you did not labour. Others have laboured, and you have entered into their labour.*

Many Samaritans from that city believed in him because of the woman's testimony, *He told me everything I have ever done.* So when the Samaritans came to him, they asked him to stay with them; and he stayed there for two days. And many more believed because of his word. They said to the woman, *It is no longer because of what you said that we believe, for we have heard for ourselves, and we know that this is truly the Saviour of the world.*

(4: 1-42)

## The Setting

In an earlier scene Jesus encountered Nicodemus. The contrast between Nicodemus and the Samaritan woman, who is Jesus' interlocutor in this narrative, is striking. Nicodemus is male, learned, respected, orthodox, theologically trained, a Jew, a man of authority, and wealthy. He approaches Jesus secretly in the middle of the night. Now we have an unnamed woman, who is a non-Jew, something of a religious and social outcast, with little education or influence. She meets Jesus openly in the full light of the middle of the day. But both she and Nicodemus need Jesus.

The story opens with Jesus deciding for reasons of safety to leave Judea and return to Galilee. Two options lie before him. He can take the longer route through the Jordan valley, or the shorter way, the customary pilgrimage itinerary, which passes along the ridge through Samaria. It is the latter path which he chooses, but his choice is not determined by geographical or convenience factors. The text reads, *He had to pass through Samaria*, which implies that Jesus' decision to move beyond Israel into the alien context of the Samaritan world is caught up in the design of God. By mid-day, Jesus is growing weary from his walking in the heat, and coming across Jacob's well at Sychar, he sits down to take a rest.[152] In the book of Genesis we are informed that the patriarch Jacob bought this land from the people of Shechem, and later made a gift of it to his son Joseph.[153] This well, so strongly associated with Jewish religious tradition, stands centre-stage throughout the narrative which follows. The disciples, who are accompanying Jesus, then go off *en masse* to buy food, leaving Jesus alone. This exit is a convenient literary device in accordance with the canons of Greek theatre; it facilitates the encounter between the two main protagonists in the drama which is about to unfold. Jesus sits on the thick, doughnut-shaped capstone of the well.[154]

A local woman, whose name we never get to know, comes to the well to draw water. This chore was usually completed in the morning or evening, usually in a group. Probably she is something of an outcast in her village community; possibly she is interested in meeting travellers. Wells play an important role in the developing story of the people of Israel. Rebecca is found by Abram's servant as a wife for Isaac by the well of Nahar. Jacob meets Rachel by the well of Haran. And Moses, after rescuing the daughters of Reuel by the well of Midian, receives Zipporah as wife.[155] In these episodes wells are focal points of life-changing relationships, experiences which are caught up in the wider plan of God. At the well of Sychar, two strangers meet. As readers we are already drawn into the story, wondering what the outcome will be.

## Jesus' Request

As is normally the case in the Fourth Gospel, it is Jesus who takes the initiative. On seeing the woman, he was expected to withdraw about twenty feet. This would indicate that it was safe and culturally appropriate for her to approach. Jesus doesn't move. She approaches anyway.[156] Tired, hot and thirsty, he asks the woman for a drink, *Give me a drink.* At first sight this seems quite a natural thing to do. He is in need, and she has access to the water of the well, having brought her rolled-up leather bucket with her. But Jesus is completely disregarding religious and cultural convention. He breaks the taboo against talking to a woman in a public place with no one else around.

Characters are described in terms of the region or religious groups to which they belong, with the risk of polarisation because of regional and religious animosity.[157] The Samaritans were considered a mixed race of semi-pagans following the importation of foreign nations after the Assyrian defeat of the northern kingdom.[158] Their relationship had been strained for centuries, since the Samaritans broke with the Jews on the return from exile in Babylon, putting obstacles in the way of the restoration of Jerusalem. Later (2nd Century BC) they had helped the Syrians against them. In 128 BC, the Jewish High Priest, John Hyrcanus, had caused their temple on Mount Gerizim to be burned down. A few years before Jesus was born, the Samaritans gained access to the Temple in Jerusalem and scattered the bones of dead people there at Passover time, defiling the place and preventing the Passover celebration.[159] Furthermore, according to Jewish standards the Samaritans were rather lax in matters of ritual purification, and there would be a risk of incurring defilement from sharing a drinking vessel. In Judaism women existed mainly for child-bearing; they could take no part in public life, act as witnesses, or be taught the Law. The Jewish attitude to Samaritan women was extremely negative.

Jesus disregards the hostility existing between the two peoples. In speaking with a Samaritan and a woman in public, Jesus is also choosing to disregard the cultural gender barrier and the Rabbinic codes. There is a remarkable freedom about him, which, as becomes evident later, his disciples find quite shocking.

Furthermore, Jesus initiates the conversation by admitting his need, humbly asking for help. He depends on her; he is the recipient of her kindness. In doing so, he affirms her dignity. The woman is clearly surprised that a male Jew[160] should flout the norms of his people and make such a request of her, a Samaritan, and a woman, and be prepared to drink out of her defiled leather bucket.[161] One senses in her voice almost a touch of delight as she makes her point.

## The Gift of God

Jesus overlooks her comment and refuses to be drawn into controversy. Instead, he maintains the initiative, and reversing the roles of giver and receiver, issues a challenging and far-reaching invitation:

> *If only you knew what God gives, and who it is that is asking you for a drink, you would have asked him, and he would have given you living water.*

In this statement the two main themes of the whole dialogue which is to follow are introduced: God's gift of *living water* (verses 11-15), and the identity of the giver (*who it is*) (16-26). There is the additional theme of her need (*you would have asked him*).[162]

The term *living water* is ambiguous. At one level of meaning, *living water* can indicate fresh, running water from a spring or a stream, in contrast with flat, insipid cistern or pond water. Since both Jews and Samaritans used the term in this way, the woman naturally takes that meaning. She focuses on the immediate, thinks in pragmatic terms, and points out some of the practical difficulties Jesus would encounter in getting this water, given that the well is deep (some 100 feet) and that he has no bucket anyway. Her local pride pricked, speaking exclusively and regionally in the plural, she poses two questions, reversing the order of Jesus' statement. And there is great irony here. Firstly, she asks from where he will get such living water. This phrase *where from* is profoundly significant for John, throughout his Gospel. Secondly, she enquires whether he thinks he is greater than their ancestor, the patriarch Jacob, who was initially responsible for the provision of this well and its abundant water supply, so plentiful that he, his sons, and his numerous cattle had been able to drink from it. At this stage in the dialogue she cannot get beyond the level of ordinary wells and ordinary water, nor can she envisage the possibility of Jesus being able to provide a water gift which surpasses the gift of Jacob, and so manifest his superiority. Locked into her own traditions, nationalistically defensive, she is not open to his word and to what is new. She cannot make a link between *living water* and Jesus.

But Jesus is really speaking about a thirst of a different order, a thirst and longing and need for God.[163] Correspondingly, he is speaking of a different kind of water. The woman needs to move into a new level of understanding. She needs to become more aware of her own thirsting; she needs to come to an appreciation of the gift on offer; she needs to come to know the identity of the one who can provide that gift.

Jesus refrains from entering into discussion about claiming ancestry from Jacob. To her twofold question, Jesus replies:

> *Everyone who drinks this water will be thirsty again, but whoever drinks the water that I shall give will never suffer thirst any more. The water that I shall give will be an inner spring always welling up for eternal life.* (4:13-14)

Ordinary water, including that from Jacob's well, quenches thirst only for a time, whereas the water which Jesus will provide slakes thirst in a permanent way. Jesus now speaks in the first person rather than the third, and his promise is extended to a wider audience than the woman, to everyone, in fact, who is prepared to accept the gift he brings. There is an inclusiveness about Jesus.[164] This water, he says, will be like an inner spring, a fountain within the believer, gushing up abundantly and inexhaustibly, an ongoing source of *eternal life*, which is the Evangelist's term for the very life of God.[165] Such water is clearly far superior to that which Jacob provided, and the giver of this water must also be *greater* than Jacob.[166] The *supplanter*, which is the meaning of Jacob's name, is supplanted. The words and promise of Jesus extend beyond an individual woman, place and moment in history.[167] In response the woman addresses Jesus with greater respect, showing some openness to his water gift and his word:

> *Sir, give me this water, so that I may never be thirsty or have to keep coming here to draw water.*

She is still thinking in terms of normal thirst and normal earthly water which will obviate the need for her burdensome daily visit to the well. She is still struggling to understand, to move beyond the present and the immediate. Progress there is, but it is tentative.

## Worship

At this juncture Jesus rescues the faltering situation by changing tack. Interest in the symbol of water fades from the narrative as other topics are introduced. Jesus invites her to go and call her husband, and she declines, with disarming honesty stating that she has no husband.[168]

Without any suggestion of judgement or condemnation, but with a compliment on her truthfulness, Jesus shows his awareness of her rather scandalous and sad private life, for she has had five husbands, and is currently living with another man. This is an indication of her restlessness and searching.[169] The surprising disclosure prompts her to regard him in a different light; she now begins to see him as *a prophet*.

A man meeting a woman at a well is, as we have seen, a typical biblical theme. At Cana Jesus revealed himself as the real bridegroom; later he was named as the bridegroom by the Baptist; now he comes to claim Samaria as an integral part of the new Israel, the Christian and Johannine community. The Samaritan woman is both an individual and a representative of her people. There is a wordplay on the double meaning of *ba'al,* which can indicate gods and husband. Jesus' declaration that the woman has no husband is, according to Schneiders, a classic prophetic denunciation of foreign worship. The true *husband/lord* of Samaria stands before her in the person of Jesus, the bridegroom, the seventh man in her life, in whose presence she will find wholeness.[170] The five husbands plus the current one, six, indicates the less than perfect worship of the Samaritans, like the six water jars at Cana. And so, as well as showing remarkable knowledge about the woman's private life, Jesus raises the central religious question about her true *husband/ba'al*. Love and worship, which touch the centre of the human heart, are linked. Her love life is bankrupt; the worship of her people is empty (*you worship what you do not know*). Her marital disorder is of a piece with the spiritual disorder of her people. This leads her to a deeper appreciation of his identity; he is a prophet.[171]

For the Samaritans, the expected Messiah would be a prophetic figure like Moses, who would both be a source of revelation and a restorer of genuine worship. So the woman raises the highly controversial issue of the correct place in which to worship God, the place where God's presence is to be found. And she does so whilst standing at the foot of Mount Gerizim, where the remains of the Samaritan temple would have been visible.[172] There was longstanding disagreement between Jews and Samaritans about the priority of the Jerusalem temple or that at Gerizim. The Samaritans held that the first site of Mosaic worship on entering the land was Gerizim. Sion became a site of worship only with David. The Samaritan tradition also shifted Jacob's vision from Bethel to Gerizim to validate it as the *House of God* and an authentic site of worship.[173]

Jesus responds, addressing her respectfully as *woman*. He looks to a future *hour* when such controversy and discussion will no longer be relevant. For a new kind of worship will replace both sacred sites. God's gift of the Spirit of truth will make it possible for human beings to worship God as Father. Jesus three times names God as Father, a seeking, searching Father; the Father who loves the world so much that he sends his Son, that the world may be saved and share *eternal life*. For true worship, knowledge of the Father is necessary, and this can come only from Jesus, who is *nearest the Father's heart,* and comes to make the Father known. Jesus will reveal him most completely in that future *hour,* when his task reaches fulfilment. The gift of the Spirit is linked to that *hour.* Through that outpouring, believers will then come to share Jesus' relationship with the Father, and will worship in the Spirit of truth. In a challenging tone Jesus indicates the inferiority of Samaritan worship in comparison with Jewish, and states that *salvation comes from the Jews*. Salvation comes from a Jewish milieu, and especially through the Judean Jesus, as the Samaritan townspeople later acknowledge. The Evangelist moves and blurs the time frames. Jesus speaks to the woman in the present, asserting the superiority of Jewish worship over Samaritan, and indicates the future *hour* within the confines of the Gospel narrative when the gift of the Spirit will become available, and a new era of worship inaugurated. He also moves into the future of the Johannine believing community; having accepted the revelation of Jesus, they know the Father whom Jesus has revealed, and so know in their *now* what they are truly worshipping. The phrase, *The hour has come,* announces the arrival of the eschatological age. *In his own person the dwelling place of God is being established in the midst of the people*.

(Mary L Coloe)[174]

This response to the woman's question is stunning in its depth and intimacy; it is probably the most significant teaching on worship in the entire New Testament.[175] She finds it difficult to assimilate fully, but it leads her to broach the subject of the awaited messianic figure. The Samaritans, who did not accept the prophetic literature, were not expecting a messianic kingly ruler, as were many of the Jews. They were anticipating a teacher, a *Taheb*, modelled on the prophet Moses,[176] who would reveal everything and restore genuine worship. It is clear that the woman has a strong faith in the future coming of this Messiah-teacher. Here she adopts the Jewish term.

The reply of Jesus to her messianic musing is difficult to translate. Usually it is put this way:

That is who I am, I who speak to you.

His response is an acceptance and confirmation of her suggestion or intuition, the disclosure that he is in fact the messianic figure to whom she has been referring, the one who fulfils the Samaritan messianic expectations. He is sitting there before her on the well, now in the present. But many scholars hold that a more accurate, though awkwardly sounding, translation would be:

I am is the one speaking to you.

Jesus is going beyond the categories within which she is moving, and is trying to lead her further. He is giving his own clarification about the identity of her interlocutor. Her hopes and expectations are again transcended, for *I am*, appearing here for the first time in the Gospel, is the formula which in the Hebrew Bible is adopted as God's self-description,[177] a formula which the prophets used when referring to the living presence of God, the God who makes himself known to his people.[178] Jesus, then, is more than a prophet and greater than a Davidic Messiah or Jacob; he is God's self-revelation enfleshed. This woman, who is also a foreigner, is the first person in the Gospel to whom he makes such an astounding self-revelation. In so doing, he challenges her again to move beyond her hopes and dreams.

## The Townsfolk

The conversation is interrupted by the return of the disciples with supplies of food. The woman hastily departs for the town. She has left behind her original antipathy, and her narrow categories, and now she leaves behind her water jar, which is useless for the water Jesus is providing.

The symbolism of *living water* she now understands. She is no longer concerned with the well or the issue of worship. She is focused on Jesus, whose true identity she is coming to realise. Filled with wonder and enthusiasm, she rushes off to bear witness about him to her townsfolk, urging them to *come and see* this extraordinary man, (who has told her everything), and expressing her hope and belief that he could be the Christ. Though she does not make a full confession, her faith has matured as the dialogue with Jesus unfolded, and she now reaches out in evangelising mission to her people, wanting them to meet him and hear what he is offering, *the gift of God, living water.*[179]

The terminology recalls the scene early in the Gospel narrative when the two disciples of the Baptiser come to Jesus; her witnessing role is not unlike his, as she fades into the background.[180] The townsfolk invite Jesus to stay with them, and as a result of his brief sojourn in their midst, large numbers of them come to believe in him on the strength of his own *word* rather than hers, and they confess him as *saviour of the world*.[181] Their coming to faith, full Johannine faith, in this non-Jewish context, is the climax of the story. *In and through the person of Jesus, the Father is seeking the Samaritan people and offering them the gift of salvation.* (Mary L Coloe)[182] Jesus has supplanted Jacob in the gift he offers – the living waters of eschatological salvation – and as the founder of a new form of worship in Spirit and truth.[183]

## Living Water

So what is this *living water* that Jesus offers as the *gift of God*? I believe that *living water* probably refers primarily to the revelation which Jesus brings, a revelation which is supremely life-giving. In the Hebrew Bible, water is found as a symbol for God's word and for divine Wisdom, which nourishes the thirsty and satisfies their needs, providing insight and knowledge.[184] In rabbinic tradition water is also the symbol of the Law. In Judaism the gift of God par excellence is the Law.[185] For the Fourth Evangelist, Jesus is God's wisdom enfleshed. He knows the mind of God, and *is close to the Father's heart*.[186] His mission is to reveal and communicate all that he has learned from the Father. In the story he reveals himself, his identity and his role to the woman and her townsfolk. He also reveals to her something about her own deeper self. The two waters, the two gifts, old and new, are contrasted.[187]

Some scholars suggest that *living water* probably refers also to the Holy Spirit.[188] In his dialogue with Nicodemus Jesus has already linked water and spirit in the new birth through which it becomes possible to enter the Kingdom and share in the gift of *eternal life*. In the Old Testament, the image of water is linked with the outpouring of God's Spirit.[189] The verb used in verse 14 for the welling up of water is reserved in the Septuagint for the coming of the Spirit on Samson, Saul and David.[190] Water and Spirit are identified later at the celebration of Tabernacles,[191] and are associated also in the scene of Jesus' death.[192] In 6:63 we are told that it is the Spirit which gives life. The Spirit is often referred to in the New Testament as the *gift of God*.[193]

In this narrative *living water* is thus a powerful and rich symbol.[194] It signifies the Spirit whom we have received in baptism, the Spirit of truth and life, the Spirit who makes us children of God, and binds us together in the Risen Jesus. The Spirit is the spring within us gushing up to eternal life. The Spirit enables us to worship God in a new and authentic way, as Father. The water is also the teaching of Jesus, his revelation and message, which can transform our mindset and outlook, and enliven our hearts, and satisfy our deepest thirsts.

## Reflections

One of the features of many of the Gospel narratives involving *Little People* is the issue of trust or faith. The story of the Samaritan woman approaches this theme in a different way, by describing a process of growth, a journey into faith. She moves slowly, finding it difficult to let go of what is familiar, and she protects her security. She struggles to understand what this unusual Jewish character is talking about. But then she catches a glimpse, her defensiveness melts away, and a whole new world begins to open up. She moves from *A Jew, Sir,* and *A prophet* to possibly the *Messiah.* She is fascinated and excited by the person who has walked into her life looking for a drink and has awakened something deep within her, and opened up new possibilities. Abandoning her jar, she rushes off to share the good news with her townsfolk, even though she doesn't yet fully understand. Her enthusiasm mirrors that of Andrew when he first met Jesus, stayed with him, and went off in search of his brother Simon Peter, telling him, *We have found the Messiah.* Her exuberance echoes that of Philip, anxious to share with Nathaniel what he had found, and bidding him, *Come and see.* It's the language of discipleship, of mission, of witness. From having nothing going for her as a Samaritan outsider, and a woman, and someone with a reputation in the town, she grows into a model disciple. She challenges us today on the quality of our discipleship, and our enthusiasm for mission.

One important aspect of this narrative is the way Jesus relates to the Samaritan woman, as woman and as Samaritan. As I mentioned earlier, relations between Jews and Samaritans were extremely frosty and hostile. Yet, Jesus walks into the heart of their territory, engages with them, and finally *stays* with them. He speaks at length with the woman, and then shares his *word* with her townsfolk, so that they come to faith in him as saviour of the world. The disciples, on returning from their shopping expedition, are deeply shocked to find him in the company of a woman. Women were generally viewed as unintelligent, incapable of coping with theology, a sexual danger. It was frowned upon to engage with them in public, especially for a rabbi. Yet Jesus ignores all the taboos and prejudices, and also her current way of life and outcast status. He respectfully engages her in serious theological conversation, and eventually reveals his identity to her, leading her to a significant level of faith. And she then becomes a witness, an apostle to her people, *the first Christian female preacher*, (Kenneth E Bailey)[195] bringing her people to him, a ministry which he accepts and to which he generously responds. The text certainly asks questions of the Church concerning the role of women. It seriously asks all of us to name and confront our own prejudices, whatever their shape, texture and colour. Jesus is an uncomfortable friend, whose freedom, grasp of the essential, and courage are refreshing, inspiring and challenging.[196]

## Concluding Thoughts

This chapter is a compendium of Gospel spirituality. It highlights in a striking manner the refreshing and disturbing newness of Jesus' understanding of the Reign of God. The passing of the years and changes in our own cultural setting can anesthetise us to the radicality of his vision and practice. He takes women seriously, treats them with respect, and responds to them no differently from his responding to men. He brings instant healing to the mother-in-law of Simon on a Sabbath. He takes her by the hand to raise her up, a gesture no rabbi of his day would admit. Similarly, he takes the hand of the deceased daughter of Jairus, a double transgression, and raises her up to restore her to her parents. He makes a point of establishing a personal relationship with the woman who has been suffering with a haemorrhage problem.

She is not allowed to melt away anonymously into the thronging crowd. He reaches out compassionately to the widow of Nain, speaking with her in her distress, incurring defilement in her service by touching the bier on which the corpse of her only son is being borne.

He notices and acknowledges the generosity of the poor widow in the temple treasury. He graciously accepts and then defends the extravagantly generous action of the woman who anoints him in the house of Simon in Bethany. He accepts the listening stance of Mary, making it clear that women can be disciples too. His dialogue with the Samaritan woman is a textbook of sensitivity, respect, and acceptance, as he patiently leads her into faith and reveals to her his identity. He accepts her missionary role as her townsfolk come to him and invite him to stay with them for a while.

For his time and place, Jesus is breathtakingly original. In order to uphold the value and dignity of women, he turns social and religious standards, traditions and expectations upside down. He dispenses with patriarchy.[197] He is not deterred by religious defilement, raised eyebrows or criticism. His style is scandalous and problematic. His action is prophetic. It challenges fundamentally the accepted mores and attitudes of his cultural milieu; it offers an alternative, proclaims a new world, which he refers to repeatedly as the Kingdom. It is prophetic also because it reveals a new understanding of God, God's inclusive love for every human being without distinction and differentiation. The freedom of Jesus, his independence, insight and assurance, his affectionate openness to all, stem from his knowing the mind and heart of God, from his listening in prayer to the God whom he called *Abba, Father,* and whom he had come to know as unconditional and compassionate love. It arises also from his commitment to his dream, the establishing of the Kingdom, God's Reign in love. The contours of this dream, to which he was surrendered, embraced wholeness, equality, acceptance, self-giving service, and generosity; there was no place for power, rank and control.[198]

The *Little People* of these stories reveal a great deal about discipleship. Simon's mother-in-law introduces the key theme of service. The woman with vaginal bleeding demonstrates faith and also great courage in approaching Jesus. The widow and the woman who anoints him highlight self-emptying and generosity. Taken together, these two incidents are such powerful illustrations of what is at the heart of the Gospel, especially as they occur in such proximity to Jesus' self-giving at the supper and Calvary. The widow of Nain reminds us of our poverty and need, the fundamental attitude of dependence on God's compassionate love. The two sisters enable Jesus to underline the importance of listening to his word. The Samaritan woman episode captures something of the excitement and thrill of encountering Jesus, and the compelling urge to share that experience with others.

# Chapter Five – The Men

## The Leper

At the end of the opening phase of Jesus' ministry, before the first block of controversy, Mark includes a story in which a man is healed.[1] The story can be viewed as the climax of this introductory section of the Gospel, or considered as an awkward appendix.[2] The man is not named; no indication of time or place is provided:

> A leper came to him begging him, and kneeling he said to him, *If you choose, you can make me clean.* Moved with pity, Jesus stretched out his hand and touched him, and said to him, *I do choose. Be made clean!* Immediately the leprosy left him, and he was made clean. After sternly warning him he sent him away at once, saying to him, *See that you say nothing to anyone; but go, show yourself to the priest, and offer for your cleansing what Moses commanded, as a testimony to them.* But he went out and began to proclaim it freely, and to spread the word, so that Jesus could no longer go into a town openly, but stayed out in the country; and people came to him from every quarter. (1:40-45)

### The Situation

The structure of the passage follows the normal pattern for healing stories: the malady, the request, the healing act, the confirmation of the healing, the response.[3] The man's infirmity, whether it was leprosy in the technical sense, or a similar unpleasant skin disease,[4] was thought at the time to be incurable. It entailed segregation from the social and religious life of the community. A leper was obliged to wear his clothing torn and his hair dishevelled, and cry *Unclean, Unclean* as he moved around. He had to live apart and was forbidden to enter any walled town or reside in a village.[5] He was thus denied access to Jerusalem and to the Temple. This was not mainly for reasons of hygiene, but because leprosy was deemed to be evidence of and punishment for sin; a leper was considered unclean in the religious sense. If he entered a house, he rendered it unclean; even a chance encounter could entail ritual contamination. His life was thus a misery, a source of physical discomfort, mental anguish, and spiritual guilt. It is small wonder that lepers were dubbed, *The first-born of death, living corpses.*[6]

## The Leper's Approach

This outcast takes the initiative in approaching Jesus, disregarding the Mosaic regulations and apparently failing to give the customary warning. He shows scant respect for the Law. This desperation is reflected in Mark's use of two verbs: *kneeling* and *begging*. He falls to his knees at Jesus' feet, and in his isolation and hopelessness implores his help, *If only you want to, you can make me clean.*[7] He asks to be cleansed, rather than to be cured. He is confident in Jesus' power to heal, but perhaps hesitant about his willingness to get involved, given the cultural inhibitions. The scene is charged with emotion. It is a tense moment. Jesus may recoil from him, and prefer respect for religious and social tradition. The challenge facing Jesus is acute.

## The Response of Jesus

Jesus makes his decision, for he is *moved with compassion.* His words and his actions express that deep feeling. He reaches out, touches him, and says, *Of course I want to! Be cured.*[8] He bridges the dreadful chasm of separation in the tone of his voice and his extraordinary gesture. The man is cured instantly. Jesus responds to the man's reckless trust, and in so doing he ignores the risk of contagion, and he incurs the stigma of ritual defilement according to the Law, something no rabbi would have been prepared to do. He makes whole this leper, publicly deemed to be a sinner, restores him to the life of the community, draws him into personal relationship and fellowship with himself, and enables him to experience the dawning Kingdom, the presence of a gracious God. The compassionate response of Jesus in touching the untouchable, and crossing the boundary between clean and unclean, was as scandalous as the leper's audacity in first approaching him.[9]

The majority of manuscripts attest Jesus' compassion. Other manuscripts read *moved with anger, with warm indignation*, and because this is the more difficult reading, and is omitted in the versions of Matthew and Luke, it is considered by some scholars, by no means all, to be the more original.[10] In this case the anger of Jesus is directed not against the leprous individual but against the power of evil which holds people bound. Or it may be a reaction to the injustice done to lepers in Israel, and to the fact that the Law and its custodians ostracised them rather than offer them help. Jesus rejects the exclusion of the leper on the basis of external criteria for purity.[11] The words and actions of Jesus remain expressions of compassion.

In the Old Testament there are only two accounts of the healing of leprosy: the cases of Miriam and Naaman.[12] These were seen as direct acts of God. One scholar notes that just as the healing of leprosy is God-like, so too is the emotion of compassion. There is strong emphasis on God's compassion in Isaiah 40-66, the New Exodus.[13]

## The Sequel

The rest of the story is a little puzzling. Jesus sternly warns him[14] and sends him away. Both verbs are strong expressions. Some scholars see this as an indication of an earlier alternative form of the story in which the indignation of Jesus was directed against an unclean spirit held to be responsible for the man's condition. Mark has combined features of this exorcism with the story of the healing. Matthew and Luke omit this verse in their versions.[15] *In this climactic episode in a series of encounters between Jesus and the powers of evil, Jesus shows his passionate commitment to the wholeness and holiness of those who are called to enter the kingdom of God.* (Francis J Moloney)[16] Then Jesus imposes silence on the man. The injunction to silence will occur frequently in Mark's subsequent narrative. Jesus probably wishes to avoid too much publicity lest his role be misunderstood and he come to be cast as a wonder-worker.[17]

Jesus then instructs the man to follow the prescribed procedures, showing himself to the priest and offering the requisite sacrifice. While it may have been possible to find a priest in Galilee, a visit to Jerusalem would take time and effort. It is paradoxical that Jesus, having himself violated the purity laws, should demand that the leper observe the legal prescriptions.[18] There is some discussion about the phrase *as a testimony to them*. It can mean as a confirmation that the leper has been healed and that Jesus is being faithful to the Law. It can also be translated as *a testimony against them;* this would be a prophetic critique or indictment of the cultic system, its ineffectiveness and lack of compassion in regard to suffering people. The strong language of the story and its position immediately prior to the next section, which contains several conflict stories, suggests to some scholars that this is the preferred option.[19]

The man ignores Jesus' command, and goes around telling everyone what has occurred.[20] The result of his missionary zeal is that crowds flock to Jesus, and this forces Jesus to avoid the towns and head for deserted places, the flow of his ministry interrupted. Ironically, the situation of the leper and Jesus are now reversed.[21] Nevertheless, people continue to seek him out, coming from afar. The chapter closes as it began, in the wilderness. *Jesus, 'the stronger one' predicted by John, has power over the dreaded leprosy, and yet he is a figure of compassion who, for the sake of a suffering human, will violate ritual laws.* (John Donahue & Daniel Harrington)[22]

## Reflections

The leper is an interesting character. Obviously, he is suffering terribly. The disease presented not only physical problems, but entailed a severe level of segregation from family, village community and friends. This would have caused a sense of loneliness and isolation. Furthermore, the affliction had a religious dimension, being considered an indication of sin, and therefore a cause of guilt and alienation from God. In his hopelessness the man comes to Jesus. His need and desperation are such that he disregards the regulations. He takes a chance, takes the risk of exposing his situation to Jesus. He shows faith, falling at Jesus' feet in supplication; but it is a hesitant faith, because he isn't sure that Jesus would be prepared to bring him healing. His later ignoring of Jesus' injunction to silence is probably understandable, but it does create problems for Jesus.

Jesus comes across again as a man of great compassion, as he reaches out warmly and touches the man. As in other stories which we have considered, he ignores taboos for the sake of a person in need. He touches the unclean, and restores wholeness. He draws the man back into society, restoring his relationships, and assuring him also of God's acceptance. He offers him a new life. Just as evil affects many areas of our lives simultaneously, the Kingdom of God is a multi-faceted reality, embracing all dimensions of an individual and of human experience. It has to do with healing, wholeness and connectedness in every aspect of life.

This story can serve as a paradigm of human experience. The man's condition is an invitation to us to acknowledge occasions and situations when we experience fragmentation within ourselves, isolation and exclusion, when relationships have broken down, including our relationship with God. It can help us locate a whole spectrum of feelings as we seek to cope with our situation. Disconnectedness is, I believe, the fundamental expression of our basic human sinfulness, our need for God. God in Christ Jesus is offering us reconciliation, healing and integration for every dimension of our being and our living. Jesus restores us to God, to one another, to our world. As disciples of Jesus we are called to be instruments of wholeness, to seek to overcome whatever divides and fragments.

# The Man with the Withered Hand

In an earlier chapter we reflected on the story of the paralysed man. That was the first in a series of five controversy stories. This block of material, which delineates the escalation of opposition to Jesus, concludes with another healing, which serves as a catalyst for a further confrontation over a religious issue, the attitude of Jesus to the Law and the Sabbath. It is this rather than the cure which is central to the episode.[23] In this passage only Jesus speaks, as he illustrates in practice the meaning of the previous controversy, when, in response to accusations of his disciples' Sabbath laxity, he claimed that the Sabbath was made for human beings, not the reverse, and that *the Son of Man is Lord of the Sabbath*. This fifth example of conflict brings the series to a climax.

Sabbath observance had long been a key feature of Judaism. In times of foreign occupation and persecution it had become a strong symbol of Jewishness, and an expression of hope for God's liberation. It looked back to creation and Exodus. In Jesus' day it had become a sign of exclusive nationalism.[24] Like most other Jews of that time, the peasants of Galilee probably observed the basic rules of the Sabbath: no secular everyday work, no buying and selling, no lengthy journeys, no lighting or extinguishing a fire, no cooking, no medical treatment of illnesses outside of life-or-death situations, and no military activity except in cases of self-defence. But they were probably not too concerned about the fine points over which special religious groups argued. There were variations between Essenes, Sadducees and Pharisees; the Pharisees differed among themselves on some points. Galilean peasants who did not belong to stringent groups would probably not have been very upset over minor acts to aid the sick on the Sabbath:[25]

> Again he entered the synagogue, and a man was there who had a withered hand. They watched him to see whether he would cure him on the sabbath, so that they might accuse him. And he said to the man who had the withered hand, *Come forward.* Then he said to them, *Is it lawful to do good or to do harm on the sabbath, to save life or to kill?* But they were silent. He looked around at them with anger; he was grieved at their hardness of heart and said to the man, *Stretch out your hand.* He stretched it out, and his hand was restored. The Pharisees went out and immediately conspired with the Herodians against him, how to destroy him. (3:1-6)

## The Context

The context for this episode is a synagogue; its exact location is not identified, but it seems likely that it is in Capernaum.[26] It soon becomes evident that it is the Sabbath day. Jesus is presented as a devout member of the Jewish community, who regularly attends synagogue, and follows the normal religious practices of his people.[27] Amongst those present for the service is a man with a withered hand. It is not clear if the physical deformity is a birth defect, the result of an accident or a disease like rheumatoid arthritis. It is perhaps a form of paralysis.[28] It would be a considerable handicap in a society in which manual labour played such an important part.

The hostility of the atmosphere in the place immediately becomes apparent, for there are people present *who were watching him to see if he would cure him on the Sabbath day, hoping for something to charge him with.* Only later do we learn that they are Pharisees, perhaps the same group as those who in the previous incident criticised the disciples for plucking grains of corn on the Sabbath. They are silent watchers, primed for accusation, seeking evidence, bent on surveillance rather than prayer.[29] The verb *watch* can mean *lie in wait for* with malicious intent. The term *accuse* is normally used of a legal charge against someone. The situation looks like a deliberate trap or set-up.[30]

There is no question about the ability of Jesus to perform a cure. It is an accepted fact. The issue is whether he will do so on a Sabbath day. The rabbis maintained that the sick and injured could be treated on the Sabbath only if life was in danger, but not otherwise. According to the strict Pharisee interpretation, to heal this man, whose life was obviously not in danger, would be a serious infringement. According to Exod 31:14 breaching the Sabbath was punishable by death. In Jesus' day this was no longer enforced, but such a charge would certainly discredit him as a prophet.[31]

## The Words of Jesus

Jesus is able to read their thoughts. Taking up their unspoken challenge, he dramatically and provocatively summons the man into the middle of the floor in full view of everyone.[32] The man has made no request to be healed, maybe because of his awareness of the Sabbath restrictions. The initiative lies entirely with Jesus. Jesus then poses a question to the congregation.[33] It highlights what the Sabbath is all about:[34]

> Is it permitted on the sabbath day to do good, or to do evil; to
> save life, or to kill?

The religious elite were interested in upholding the Sabbath observance and in defining the nature of *work* so as to determine exactly what was forbidden. Jesus argues from a different angle. To heal is to *do good*; to leave in distress and infirmity without offering relief is *to do evil*. In forbidding healing, the rabbis admit that on the Sabbath, normal moral values are reversed, because it is forbidden to do good and prescribed to do evil. For Jesus, on the other hand, one must do good at all times and in all circumstances. Inaction in the face of glaring human need would be to opt for evil rather than good and so would be against God's will. The purpose of the Law is to give life; when misinterpreted, its true intention is denied and it becomes an instrument of death. The Pharisee attitude tends towards destruction rather than life-giving, so it is really Jesus who upholds the Law.[35] The Sabbath was meant to be a celebration of creation and redemption.

Another element to bear in mind is Jesus' sense of mission. He believed that he was engaged in the final battle against evil, and this imposed haste and urgency. Every healing was a blow against Satan. Evil is at work every day of the week. His struggle against the forces of evil is likewise a constant affair, a crusade which cannot be interrupted. Once again the real issue is the failure of Jesus' foes to realise that his coming inaugurates a new situation in which the laws of the old age are not absolutely binding.[36] But Jesus' question has bearing not only on the welfare of the disabled person in front of him. It shows that he is aware of the hostile Sabbath intentions of his adversaries, bent on evil and death.

The Pharisees say nothing in reply; they opt for stony silence. Jesus has placed them in an impossible situation, though they could at least have pointed out that the man was not in danger of death. Jesus, however, does not manifest quiet satisfaction in getting the better of the opposition. Rather, he is deeply angered; their *hardness of heart* saddens him. He is angry because their attachment to legal minutiae makes them blind and insensitive to what is happening in their midst with the coming of the Kingdom, and closed to the well-being of the man whose healing they would wish to block. They seem unable to embrace the image of a God who wants mercy, compassion and love. Jesus detects in their silence an expression of malice, a refusal to acknowledge the truth.[37]

He is distressed by their obtuseness, their *hardness of heart,* a frequent lament of the prophet Jeremiah concerning Israel. *Hardness of heart* is the rejection of God's presence and activity; here it manifests itself in the Pharisees' lack of openness to Jesus, and their malicious schemes for his destruction.[38] The combination of anger and grief in Jesus is powerful: their hardness of heart causes him deep pain; it is out of this pain that his anger springs.[39] Such hardness is a condition which Jesus will repeatedly struggle to break through.

## The Healing

The healing is told very simply. Jesus commands the man to stretch out his hand. The man does so without hesitation, and thus manifests his faith in Jesus. His hand is immediately restored to normal functioning. He is cured simply by the word of Jesus. Apparently, to heal by word rather than by touch was not against the Law, so Jesus is in fact blameless! He does not break the Sabbath.[40] The healing is a symbol of the fullness of life which Jesus brings, an indication of the presence of the Kingdom.

## The Sequel

The reaction is immediate. It is not one of wonder, astonishment, or appreciation, as is frequently the case in such stories, but of hostility. It is also not without irony, given the life or death terms in which Jesus has focussed the Sabbath issue. The Pharisees leave the synagogue at once, and engage in plotting with the Herodians against Jesus, discussing how to destroy him. The former aimed at a high level of religious purity; the Herodians were supporters of Herod Antipas, possibly some of his officials, and were a political not a religious grouping. They collaborated with the secular foreign power, and normally would have nothing in common with Pharisees. The latter, in seeking their support in order to turn Herod against Jesus, were acting unscrupulously, since they were their natural enemies. Perhaps the Herodians were open to co-operate through fear that Jesus was politically dangerous. The Pharisees ally with the supporters of the man who was responsible for the death of the Baptist, in order to effect the death of Jesus too. Mark closes the episode on this intensely antagonistic note, with religious and secular groups conspiring together, ironically bent on the destruction of his life, unable to acknowledge that Jesus was from God, and was God's agent.[41] Opposition to Jesus is now intense and open; he is seen as a threat. From now on Jesus lives and works in the shadow of the cross.[42]

## Reflection

The man in this story does not speak a word. He does not ask Jesus for healing. He is probably somewhat surprised and embarrassed at the dialogue erupting around him. But when Jesus calls him out into the centre of the floor, he responds. When Jesus then invites him to extend his hand, he does so. In this way he shows faith in Jesus' power and will to heal.

His situation is the occasion for a discussion about a serious issue of discipleship, an issue which will raise its head again as the Gospel story proceeds. It highlights the danger of legalism, small-mindedness, and endemic resistance to change. A perplexing phenomenon common in religious circles is a tendency to rigidity. History, and current experience, suggest that there is an ongoing danger of concentrating on things, regulations and practices, to the detriment of people. Genuine perspective can easily become distorted. This issue is as vibrant and dangerous today in Christianity as it was with the Pharisees of Jesus' time. Frequently, the key issue has to do with an understanding of God, the God of Jesus.

Jesus in the episode demonstrates a different standpoint. For him the healing and wholeness of human beings is paramount. It is not something to be programmed into a restrictive timetable. His awareness of the Father's goodness and passion for life gives clarity to his values and his judgement, and is liberating. It is, however, challenging and controversial. The story highlights another aspect of his character, as he reacts with frustration, anger and sadness at the *hardness of heart* of his adversaries.

# Father and Son

This compelling episode takes place in Mark's narrative after the Transfiguration of Jesus. On the way down the mountain after that remarkable experience the disciples raise the question about Elijah's expected coming, and are informed that he has already come, presumably in the person of the Baptist. On reaching the rest of the group of disciples, Jesus and his three companions encounter a scene of confusion.[43] The text reads as follows:

> When they came to the disciples, they saw a great crowd around them, and some scribes arguing with them. When the whole crowd saw him, they were immediately overcome with awe, and they ran forward to greet him. He asked them, *What are you arguing about with them?*

Someone from the crowd answered him, *Teacher, I brought you my son; he has a spirit that makes him unable to speak; and whenever it seizes him, it dashes him down; and he foams and grinds his teeth and becomes rigid; and I asked your disciples to cast it out, but they could not do so.* He answered them, *You faithless generation, how much longer must I be among you? How much longer must I put up with you? Bring him to me.* And they brought the boy to him. When the spirit saw him, immediately it threw the boy into convulsions, and he fell on the ground and rolled about, foaming at the mouth. Jesus asked the father, *How long has this been happening to him?* And he said, *From childhood. It has often cast him into the fire and into the water, to destroy him; but if you are able to do anything, have pity on us and help us.* Jesus said to him, *If you are able! – All things can be done for the one who believes.* Immediately the father of the child cried out, *I believe; help my unbelief!* When Jesus saw that a crowd had come running together, he rebuked the unclean spirit, saying to it, *You spirit that keep this boy from speaking and hearing, I command you, come out of him, and never enter him again!* After crying out and convulsing him terribly, it came out, and the boy was like a corpse, so that most of them said, *He is dead.* But Jesus took him by the hand and lifted him up, and he was able to stand. When he had entered the house, his disciples asked him privately, *Why could we not cast it out?* He said to them, *This kind can come out only through prayer.* (9:14-29)

## The Approach to Jesus

Jesus' disciples are in the midst of a large crowd,[44] and are discussing or arguing with some scribes. The people have presumably been waiting for Jesus, anthemselvesd on catching sight of him, they excitedly rush up to greet him.[45] Jesus then asks the disciples what the argument with the scribes is all about.[46] It could well have concerned the correct procedure for exorcising demons.[47] It was, more likely, the disciples' failure to solve the problem and remedy the situation. The question remains hanging in the air, for a man from the crowd interrupts, explaining that he has brought to Jesus his son who is possessed by a spirit of dumbness. He has come to Jesus out of a mixture of desperation and hope; clearly he has some faith in Jesus' healing power.[48] In his absence the disciples have been unable to cast the spirit out. The man gives a vivid description of the boy's plight: the spirit takes hold of him and throws him to the ground, where he foams at the mouth, grinds his teeth and goes rigid. The symptoms indicate a form of epilepsy, typically interpreted in terms of demon possession.[49] Jesus is wearied and exasperated by the lack of faith which surrounds him, especially that of his disciples,[50] but commands that the boy be brought to him. As this happens the spirit throws the boy into convulsions. Jesus asks the boy's father how long this has been taking place, and is informed that the boy has been afflicted in this way since childhood; the spirit has attempted to destroy the boy by throwing him into fire and water. The situation is manifestly serious; it cannot but have caused deep anguish and suffering to the parents.

The man then pleads:

*But if you are able to do anything, have compassion on us and help us.*

In the Gospels there are many requests for mercy, but this is the only occasion when the technical term for compassion occurs as part of a request. The man appeals to the compassion of Jesus for both the boy and himself, and doubtless for family and friends too.

## Jesus' Response

In reply, Jesus repeats the conditional *if*, highlighting the lack of faith evident in its use, a hesitancy possibly caused by the failure of Jesus' disciples to provide help. Jesus states clearly that everything can be done (by God) for the one who trustingly believes.[51] In the first place this refers to Jesus, who trusts in God; *his immediacy with God is the source of his miraculous authority, God's power is available to him.* (Francis J Moloney)[52] It then refers to the distraught father.[53] Acknowledging the inadequacy of his faith, he responds to Jesus' challenge with a further plea:

*I believe; help my unbelief!*

It is a heartfelt cry, echoed down the ages by many struggling with a wavering faith, *one of the most memorable and beloved statements in the New Testament.* (John Donahue & Daniel Harrington)[54] He is torn between faith and unbelief.[55] This second request concerns himself alone. Jesus responds compassionately to both requests simultaneously.[56] With solemnity and his customary personal authority he commands the evil spirit to leave the boy definitively. There is a final convulsion which leaves the boy like a corpse. But Jesus takes him by the hand, and raises him up.[57] There are overtones of resurrection here; *the Christian language of resurrection rings out as the miracle story comes to a close.* (Francis J Moloney)[58] This episode is a further example of God's victory in the cosmic struggle with evil, effected through the ministry of Jesus. There is no response from the father or the crowd, as is normally the case in the miracle story format. The story ends rather abruptly.

## The Sequel

When Jesus and the disciples are later in the house[59], the puzzled disciples ask him privately why, after their earlier successes, they had not been able to conduct an exorcism this time. Jesus replies that this type of demon can be expelled only by prayer.[60] He does not refer to faith, though prayer is clearly an expression of faith.[61] In the wider context of the Markan narrative the disciples were perhaps becoming overconfident in themselves, presumptuously forgetting the need to trust completely in God, the source of any power, and neglecting to turn to God in prayer. Their struggling journey into faith continues as the narrative unfolds.[62]

## Reflections

In this episode we meet a frustrated Jesus. He is uncomfortable with excited crowds, disappointed with the performance of his disciples, and ill at ease with the man's lack of faith. On the other hand, he is clearly moved by the man's description of the dreadful plight of his son. The man hit the right note in appealing to his compassion. Jesus challenges the man's hesitant faith, pushing him to go further in his trust in God's mercy and power. In response to the man's passionate prayer for deeper faith, he casts the devil from his son. This is what his mission is about. As in other stories, he then takes the boy's hand and lifts him up. The gesture and the wording are deliberately symbolic of risen life too. The father in the story is a touching figure. One senses the depth of his anguish, his concern for the welfare of his son, the pain of his own suffering over the years. There is desperation in his appeal. His hesitancy is perhaps understandable, given the milling crowds and the ineffectiveness of the disciples' intervention. But he rises to Jesus' challenge with that beautiful plea, *Help my unbelief.*

We can readily identify with this father. All of us have people about whom we are deeply concerned. We doubtless bring them to Jesus in prayer, entrusting them to his compassion. It is important that we seek to involve him in these situations. He may not bring healing in quite the way we would wish, but he will help them and us to cope better. And we make our own the father's prayer, *Help my unbelief.* I think that we are constantly in that situation of believing and not believing at the same time, or believing and yet not fully understanding. We grapple with our doubts and questions and faltering faith. The major challenge which faces readers of the Gospel is highlighted in the question, *Do you believe?* which Jesus puts to Martha when he goes to Bethany to raise her brother to life.[61]

# The Unnamed Blind Man

In Mark's Gospel there are two stories in which Jesus brings healing to a man suffering from blindness.[64] Each story has its own peculiar fascination. For the Evangelist these are not simply two separate incidents; he uses them as part of a wider picture. The *Little People* are caught up in Mark's treatment of the nature of discipleship.

## The Context

As Mark's narrative has unfolded, it has become clear that the disciples of Jesus are struggling to cope with their Master. They have found it difficult to understand his parables. They have panicked in the storm on the lake, despite his being with them on the boat. On returning from their missionary experience, they excitedly recount to Jesus all that they have done and taught, perhaps attributing their success to their own efforts and skills, losing sight of their dependence on him. At that juncture, perceiving that they need a break and a rest after their exertions, Jesus suggests that they should head off by boat for a quiet place. The local people, however, guess where they are bound, and reach the place before them. On stepping ashore and seeing the crowds, Jesus is moved with compassion for them, and proceeds to teach them at some length. After some time the disciples approach Jesus, suggesting that he should send the people away so that they can find food and are disconcerted when Jesus intimates that they should provide the food themselves. Then, after Jesus has multiplied the loaves and fishes, sent the crowds away, and enjoined that they set out across the lake again, they are overcome with terror at the sight of him, as he comes to join them, walking on the water. Mark comments:

> At this they were completely dumbfounded, for they had not understood the incident of the loaves; their minds were closed. (6:52).

Not long afterwards they have problems in fathoming the meaning of Jesus' radical comment in his controversy with the religious leaders about ritual defilement. Jesus asks them, *Do you also fail to understand?* (7:18) Later, when the crowds gather again and have nothing to eat, the compassion of Jesus and his desire that they be fed provokes the following reply from his disciples, *How can one feed these people with bread here in the desert?*

They have short memories! Jesus uses the seven loaves which they have brought with them to feed the 4000. (8:1-10) After this second multiplication of the loaves, the Pharisees ask Jesus for a sign from heaven; they are unwilling to accept the signs he has given. So Jesus and the twelve cross the lake again, and the disciples become worried because they have forgotten to bring with them adequate bread supplies; they have only one loaf. Jesus administers a trenchant rebuke:

> *Why are you talking about having no bread? Do you still not perceive or understand? Are your hearts hardened? Do you have eyes, and fail to see? Do you have ears, and fail to hear?* (8:17-18)

The disciples are deaf and they are blind. The next section of the Gospel as far as Jesus' arrival in Jericho addresses this situation, as Jesus vainly seeks to remedy their inadequacy. The two stories in which Jesus brings sight to blind men are central to this theme.

When introducing the story of the Syrophoenician woman, I pointed out the interesting structure which Mark creates for chapters six, seven and eight. He devises two parallel blocks. The first section commences with the feeding of the 5000 and the crossing of the lake, followed by a controversy between Jesus and his opponents about cleanliness and the old traditions. Finally, there are the two stories of the Syrophoenician woman, in which there is a reference to bread, and the healing of a deaf mute. This pattern is then immediately paralleled in the subsequent section. In this sequence 4000 are fed; there is a brief lake crossing, a controversy (the demand for a sign), a reference to loaves of bread, and a healing, this time of a blind man.[67]

The episode which we shall now consider, which is found only in Mark, looks both ways, serving as a bridge passage, or a hinge.[68] It brings to a conclusion the second sequence of events which begins with the feeding of the 4000, and is in parallel with the conclusion of the first sequence, the cure of the deaf mute.[69] Taken together these two cures fulfil the prophecy of Isaiah, that the deaf will hear and the blind will see, as we saw in Chapter three. Looking forward, the passage under consideration introduces the next main section of Mark's story, sometimes called *The Journey Narrative*. This is thus framed by two incidents in which Jesus cures a blind man, the second being the story of Bartimaeus in Jericho, *from blind to blind*. In this section Jesus seeks to lead his disciples from blindness to vision and the insight of faith; he strives to educate them about his identity and role, and about the true nature of discipleship. With this background, we can approach the text:

They came to Bethsaida. Some people brought a blind man to him and begged him to touch him. He took the blind man by the hand and led him out of the village; and when he had put saliva on his eyes and laid his hands on him, he asked him, *Can you see anything?* And the man looked up and said, *I can see people, but they look like trees, walking.* Then Jesus laid his hands on his eyes again; and he looked intently and his sight was restored, and he saw everything clearly. Then he sent him away to his home, saying, *Do not even go into the village.* (8:22-26)

This story is often referred to as a two-stage miracle. It is the only miracle story in the Gospels in which Jesus is not immediately successful, which is possibly the reason why Matthew and Luke omit it. Perhaps the case was particularly difficult, and yet the power of Jesus wins through in the end. Or the story may be intended as a symbol of the gradual process of the disciples into faith; until the resurrection they remain only half-seeing. Thus the story is to be understood in conjunction with the following incident at Caesarea Philippi, when Peter makes his profession of faith in Jesus as Messiah, but then refuses to accept Jesus' understanding of that title and role.

## The Setting

The setting is Bethsaida, a small fishing village on the North Eastern shore of the lake, just over a mile from where the Jordan flows into the lake. It was situated about four miles from Capernaum, and was in the territory of Philip. He developed a thriving city a mile and half inland which was called Bethsaida Julias, named after the daughter of Augustus. The old village, with a mixed Jewish and Gentile population, continued to exist as a lakeside port. It was a prosperous little town rather than a village, with about 200 inhabitants.[66] Since Jesus arrives by boat, it is probably the old fishing village which is intended.[67] Unnamed people bring a blind man to Jesus, asking that he touch him.[68] They show faith in bringing him to Jesus, as well as concern for their friend. It is assumed that contact with Jesus is curative. The structural and verbal parallels with the earlier incident of the deaf mute are close.[69]

## The Response of Jesus

Jesus takes the man by the hand, and leads him outside the village away from the others, as in the parallel story. Whilst this may be a way of avoiding a public spectacle, it also illustrates the sensitive thoughtfulness of Jesus, as he walks with the man, establishing a personal relationship, and enabling trust and confidence to develop. There are echoes of the way the prophets refer to God's taking Israel by the hand in the Exodus, a pattern to be repeated in the new Exodus.[70] They stop, and Jesus spits into his eyes and lays his hands on him. The NRSV translates this more delicately, *When he had put saliva on his eyes.* This complex ritual is almost magical.[71] In the earlier story of the deaf-mute Jesus spits on his own fingers and touches the man's tongue with his moistened fingers. There is evidence of such actions and healing practices in the ancient world.[72] Next Jesus asks the man whether he can see anything. This question is echoed later when Jesus asks his disciples about their insight into his identity. The parallel may well be deliberate.

The man is beginning to see, but still cannot distinguish objects too well; his vision is blurred. To Jesus' question, *Can you see anything?* he replies, *I can see people, but they look like trees, walking.* The man has regained his sight well enough to make out people moving in the distance, but the blurred images look more like trees than humans. Perhaps he is peering into the distance to see his friends, since Jesus has led him away from them.[73]

Jesus then touches the man's eyes again without using spittle, and he comes to complete sight. *He looked intently and his sight was restored, and he saw everything clearly.* The complete and lasting nature of the cure brought about by Jesus' second intervention is clearly indicated, and three different verbs are used together to convey this.[74] Thus the man makes a journey from no sight through partial vision to full sight.

## The Sequel
There is no reaction from the man, his friends or the bystanders. Jesus sends him home, with instructions not even to go into the village, which implies that the place is not his home. Presumably the purpose is to avoid the matter getting widely known lest false messianic expectations be aroused.[75] The man disappears from the scene, his part in the story completed.

The story is very significant for Mark. It is placed immediately after the blindness of the disciples has been rigorously highlighted, their need to be led into sight and understanding.[76] The man is brought to sight in two stages; firstly he sees, but only partially; then he comes to full sight. The story is symbolic, and sets the scene for the section 8:27-10:52, and for the rest of the Gospel.

150

The next scene in Mark's narrative is the incident at Caesarea Philippi. There Jesus quizzes his disciples about the current views concerning his identity, and is informed that some people believe him to be the Baptist, others Elijah, and others one of the prophets. Genuine insight is lacking. Jesus then asks them about their own opinion. Peter speaks up, stating, *You are the Messiah.* At last, a sign of real understanding and perception! But Peter omits Son of God. Jesus then articulates for them his view of his messianic mission, speaking of his passion and death for the first time. This is too much for Peter, and he strongly objects. Taking Jesus to one side, he seeks to deter him from such a course and to persuade him to adopt a different path. Jesus sternly reprimands him for thinking in a human way, and being closed to God's plan. Peter sees, but only partially. The disciples will not, in fact, finally see clearly until after Jesus' death and resurrection. The parallel between the healing of the blind man and the Caesarea Philippi incident which follows, is deliberate.[77]

## Reflection

This fascinating story is a further incident in which a group of people show their concern for a suffering friend, relative or neighbour by bringing him along to Jesus seeking a cure. Clearly, they are people of faith; they believe that Jesus can and will respond by healing the man. It is interesting that they ask Jesus to touch him. The faith of the man himself is not made explicit, but as the story develops it is clear that he is open to the actions of Jesus, and co-operative, which implies his faith. Their faith is not misplaced.

Jesus' desire to avoid a public display is again evident. His sensitivity and kindness is apparent in his taking the individual by the hand, and walking with him, thus establishing a relationship. In this story more than many others, a rapport seems to have been established between the invalid and Jesus. The unusual procedure which Jesus adopts no doubt facilitates this, and builds confidence. There is even a little dialogue at the halfway stage. We can imagine the man's joy when finally he is able to see clearly, and can himself choose the route to take in order to avoid passing through the village. He is free, responsible and independent again, and has glimpsed the meaning of Kingdom.

Blindness is a terrible affliction, a great burden to bear. The gift of sight is one of the most wonderful gifts with which most of us have been endowed. Effortlessly, our eyes catch the beauty of the world around us, in its bewildering variety of hue, shape, texture and movement.

We can distinguish the shades of green in the trees, the shades of grey in the clouds. We can appreciate the bright and subtle colours of the flowers and birds. We can appreciate the skill of artists as they seek to capture and hold such beauty in oil and pastel and water. We can stand in bewilderment in a clothes shop, or when choosing curtains or wallpaper or paint for our home. We can scan people's faces, sensitive to details of uniqueness and mood, the warmth in a smile, the twinkle in an eye, the sadness on a brow. We can contemplate the play of light and shade. Sight brings such richness and meaning to our lives. As we imagine the joy of the man in the story, a joy shared by his friends, perhaps we can pause to thank God that we can see, and resolve not to take this wonderful gift for granted.

# Blind Bartimaeus

The healing of blind Bartimaeus is the last of Jesus' cures in Mark. The story is to be taken in conjunction with the earlier episode of the two-stage cure of the blind man outside the village of Bethsaida before the journey to Jerusalem began. The two stories frame the section of the Gospel narrative in which Jesus has been attempting to open the eyes of the disciples to the meaning of his Messiahship and the nature of discipleship. This episode forms a dramatic contrast to the disciples' persistent misunderstanding, and foreshadows the second stage of their coming fully to inner sight after the resurrection, when they will *see* Jesus in Galilee:[78]

> They came to Jericho. As he and his disciples and a large crowd were leaving Jericho, Bartimaeus son of Timaeus, a blind beggar, was sitting by the roadside. When he heard that it was Jesus of Nazareth, he began to shout out and say, *Jesus, Son of David, have mercy on me!* Many sternly ordered him to be quiet, but he cried out even more loudly, *Son of David, have mercy on me!* Jesus stood still and said, *Call him here.* And they called the blind man, saying to him, *Take heart; get up, he is calling you.* So throwing off his cloak, he sprang up and came to Jesus. Then Jesus said to him, *What do you want me to do for you?* The blind man said to him, *My teacher, let me see again.* Jesus said to him, *Go; your faith has made you well.* Immediately he regained his sight and followed him on the way.

## The Setting

As their journey continues, Jesus and the disciples reach Jericho, a prosperous town on the main route to Jerusalem, which was still some 15 miles distant. It stood 6 miles north of the Dead Sea, and had the character of a *garden city,* a place with ready access to water and a good climate. It was an agricultural centre, a crossroads, and a winter resort for the Jewish aristocracy. Herod the Great had built a winter palace there. At 850 feet below sea-level, it was the lowest inhabited place in the world, and had been inhabited since around 8000BC; Jerusalem was 2500 feet above sea-level.[79]

## The Request

As Jesus leaves the town, accompanied by his disciples and a large crowd, Bartimaeus, a blind beggar, is seated at the roadside. Since this was on the pilgrim route to Jerusalem at Passover, a time for almsgiving, it was doubtless an advantageous spot. As a blind man, condemned to begging for survival, he was a nobody.[80] The fact that he is named, firstly in Greek and then in Aramaic, suggests to some scholars that he was known in early Christian circles.[81] On hearing that it is Jesus who is passing by, he determines to seize his opportunity and cries out, *Son of David, Jesus, have pity on me!* It is unclear what he may have had in mind in calling Jesus Son of David. He may simply have been indicating Jesus' Davidic ancestry. This title was a fairly common messianic title in later Jewish literature (though not in the Old Testament), but Mark normally shows little interest in it. In contemporary Jewish traditions it was associated with Solomon, the only reigning king to be called by this title in the Hebrew Bible, who was famous for his exorcisms and healing qualities.[82] Although the title is not adequate, there is irony in a blind man having greater perception than the fully-sighted.[83] The title will be picked up again as an acclamation in the subsequent story of the entry of Jesus into Jerusalem.[84] It recurs in a later controversy.[85] It resurfaces in the Sanhedrin and Roman trials, and in the mockery on the cross, transposed into the theme of *Messiah*, King of the Jews. At a redactional level Mark intends these connections.[86] The emphasis, however, should not be placed on the man's confession, but on his recognition that Jesus could bring him healing.[87]

The crowds, probably mainly pilgrims, who are milling around and less insightful than he, and possibly the disciples too, tell him to hold his tongue.[88] The same verb is used elsewhere in Mark.[89] It has usually been Jesus who imposes silence when his messiahship is acknowledged. This time he does not, maybe because his passion is near, and others do! They consider the man a nuisance, and presume that Jesus cannot be bothered with such folk. Far from being dissuaded, the man cries out with strong faith for mercy all the more loudly and insistently, repeating the title.[90]

## The Response of Jesus

Jesus stops and has Bartimaeus called to him. The people change their tone and tell him encouragingly, *Courage, get up; he is calling you.* Jesus does not take him aside privately, but calls him openly to him. The man's trust and hope are palpable as he immediately throws off his cloak, or, if it is lying on the ground to receive donations, which, in that climate is the more likely case, he pushes it aside as irrelevant,[91] springs up and comes to Jesus. Like others called previously, he abandons everything he has.[92]

Jesus, in words recalling the recent incident involving the sons of Zebedee, when, blind to the values of Jesus, they sought power and authority, puts that gently provocative question:

*What do you want me to do for you?*

The reply comes unhesitatingly and predictably:

*Rabbuni, I want my sight back.*

The man is aware of his need and helplessness, and finds hope in the person of Jesus, turning to him for help. It seems that at one time he had been able to see. Only Jesus can bring fresh sight. The form of address, *Rabbouni, my Master,* used only here and in John 20:16, is more reverential than simply, *Rabbi*. Bartimaeus is cured because of his trust, his energetic faith, *Your faith has saved you*. There is no reference to Jesus touching him, as in the earlier parallel story. The word of Jesus brings immediate and complete healing, body and soul.[93] *Blind Bartimaeus joins the Syrophoenician woman and the father of the epileptic boy in presenting himself to Jesus, bringing nothing except faith, and thus comes to full sight.* (Francis J Moloney)[94]

Jesus tells him to go; he now has that freedom and independence. But he chooses to follow Jesus on the road to Jerusalem and to the cross - a symbol of discipleship (*the way*), which also expresses something of the deeper significance of his being *saved*. He *is presented to the reader as a disciple prepared to follow in trust the way of Jesus through the cross to resurrection*. (Francis J Moloney)[95] His faith, even if the title Son of David is not entirely adequate, sets him apart from the crowd, who are not able to see the truth about Jesus. It also stands in contrast to the failure of the disciples in the previous incident, and throughout this section of the narrative, who show such little insight into the true identity and role of Jesus. *His faith in Jesus' power, his confession of his authority, and his willingness to follow him all mark him out as a disciple.* (Morna D Hooker)[96] It is also clear that only Jesus can lead people into sight and insight. The story foreshadows the second stage of the healing of the disciples' sight.

*The story of the calling of Bartimaeus serves as a paradigm for Jesus' power to heal, restore and give sight to those who respond to his call to follow him on the way to the cross.* (R Alan Culpepper)[97]

Bartimaeus is now able to see; with physical sight comes the insight of faith. The verb *see* is used on Calvary. When the centurion sees the dead Jesus, he *sees* the ultimate truth of his identity, and confesses him as *the Son of God*. The theophany of the cross makes such faith vision possible. At the empty tomb the heavenly envoy proclaims the Easter kerygma, and tells the women to inform the disciples that if they go to Galilee they will *see* the risen Jesus. The healing of Bartimaeus prefigures the full healing of Peter's blindness which will take place after the death and resurrection of Jesus. *Along with the other disciples he will finally see that Jesus the Messiah is also necessarily Jesus the crucified and risen Son of Man. Only then will he see and understand Jesus as Son of God.* (John P Meier)[98]

## Reflection

Bartimaeus is presented as a man of considerable faith. The antagonism of the crowd does not deter him in his quest to meet Jesus and find healing. His determination, in fact, grows. There is strong emotion in his throwing aside his cloak, and in his response to Jesus' question. He longs to see again. His response to Jesus' cure in opting not to go home but to follow Jesus on the way to Jerusalem means that he has an ongoing role in the narrative. He is a model of what discipleship is about.[99] And he is a challenge to us in our lives today.

The compassion of Jesus is again evident.[100] When he hears the man's impassioned cry, he stops and gives him his attention, overruling the crowd's attempts to silence him. Calling him to come to him, he immediately communicates his willingness to respond. In asking Bartimaeus what he wanted, he was acknowledging the man's responsibility for what lay in the future, the consequences of being healed. Jesus must have warmed to his single-mindedness and enthusiasm, as he fell in behind him on the journey.

This story invites us to ponder our understanding of Jesus, our faith in him, expressed in our practical living. In our lives we have listened to sermons and attended lectures. We have read articles and books, received counsel and advice. We have spent time in prayer. We have engaged in conversation and discussion. Opportunities for enlightenment have been numerous. How rich is our vision, how deep our understanding, how strong our commitment? Perhaps, like the disciples, we stumble along, sometimes in the light, sometimes in the shadows. There are things about Jesus which perhaps are something of a puzzle. There are aspects of discipleship with which we struggle. Though we are not blind, our sight is impaired and partial still. Like Bartimaeus we ask Jesus to enable us to see, to see more clearly and more truly. We pray for firmer faith and stronger commitment in following him.

# Concluding Thoughts

Jesus warmly reaches out to the leper and touches him. In this he again disregards taboos, and incurs ritual defilement according to the Law by touching the unclean. For Jesus what is important is to bring healing, and to restore the man to life. Similar compassion is seen in his treatment of Bartimaeus. Jesus hears his cry, and overrules the crowd's attempt to keep the man at a distance and on the margins. There is a warmth in his question, as he restores his sight. The father of the epileptic boy appeals, with some hesitation, to his compassion, and, after urging him to greater trust, Jesus accedes to his request, reaching out to lift the boy to his feet. With the first blind man, we glimpse his sensitivity. Jesus is not a healing machine; he establishes relationships, treating people as individuals of value.

At the same time the stories reveal other aspects of the human Jesus. He reacts with frustration and anger at the hardness of heart of his adversaries in the synagogue, challenging their restricted viewpoint. In the scene after the transfiguration he is uncomfortable with the madding crowd and frustrated by his stumbling disciples. Yet, he manifests his clarity of conviction, and his desire to lead people out from their narrowness.

The *Little People* are an interesting bunch. The leper is determined; he disregards the rules in order to encounter Jesus. He is desperate, understandably. He is confident in Jesus' ability to cleanse him, but hesitant about his willingness, given the legal situation. In the end he demonstrates a disregard for Jesus' recommendations, creating problems for him. The man in the synagogue must have felt confused by the argument raging around him, but when invited to extend his hand, he has faith enough to do so. The father of the epileptic boy is another of those who come to Jesus seeking healing for a dear one. One cannot but empathise with him in his anguish, and in his hesitant faith. He perseveres and his faith wins through. In Bethsaida other people approach Jesus seeking a cure for a friend, asking Jesus to touch him and restore his sight. Their faith is clear and unhesitating. Like the leper Bartimaeus seeks healing for himself. He is insistent when the crowd bid him keep silent. He desperately wishes to see again. Like Legion earlier, his reaction to being cured is to wish to join Jesus as a disciple. He is allowed to do so, following him along the way, now a genuine disciple. Taken together, these stories illustrate different facets of faith, especially the need for persistent faith, a faith that can overcome obstacles.

# Chapter Six – The Passion and Resurrection

The *Little People* feature quite prominently in the accounts of Jesus' Passion and Resurrection. Whereas in the narrative of the ministry few are named, here several names are provided. In Mark's Gospel there is Simon of Cyrene, who is pressed into helping Jesus to carry his cross to Calvary. There is the Gentile centurion, who after Jesus has died, makes a profession of faith. A group of women are present on Calvary and at the burial of Jesus by Joseph of Arimathea. The *Little People* perform for Jesus the services which his disciples ought to have rendered, but they were nowhere to be seen! The women go to the tomb of Jesus early on the Sunday morning, and find the tomb empty. In John's Gospel, there is the beautiful encounter there between the Risen Jesus and Mary of Magdala.

## The Passion

### Simon of Cyrene

By this time in Mark's narrative, Jesus has been arrested in the garden as a result of Judas' treachery. The disciples have all fled, including the elusive youth who leaves his garment behind. As predicted by Jesus, Peter has denied his Master three times, the third time with curses and a solemn oath. A kind of trial before the Sanhedrin has followed, leading to the decision that Jesus should die. The Jewish religious leaders have subsequently handed Jesus over to the Roman procurator, Pilate, who eventually yielded to public pressure, condemneding Jesus to death. After being scourged, and crowned with thorns, and abused by the soldiery, Jesus is finally led out for crucifixion:

> Then they led him out to crucify him. They compelled a passer-by, who was coming in from the country, to carry his cross; it was Simon of Cyrene, the father of Alexander and Rufus. Then they brought Jesus to the place called Golgotha (which means the place of the skull). *(15:20-22)*

It was the Roman and Jewish custom that crucifixion should take place outside the city walls, near a busy road.[1] The usual Roman procedure was that the upright was permanently in position, and the person condemned was required to carry the crossbeam (the patibulum) like a yoke to the place of execution. Jesus was not able to do this. After a while it became necessary to requisition a stranger. The Romans, as the army of occupation, exercised their right to enlist someone for forced labour. The inference is that Jesus was so exhausted by the scourging and torture that he was too weak to carry the beam himself; this may also be implied by his speedy death.

The person forcibly pressed into service was called Simon. Whilst it is not impossible that he was a Gentile, it is most likely that he was a Jew, either coming on pilgrimage for the feast from Cyrene, a city in Libya, N Africa, and residing temporarily outside the city, or a repatriated *diaspora* Jew now locally resident.[2] There was a large Jewish colony in Cyrene comprising four administrative districts. In Jerusalem there were synagogues where services were conducted in Greek, including one for Cyrenaeans.[3] Simon's sons, Alexander and Rufus, were presumably well known to Mark's community as Christians.[4] Mention of them serves as guarantee of the detail's authenticity. The reference to the *country* is vague; it could indicate that he was coming in from the fields, or simply from his home or residence outside the city. It cannot therefore shed light on the question as to whether it was a feast or not, and so be used in the discussion over the dating of the crucifixion.[5]

Although Simon probably did not embrace the cross freely or willingly, he is put forward by Mark as a symbol or model of genuine discipleship. The same verb for carrying the cross is used earlier when Jesus is spelling out the meaning of discipleship after the incident at Caesarea Philippi.[6] Given that the other disciples have taken flight, it is Simon alone who carries the cross.[7] *Where the principal 'Simon' (Simon Peter) is glaringly absent, another Simon has appeared to become the point of entry into the story for all subsequent disciples.* (Brendan Byrne)[8] As readers we make the connection.

## The Centurion

After Jesus has reached Golgotha with Simon's help, he is crucified. The soldiers divide his clothes amongst them, as was the custom. Above the cross an inscription is fixed, *The King of the Jews.* Two bandits suffer the same fate, one on either side of him. The passers-by mock Jesus, suggesting that he should save himself and come down from the cross. The chief priests and scribes do likewise, saying, *He saved others; he cannot save himself. Let the Messiah, the King of Israel, come down from the cross now, so that we may see and believe.* Even the two who were crucified with him taunt him. A period of darkness descends dramatically over the whole earth.[9] Jesus cries out, *My God, my God, why have you forsaken me?* His sense of isolation is absolute. Jesus utters another loud cry before breathing his last. *This wordless scream is Mark's final and dramatic statement on the crucifixion.* (Francis J Moloney)[10]

In the immediate aftermath of the death of Jesus two important things take place, which indicate the theological significance of what has happened, and point to the beginning of the new age:

> And the curtain of the temple was torn in two, from top to bottom. Now when the centurion, who stood facing him, saw that in this way he breathed his last, he said, *Truly this man was God's Son!* (15:37-39)

The first is the tearing apart of the curtain of the Temple. The passive verb indicates that this is God's action, which breaks God's silence.[11] A link can be made between this tearing in connection with Jesus' death, and the tearing apart of the heavens at his baptism. On the earlier occasion the Father responds to Jesus' associating himself with sinful humanity by proclaiming him *beloved Son*; now, at Calvary, it is a Gentile executioner who acknowledges his true identity. For Mark, the death of Jesus is the decisive and ultimately fatal blow to the reign of Satan, making possible the transforming advent of God's Kingdom.[12]

There were in fact two temple veils. One hung at the entrance from the outside court to the Holy Place (the outer veil), and would have been visible to people outside. The other separated the Holy of Holies from the Holy Place (the inner veil), through which the High Priest alone was allowed to pass once a year (at *Yom Kippur*).[13] This was very significant. Mark is not specific, but probably intended the inner veil.[14] The Temple has featured often during Jesus' final days. His action in cleansing the Temple,[15] coupled with the incident of the barren fig tree which frames it, was a prophetic sign of coming judgement and destruction, a condemnation of corrupt and fruitless worship. Jesus clearly foretold the Temple's destruction.[16] Ironically, the words of those who falsely accused Jesus during the trial, and of the passers-by who mocked him on the cross, are brought to realisation, and a new temple not made by hands, the Christian community, constructed on the rejected cornerstone and open to all, is about to come into existence.[17] Jesus is vindicated by God.

The rending of the curtain is thought to symbolise the end of the Temple cult and sacrificial system, and the Old Testament dispensation as a whole. The Temple no longer has any religious significance. The special character which made the place a holy sanctuary is now obsolete. The presence of God is no longer there. It is also a sign of what was yet to come, the future destruction of the Temple by the Romans, which had probably already taken place by the time the Gospel was written. This is seen as God's wrathful judgement of the People for their rejection of their Messiah.[18]

160

The tearing of the Temple veil also symbolises the removal of the barrier between God and humankind. Everyone now has unrestricted access to the presence of a gracious and forgiving God, and the possibility of entering into a new relationship with God, including the Gentiles, as the following episode eloquently illustrates.[19] The dividing wall between Jew and Gentile has been broken down through the blood of Jesus.[20] A curtain that is torn from top to bottom is at the same time an irremediable destruction and a decisive opening.

The second event to follow Jesus' death is the centurion's statement, *Truly, this man was God's Son.* An officer of centurion rank has not been mentioned previously in the passion narrative. His being in charge of the execution is confirmed later, when he is summoned by Pilate to verify Jesus' death.[21] His reaction at the cross springs from what he *saw* as he stood there facing Jesus. *Seeing* has been a key term throughout the second part of the Gospel narrative. Some are of the view that the focus of the *seeing* is the cry of Jesus, his actual death and possibly his last words. Others would include the darkness and the rending of the Temple veil, the latter being an indication that Jesus was so close to God that the deity had begun to destroy the sanctuary of those who had been responsible for handing him over to the Romans and had also mocked him.[22] This, however, would take away from the centrality of the crucified Jesus. It is the death of Jesus which brings this Gentile to faith.[23]

In the course of Jesus' ministry neither his preaching nor his mighty works have succeeded in penetrating the blindness and incomprehension of his disciples or the people generally. Jesus was condemned by the religious leaders of his people for blasphemy on the grounds of his messianic claim, and Pilate committed him to crucifixion as a would-be king.[24] It is in that total losing of self in death, that complete self-gift in the service of others, that his divine sonship and the nature of his messiahship – his deepest reality – are revealed and can be understood. It is in the crucified Jesus that the Son of God can be found.[25] This is the high point of the Gospel.[26] The centurion's seeing is the gift of God.[27]

Though the Greek text does not contain the definite article before *Son*, it is generally agreed in scholarly circles that Mark intended the centurion's comment to be understood in this way, as *the* Son of God.[28] The gospel began with the presentation of Jesus as the Son of God, and he was proclaimed as such by the heavenly voice on the occasion of his baptism, and at the transfiguration.[29] The evil spirits were quick to recognise this.[30]

The issue was starkly raised during the Jewish trial, when Jesus answered *I am* to the question whether he was the son of the Blessed One. However, the centurion's confession is the first time in the course of the gospel narrative that a human being has realised and proclaimed Jesus' true identity, which could not be penetrated before the Son of Man underwent his passion and death. The mocking religious leaders invited Jesus to come down from the cross so that they might *see and believe*. It is the death of the Jesus who remained on the cross which leads the centurion to *see and believe*.

The centurion's exclamation is an unqualified profession of faith, and comes as the climax not only of the passion story, but of the whole gospel.[31] The centurion is also the representative of Gentile Christianity which saw the significance of Jesus as the Son of God revealed *par excellence* in the drama of the cross. Jesus' promise during his final discourse that the Gospel would be preached to all nations has begun to come true.[32]

These two Calvary signs proclaim symbolically the reversal of the situation of failure; they are a prelude to resurrection. They indicate that God is not absent, and that God will fully vindicate Jesus, as he had predicted. The reader suspects that there will be a reversal for the failed disciples also.

## The Women at Calvary
It is only after the death of Jesus that Mark makes mention of the presence of some women at the scene:

> There were also women looking on from a distance; among them were Mary Magdalene, and Mary the mother of James the younger and of Joses, and Salome. These used to follow him and provided for him when he was in Galilee; and there were many other women who had come up with him to Jerusalem. (15:40-41)

They are new characters in the story, not having featured previously. The two Marys[33] will be mentioned again as present for the burial of Jesus, and later, with Salome, at the empty tomb, where they will be the recipients of the news about the resurrection. The introduction of their names without explanation may indicate that, along with their sons, they are known to the Christian community. They are eyewitnesses to what has happened. At Calvary they are described as looking on *at a distance*. This is historically plausible, for in the time of Pilate, friends were usually permitted to come fairly near the victim, but still kept some distance away.

Back in Galilee, these three women went around with Jesus and saw to his needs.[34] Besides the three named women, Mark refers to *many other women* who have made the journey up to Jerusalem with Jesus, but are not present on Calvary. He does not state that they too have provided for Jesus in Galilee, though this is probably his understanding.

In his description, Mark uses the language of discipleship; they *follow*; they are *with* Jesus; they *serve.* These are key words in Mark's story.[35] The terms apply to the three and by implication to the wider group.[36] As followers and servants, during the ministry in Galilee, they have taken care of Jesus' material needs, particularly for food and drink, but this is not to be understood as the sum total of their discipleship. Clearly, they are authentic disciples in the full sense of the term.[37] And they are numerous. This opens up fascinating perspectives for our understanding of the historical ministry of Jesus and his unconventional inclusiveness.[38]

In considering the significance of the three women for Mark's story there are two points of view. Firstly, some consider that their faithfulness in being present at the cross contrasts with the lack of faithfulness of the male disciples, who have all panicked and fled, and particularly Peter, who has dissociated himself from Jesus.[39] Like the woman who anoints Jesus earlier, they do what they can, this time in harrowing circumstances. Watching *with him*, they are silent witnesses to Jesus' suffering and self-giving as *a ransom for many*.[40] And in spite of everything, they are *hanging in* there; they are present.

On the other hand, some point out that for the Evangelist the contrast lies between the centurion standing by the cross who makes a confession of faith, and the distant women who remain silent, and express no evaluation. Mark would see something lacking in the quality of their discipleship. *Observing the crucified sympathetically but from a distance was insufficient to guarantee the fidelity demanded of disciples.*[41] Earlier, after the arrest of Jesus, Peter followed *at a distance*, prior to his denials and subsequent flight. The women are also *at a distance.* Perhaps, in a similar way, there are limits to their association with the crucified.[42]

## Joseph of Arimathea

Mark's passion narrative closes with a brief account of the burial of Jesus. After the death of the Baptist in Herod's prison, his disciples came, took away his body and buried it in a tomb.[43] In the case of Jesus this service is performed by a stranger:

When evening had come, and since it was the day of Preparation, that is, the day before the sabbath, Joseph of Arimathea, a respected member of the council, who was also himself waiting expectantly for the kingdom of God, went boldly to Pilate and asked for the body of Jesus. Then Pilate wondered if he were already dead; and summoning the centurion, he asked him whether he had been dead for some time. When he learned from the centurion that he was dead, he granted the body to Joseph. Then Joseph bought a linen cloth, and taking down the body, wrapped it in the linen cloth, and laid it in a tomb that had been hewn out of the rock. He then rolled a stone against the door of the tomb. Mary Magdalene and Mary the mother of Joses saw where the body was laid. (15: 42-47)

The story of the burial confirms the reality of Jesus' death, and also prepares for the events of Easter. It serves therefore as a bridge passage. The basic tradition is that Jesus was buried in a place that could be remembered. The opening time reference *it was now evening* is imprecise, since for the Jews sunset marks the beginning of another day, and according to Jewish law burial should take place before sunset, which usually occurs at around 6pm. Since the actions later described would take about two hours, late afternoon is probably intended, no earlier than 4.30pm.[44] The second indication of time is *it was Preparation Day, that is, the day before the Sabbath.* This is problematic, as it seems to imply that the day of Jesus' death was not Passover, but its eve, as in John's Gospel. This would conflict with Mark's own chronology so far, whereby the final supper which Jesus took with his disciples was a Passover meal.[45] Perhaps the stress on the oncoming Sabbath reflects the intensified sense of Jewish outrage at the possible profanation of a sacred day; this was likely to increase the possibility that to avoid trouble the Romans might consent to have the bodies taken down.[46]

Joseph of Arimathea is unknown apart from this act of service. Arimathea (usually identified as Ramathaim) could have been the place where he resided, but was probably his birthplace.[47] He is a non-Galilean. In the absence of disciples or friends, he comes forward, and approaches Pilate, requesting permission to bury Jesus. He is described as *a respected member of the council,* which probably means the Sanhedrin; Mark has indicated that the whole Sanhedrin condemned Jesus as deserving death.[48] It is likely that for Mark he is not a disciple of Jesus, but a pious, observant Jew *waiting expectantly for the kingdom of God*, the fulfilment of God's promises.[49]

Since the Law required that a criminal's corpse should not be left to hang on the cross after sunset, especially if the next day was a Sabbath,[50] his request is an expression of his desire to fulfil God's will, and is an act of piety. In Jesus' time, the burial of corpses was taken very seriously, and was seen as a necessary good which overshadowed any ritual impurity.[51] His action was risky and courageous, since such an approach could have associated him, an influential figure, with Jesus, thereby possibly leading him to be tainted with treason.[52] However, the fact that he was a member of the Sanhedrin which had handed Jesus over would probably count in his favour. Jesus' unusually quick death is a surprise for Pilate,[53] perhaps arousing some suspicion, so he verifies the facts with the centurion. The death of Jesus is confirmed by the centurion, which leaves Pilate free to grant Joseph's request, and allow the corpse to be handed over.

Joseph then buys a *sindōn*, a piece of fairly good, durable linen, probably a sheet. Apparently, it was possible to buy a linen sheet on a feast day or Sabbath, provided the matter was urgent, and the financial aspects were discussed later.[54] Joseph was probably a man of some means. Mark states that it was Joseph who took the body from the cross, presumably with servants to help him. This implies that the Romans did not insist on the petitioner having to wait until they themselves took the body down and formally handed the body over. Joseph then tied or tightly wrapped the body in the cloth. The burial is hurried; there is no mention of washing or anointing the body, nor is there any indication of lamentation. The women followers of Jesus do not get involved.

Joseph then *laid him in a tomb which had been hewn out of the rock.* For burial the Jews used tombs hewn from out of the rock, or natural caves. Tombs were tunnelled into the soft limestone rock vertically and horizontally, the former being more common for private burial. The body was placed on shelves or slabs, and the entrance was closed with a rectangular block of stone, or rounded slab, normally to prevent animals or grave robbers from gaining entry. After a year or so the bones would be gathered and placed in a stone ossuary. Joseph is said to have rolled the stone, which suggests a horizontal type.[55] There is no indication as to who owned the burial place or why Joseph was free to use it.

Jewish tradition from the prophets to the Mishnah insisted that one found guilty according to the Law should not have an honourable burial.[56]

A Sanhedrin member who had voted for Jesus' condemnation for blasphemy would not have given him such a burial. Probably there were common burial places for convicted criminals maintained in readiness by the courts, hollows quarried into the rock walls outside the city near the place of execution. A distinguished Sanhedrin member may have had access to them. This, however, was not an indistinguishable common grave, a mass grave. After decomposition the bones could be gathered and reburied in the ancestral grave, as was the custom with normal burials. Joseph, as a pious law-observant Jew, could have placed Jesus in one of these.[57]

Mark presents Joseph in a positive light. He takes the place of the disciples in their absence, and at personal cost associates himself with the crucified Jesus.[58] Historically, he was probably acting not out of devotion to Jesus, but so that the Law would not be broken.[59] The burial of Jesus was, technically, a dishonourable burial.[60] *The Christian Gospel has preserved and treasured the memory of this courageous and observant Jew whose action sheds a ray of decency on the otherwise unrelieved cruelty that surrounded the events of the Passion.* (Brendan Byrne)[61]

## The Women at the Burial

Mark concludes his account of the burial of Jesus with the statement that *Mary Magdalene and Mary the mother of Joses, saw where the body was laid* (15:47). On Calvary, the latter was named as the *mother of James the younger and Joses.*[62] The women do not seem to cooperate actively in Jesus' burial. Their lack of involvement perhaps supports the view that Joseph was not acting as a friend or disciple. There is no mention of any lamentation, which was the custom. The women simply observe; they are witnesses to what is happening.[63] They know the location of the grave. They will be key players in the next phase of the drama.

## Reflections

The role of the *Little People* recalled in this chapter is mixed and perplexing. History and redaction are in conflict. From a historical point of view, Simon and Joseph are not sympathetic to Jesus. Simon is forced to carry his cross; he has no option. Joseph buries him out of faithfulness to the Law. From Mark's more positive editorial perspective the two fulfil discipleship roles, taking the place of the Twelve who have taken to their heels and fled the scene. Because of this flight the women appear in a good light, for they do not run away. They remain faithful; they are there when it matters.

That is what discipleship is about. Yet, it would seem that, for Mark, their discipleship has its limitations: they stand *at a distance;* they make no faith confession; they play no active part at the burial. The hero of the piece is the Gentile centurion, who has not stumbled across Jesus before that Friday, and who has officiated at his execution, a gruesome task. It is he who proclaims Jesus as Son of God, the first human being to perceive his true identity. His insight is derived from seeing the way in which Jesus dies.

I think we all struggle with our response to Jesus. We know the words which define his identity, but the depth of their significance eludes our grasp. We continue our life's quest of seeking to know the Risen Jesus himself. And we can probably create an accurate list of the requirements of discipleship, spelling them out precisely. Yet, it is only in the daily living that the full implications become evident, and we often fall short. We can take heart from the words of Jesus concerning the woman who anointed him in the house of Simon the leper, *She has done what she could.* In the final analysis true discipleship is not an achievement, but a gift; it is the gift of a gracious and faithful friend.

# The Resurrection

### Sunday Morning, in Mark

The distress and darkness of the story of Jesus' passion and death is lightened by the rich symbolism of the tearing of the temple veil, and by the climactic comment of the centurion. These are powerful hints that the vindication hoped for by Jesus will be realised. Mark proclaims this vindication in his narrative of the Empty Tomb. The theme of the failure of the disciples is also taken up again, as the ever faithful Jesus invites the women to instruct them to meet him again in Galilee. The original Gospel then ends rather abruptly at 16:8, without any account of Jesus' appearances. According to the vast majority of scholars the remaining verses, alternative endings found in some manuscripts, were added later by scribes in order to fill the gap:[64]

> When the sabbath was over, Mary Magdalene, and Mary the mother of James, and Salome bought spices, so that they might go and anoint him. And very early on the first day of the week, when the sun had risen, they went to the tomb. They had been saying to one another, *Who will roll away the stone for us from the entrance to the tomb?* When they looked up, they saw that the stone, which was very large, had already been rolled back.

As they entered the tomb, they saw a young man, dressed in a white robe, sitting on the right side; and they were alarmed. But he said to them, *Do not be alarmed; you are looking for Jesus of Nazareth, who was crucified. He has been raised; he is not here. Look, there is the place they laid him. But go, tell his disciples and Peter that he is going ahead of you to Galilee; there you will see him, just as he told you.* So they went out and fled from the tomb, for terror and amazement had seized them; and they said nothing to anyone, for they were afraid. (16:1-8)

## The Setting

Mark carefully links the Easter story with his description of the death and the subsequent burial of Jesus. The women are named as Mary Magdalen, Mary the mother of James, and Salome. They were present on Calvary at a distance.[60] Not having obtained spices on Friday, and having observed the Sabbath faithfully, the women go on Saturday evening to buy some, presumably with a view to using them next morning. Early on that Sunday morning, after the rising of the sun,[66] they make the journey to the tomb in which Jesus was buried. Its location they know because of their presence at the burial. Because of the hurried nature of Jesus' burial, and also because it was *dishonourable*, their intention seems to be to rectify the omission.[67] Presumably, they were also motivated by grief and loving devotion; perhaps they also sought some sort of closure.[68] As readers we recall the anointing of Jesus in Simon's house at Bethany, which he interpreted in terms of an anticipation of his burial. It was not unusual in that culture for relatives to visit the grave for three days after burial; in fact, mourning was at its height on the third day. Perhaps it was unrealistic of the women in such a climate to think of anointing a corpse after three days, but love and concern often override practical considerations.[69] It is clear that the possibility of Jesus' resurrection never entered their heads.

## The Appearance

While on the way, the women wonder how they will manage to roll the stone away from the tomb entrance, given its size. As a good storyteller, Mark is creating dramatic tension and excitement, preparing for the amazing and totally unexpected surprise which follows. For, on arriving, they find the tomb open, the large stone rolled away.[70] The passive verb indicates the action of God; the women look up and *see* what God has done.[71] Having moved inside, they find *a young man* in a white robe, the traditional attire of heavenly beings; this figure is presumably an interpreting angel.[72]

He is seated on the right. The women are overcome with amazement and fear at this unexpected occurrence; the verb indicates deep feelings of awe at the numinous, the reaction which normally accompanies heavenly manifestations.[73]

After seeking to dispel the women's fear, the role of the angelic youth is to proclaim the Easter message:

> *Do not be alarmed; you are looking for Jesus of Nazareth, who was crucified. He has been raised; he is not here. Look, there is the place they laid him.*

The death of Jesus is not the end of his story.[74] He has been raised. His faithful God and Father has not forsaken him, but has vindicated him, as Jesus had foretold, reversing his apparent failure, and conquering death. Jesus is named as *Jesus of Nazareth* (the *Nazarene*), as at the outset of Mark's narrative. In this way the Evangelist draws together his entire story, and indicates that *the Jesus whom God has raised from the dead is no other Jesus than the one with whom he began his story, namely the Jesus who is God's beloved Son.* (Jack Dean Kingsbury)[75] The startling antithesis and contrast between *was crucified*, and *was raised* by God is typical of the kerygmatic formulas of the Early Church.[76] The insight of the centurion into the true identity of Jesus is confirmed. The formula rings out like a triumphant shout of victory. Through *the angel/young man*, God proclaims the resurrection of the Son. After the proclamation comes a reference to the emptiness of the tomb, the reason for which is now evident.

### The Commission

But Jesus' death is not the end of the story for the disciples either. The messenger continues:

> But go and give this message to his disciples and Peter: *He is going on before you into Galilee; there you will see him, as he told you.*

The women are sent on mission to the disciples, leaving the empty tomb behind. In spite of their failure and flight, their choice not to *be with* him, their unwillingness to accept the shame of belonging to him, they are still considered to be his disciples. In spite of his threefold denial, his emphatically sworn choice no longer to *be with* Jesus, Peter is still singled out for special mention. The Risen Lord remains faithful; he has forgiven them, he calls them back to him once more in Galilee, where it had all begun, where they had been with him, been taught by him, witnessed his mighty deeds, and had experienced mission. On the way from the supper room to Gethsemane, as in the prophet Zechariah's words, Jesus foretold his death and the fact that they would be scattered, he had also promised that he would go before them shepherd-like to Galilee.[77] The words are here repeated, with the additional assurance that they will *see* him there.[78] If the disciples respond to the message by following Jesus to Galilee, they will see him, see him with new eyes, come to genuine faith and clearer understanding. The scattered sheep will be gathered again, the journey of discipleship will begin anew, mission will be undertaken, especially to the Gentiles.

### The Sequel

The final verse of the gospel narrative is something of a puzzle:

> So they went out and fled from the tomb, for terror and amazement had seized them; and they said nothing to anyone, for they were afraid.

The women, who had remained true and stood by Jesus when all the men failed, are now overcome by fear and astonishment, and they too take flight. Their fear is connected with the appearance and message of the *young man*. In the face of God's action, a reaction of fear is not unnatural, and is a common biblical feature. They are unable to cope with the experience and the news.

Their ongoing silence, however, is more problematic. Many scholarly explanations have been put forward. A frequently adduced view is that perhaps Mark is seeking to underline the mystery and awesomeness and supernatural character of resurrection.[79] Perhaps he wishes to emphasise our human inadequacy in the face of God's action. Maybe he wanted God to have the last word, the God who bestows the gift of Easter faith.[80] *Throughout the gospel men and women have been blind and deaf to the truth about Jesus, and now at the end, when the divine message is delivered to the women, they are struck dumb, and fail to deliver it.* (Morna D Hooker)[81] It is Mark's final irony. Frequently, Jesus has told folk to say nothing about the truth they have glimpsed, and they have disobeyed. Now that their time has come to report what has happened, the women are silent! Even the women fail; *their disobedience and fear demonstrate their inability to believe the good news.* (Morna D Hooker)[82] The verse with which the Gospel ends *drives home with considerable force the women's sharing in one of the fundamental aspects of the disciples' failure to follow Jesus to the cross – fear.* (Francis J Moloney)[83]

It is clear from the other Gospels and from Paul that the early Christian communities were aware of the appearances of the Risen Jesus. Their faith

170

was founded on this. Mark seems to have changed the story. The reader will presume that, like his other predictions and promises, this promise of Jesus, reiterated by the *young man* at the tomb, will also come true. The Christian reader knows that it did, otherwise there would be no Gospel and no believing and celebrating Christian community. Mark takes all initiative away from human beings, and places it with the overspilling goodness, incredible faithfulness, and gratuitous love of God.[84] It is the Father's transforming action which has vindicated the Son's generous and loving self-gift in death; it is the Father's action which has transformed the fearful and failed disciples and brought the Christian community into existence. Mark proclaims and articulates the faith of this community in the opening verse and prologue of his Gospel. His story challenges us, centuries later, to accept Jesus' way, and in our struggles and failures assures us of God's ongoing faithfulness, trustworthiness, and transforming power. By ending as he does, Mark *leaves his readers, who may have thought that the story was about somebody else, with a decision to make...* (M Eugene Boring)[85]

## Reflections

In some ways, the ending of Mark's Gospel is bleak. Both women and men fail; they are indeed *fallible followers*. We admit that we probably find ourselves in their company. We can, however, take heart, for the God behind the story is always faithful. And the Jesus He calls his *Son, the Beloved,* is faithful too. Throughout the meandering story subsequent to his lakeside encounter with the two pairs of fishermen, Jesus has remained true to his disciples, despite their fragility, dullness, and capacity to get it wrong. Beyond the tragic mess and failure of passion-tide, he summons them back to Galilee to start again. In the Hebrew Bible, God is understood above all as faithful love. This is the God made known in Jesus. This is how the darkness of Calvary is transformed into the bright dawn of Easter day. This is how our own shadows and darkness too will be transformed, as God's faithful love is revealed in our own life experience as fallible disciples of Jesus.

## Sunday Morning, in John

Given the sombre tone of Mark's presentation of what happened at the tomb of Jesus, I believe it would be good to conclude by reflecting on John's version of the events.

One of the characters present at Calvary and the tomb in all the Gospel accounts is Mary of Magdala. In the Fourth Gospel her role is symbolic, inspiring and very significant.[86]

### The First Visit

The setting is the garden in which Jesus was buried in a new tomb by Joseph of Arimathaea and Nicodemus with lavish style worthy of a king.[87] It is the first day of the week, early in the morning and still dark. The engulfing darkness mirrors Mary's inner disposition as she makes the journey to the tomb, grieving and devoid of hope. She is alone. The purpose of her visit is not specified. She probably comes with aching heart to mourn her beloved Jesus, overcome by the brutal reality of death. She is caught up with mortality.[88] To her horror she sees that the stone has been rolled away from the entrance, and she assumes that the tomb is empty. Her initial distress intensified, she rushes off to find the two leading disciples of Jesus, Simon Peter and the enigmatic Beloved Disciple, and tells them the dreadful news:

> They have taken the Lord out of the tomb, and we do not know where they have laid him.

She jumps to the conclusion that the body of Jesus has been stolen. Grave robbery was not uncommon; people sometimes sought valuables in the tomb, and there was the possibility of hate crime.[89] She does not intuit God's action or imagine the possibility of resurrection.[90]

Peter and the other disciple run to the tomb.[91] The Beloved Disciple reaches the tomb first. He bends down and through the low opening is able to see the linen cloths lying on the ground, but deferentially he waits until Simon Peter arrives. Peter rushes in and sees the cloths and also the head napkin, folded and left on one side. The other disciple then follows him into the tomb. He is able to decode the message conveyed by the empty tomb and the cloths, especially the folded veil, and perceives the action of God in this place. He *saw and believed*, we are told, and then the two depart. It would seem that Mary accompanied them back to the tomb or followed closely behind. When they leave, Simon Peter still unbelieving, and the Beloved Disciple taciturn in his belief, she remains, now centre stage, standing near the tomb in considerable distress.[92] The scene is set for a remarkable encounter.

### The Second Visit

John's text reads as follows:

> But Mary stood weeping outside the tomb. As she wept, she bent over to look into the tomb; and she saw two angels in white, sitting where the body of Jesus had been lying, one at the head and the other at the feet.

They said to her, *Woman, why are you weeping?* She said to them, *They have taken away my Lord, and I do not know where they have laid him.* When she had said this, she turned around and saw Jesus standing there, but she did not know that it was Jesus. Jesus said to her, *Woman, why are you weeping? Whom are you looking for?* Supposing him to be the gardener, she said to him, *Sir, if you have carried him away, tell me where you have laid him, and I will take him away.* Jesus said to her, *Mary!* She turned and said to him in Hebrew, *Rabbouni!* (which means Teacher). Jesus said to her, *Do not hold on to me, because I have not yet ascended to the Father. But go to my brothers and say to them, 'I am ascending to my Father and your Father, to my God and your God.'* Mary Magdalene went and announced to the disciples, *I have seen the Lord; and she told them that he had said these things to her.* (20:11-18)

The resurrection narratives in the different Gospels follow the same basic literary pattern which contains five constituent elements: an initial situation of loss, the unexpected presence of the Risen Jesus, doubt or failure to recognise him, recognition, commissioning.[93] This is a useful working framework, and the Magdalen story is a good example of this template. Sandra Schneiders proposes three different structural elements: weeping, turning, announcing.[94] I prefer searching or seeking to weeping. Searching is a more dynamic term; it moves the narrative forward.

### Searching

The bereavement, grief, weeping element is clearly a key feature of the early part of the story, reflecting Mary's intense sense of loss. There is a persistent emphasis on emptiness and absence. Twice Mary is asked the reason for her weeping; firstly by the two angelic figures seated at either end of the burial shelf, secondly by the gardener. Her reply to the angels echoes her earlier words to the disciples, except that she speaks in the singular rather than the plural, which highlights her personal relationship, perhaps suggesting a little possessiveness.[95] She clearly does not suspect that Jesus has been raised.

Mary peers into the tomb. Later the *gardener* asks her, *Who are you looking for?* This is a question which recalls that posed by Jesus to his earliest disciples.[96] And this highlights the reason why she is weeping. Mary of Magdala has found love and meaning in Jesus, as is evident from her presence at the cross, and her solitary journey to the tomb in the dark. And now Jesus has been taken away, not only personally in death, but his corpse as well. She searches for him desperately, with grim determination.

She will not abandon her search. Her plea to the gardener is wrung from one clutching at straws:[97]

> *Sir, if you have carried him away, tell me where you have laid him, and I will take him away.* (20:15)

But she is searching for the wrong thing, a dead body, and she is searching in the wrong place, a garden tomb. And when the real object of her search arrives on the scene, Mary, blinded by her tears and preoccupied about grave robbers, fails to recognise him, mistaking him for the gardener. The irony is intense. She remains in unbelief and confusion.

### Turning

Twice the Evangelist mentions Mary's turning. After the angels have addressed her, she turns away from this sign of God's action in the tomb, and turns back to her quest for a dead body and the past with which it is associated. It is then that she comes face to face with the gardener. The Risen Jesus then speaks her name, *Mary!* The power of a name! The surprise of a voice no longer silent! Here the Good Shepherd is calling his sheep by name, and she recognises his voice.[98] It's such a magical, numinous moment, the moment of recognition, the moment of transformation. The text states that at that point she *turned,* a gesture symbolising the inner change which is taking place, her movement into faith. Instead of the corpse she was seeking, there stands before her a real, living person, her Jesus, her Lord. She cries in joyful response *Rabbouni! My Teacher!* She cries with great spontaneity and transparent affection. She wants to hold on to this moment forever, and never let Jesus go, for he is her meaning, he it is who enables her to discover her true self, he is her love and her life, and she has found again the one she sought.[99]

But no, Jesus has not returned as he was before. The old familiar name does not capture his true identity. The old way of relating cannot be resumed. This is not the Jesus of the past. Mary's touching or holding on to him, natural as it is, expresses her misunderstanding of the nature of his presence.

Through being *uplifted,* Jesus has returned to the Father and is now the glorified Risen One. He is truly alive and present, but in a new and vastly different way. Mary needs to come to understand this; further growth is required; her faith journey must continue; another threshold remains to be crossed.[100] From the Father's side he will send the Spirit, the Paraclete, bringing his mission to completion. It will be through the Spirit that Jesus will remain, abide, with her and his followers on into the future. This Jesus had promised at the Supper.

Now she must indeed turn; she must loosen her embrace, let go and move forward into the future, into a new way of being and living.[101]

### Announcing

The final stage of the narrative consists in Mary's commissioning by the Risen Jesus:

> *Go to my brothers and say to them, I am ascending to my Father and your Father, to my God and your God.* (20:17)

The imperative is strong and decisive. Mary has received the revelation of Jesus, and is formally sent on mission, sent as *the apostle to the apostles*, commissioned to bear witness, and to announce the new situation which is unfolding. The phrasing of the message is carefully balanced (recalling Ruth 1:16, and the covenant formulas of Jeremiah 31:3, and Ezekiel 36:28). It emphasises at the same time the otherness of Jesus and his closeness and belonging. As a result of his being *lifted up*, his followers are for the first time referred to as his brothers and sisters, able to call His Father their Father. The purpose of his coming in the first place, his being sent, is now fulfilled; they have become children of God. The Risen One draws them into the mystery of the Father's enduring love, the mystery of *abiding*. Through the event of the *hour* the new covenant community is coming into being, the new family of God is coming to birth.

Mary obeys the word of Jesus. She once more leaves the garden tomb, retracing her steps. This time she is not the harbinger of perplexing and disconcerting news about an empty tomb. She has been the first to encounter the Risen Lord; she has come to faith. The purpose of her journey is to announce to the disciples the Easter kerygma so full of promise, *I have seen the Lord!*[102] Her words will resound beyond that intimate circle, and draw others into the experience, enabling them to find meaning, true selfhood and lasting love in relationship with the Risen Jesus. Within the narrative itself, her proclamation and witness to the other disciples sets the stage for the appearance of the Risen One in the room where they are fearfully taking refuge, and for the outpouring of the life-giving and transforming Spirit, the gift which brings Jesus' mission to fulfilment.[103]

## Reflections

### Searching

As I suggested earlier, although the story is about Mary of Magdala, her coming to faith, her foundational apostolic witness, her pivotal role in the early community, it is possible for us today to find ourselves in the narrative.

The question of the gardener, really the Risen Jesus, is challenging and fundamental, *Who are you looking for?* It echoes a question put by Jesus to the two disciples of John the Baptist who were following him down the path right at the beginning of the story, *What are you looking for?* Who, what are we looking for? Mary, like all of us, had been seeking meaning, friendship, fulfilment, hope, aliveness. She had found them in Jesus. The *what* was in fact a *who*. In our case, in our life's search, the *what* and the *who* perhaps do not always coincide; they can be prised apart. Like Magdalen in the garden we can be looking for the wrong thing, looking in the wrong place. We can fail to recognise what we are looking for, even when it is there before our eyes.

Our world today is, I feel, increasingly becoming a world in which it is what we have that matters, that conveys identity, bestows worth. The advertising agencies exploit this so effectively: magnificent houses, shining cars, brilliant technological gadgets, fashionable clothes, exotic holidays etc. Our lives can be dominated by *whats*: systems, reports, assessments, schedules, targets. In education and the health service there is intense pressure towards *whatification*, to coin a term. We can become bogged down in things, busyness and trivia. As Christians, we can quite easily get caught up in this flood tide, and lose focus and perspective. As a Church, over the centuries, we have developed new *whats*, theologies, structures, liturgical forms, regulations, which have often blurred our vision of the *who*.

Our deepest human *whats*, our fundamental thirsts, needs, and longings, coalesce into a *who*. *Who are you looking for?* It is Jesus who alone can satisfy what is at the core of our being, who can set us free, and give us life in its fullness. And the *who,* that is Jesus, pushes us towards other *whos*, our brothers and sisters, our young people, the people we seek to serve. We must, in life and ministry, maintain and promote the primacy of the *who*. Christian spirituality is fundamentally relational.

### *Turning*

In the journey of Christian discipleship there is the constant element of turning and letting go. We cannot stay as we are, locked into sameness. Like Magdalen we often find that we want things to remain as they were; we find it hard to turn away, let go and move on. The old and the familiar and the tried cast a holding spell. Yet, Jesus, as he calls our name, frequently asks us to embrace the new, to risk the unknown, to step forward.

It's possibly something like a child reluctantly coming forth from the security of the womb into a new world. The child has no idea of the wonders and new possibilities which await it until the birthing process is complete.[104]

*Do not cling.* Openness to respond to God's call, obedience for mission, can really hurt. We may have to move geographically, leaving hills, open fields, the singing of early morning birds, for the noise and dust of the city, or vice versa. It may be a question of changing job or responsibility, or coming to terms with new organisational changes and personnel in our place of work. It may simply be the need to relinquish pet ideas or preferred ways of doing things, sacred and comfortable routines. It may be shifts in significant relationships. It may be the need to welcome the changes which are part of the ageing process. The following of Jesus demands poverty of spirit and inner freedom, as we prepare for the ultimate letting go. What is true for us as individuals can apply to us as communities too. Becoming fully alive demands the dynamic of turning and letting go.

In turning away, we turn towards, and we encounter Jesus, the Risen One. He remains the answer to our quest. It is *He* who enables us to find our true selfhood as individuals, our true identity as community. It is *He* who is the love of our life. It is *He* who is the centre. It is our relationship with *Him* which colours everything else; the way we see ourselves (our self image), the way we live our sexuality, our attitude to possessions and status and success, our seeking to discern the demands of love in our lives and ministries, and to respond to those demands. If *He* isn't there, we are back sitting around a tomb, dreaming of the past, gazing sadly into emptiness.

### Announcing

Having been found by Jesus, like Magdalen we are sent on mission. Our experience must be shared with others. We are to tell them that God is our loving Father and their loving Father. We are to tell them that, *I have seen the Lord.* Jesus is risen, is alive, is central to our lives, is present with us; we are his friends, his brothers and sisters. This is our message as we seek to share our *who*.

And how are we going to communicate this gladdening news? We are bearers of his revelation, his life-giving word. Evangelisation, catechesis, education are at the heart of Christian mission. Theological ideas are important, and liturgical sensitivity, and technological proficiency. But we are sent above all to bear witness in our daily living to the reality of the Risen Jesus as someone whom we know as saviour and friend.

This comes across through the sparkle in our eyes, the warmth of our smile, our genuine welcome, acceptance and hospitality, the song in our heart, the lightness of our step, the gentleness of our compassionate touch. It is communicated through the excitement of our vision, our enthusiasm for what we are engaged in, our freedom and flexibility, the simplicity and generosity of our self-giving and service. Basically it all has to do with who he is for us and who we are for him. *I have seen the Lord.*

As Mary left the garden, walking swiftly into her unexpected future, I imagine that she noticed for the first time that day that the birds were singing, the sun was warm on her back, and a gentle breeze was caressing her hair. A deep peace pervaded her being, and she was aching with joy and love.

# Concluding Thoughts

In this final chapter we have reflected on the part played by the *Little People* in the events which form the climax of Jesus' life and ministry, his passion and resurrection. As Mark presents the story they play a mixed role. On the positive side, Simon helps Jesus to carry the crossbeam to the place of execution outside the walls of the city. Some women disciples, good friends of Jesus, stand by some distance from the cross. They are faithful, whereas the Twelve have fled and abandoned their Master. On the death of Jesus, a Roman centurion professes his conviction that Jesus is God's Son. Then a prominent Jew, named Joseph, comes forward and organises the burial in a tomb nearby. The women are still present, taking note of what is taking place. On the Sunday morning they make their way back to the tomb of Jesus in order to mourn his passing, and to offer his corpse the service of anointing.

On the other hand, their standing *at a distance* and their silence on Calvary, and the fact that they do not get involved in Jesus' burial, suggests that the quality of their discipleship leaves something to be desired. This is highlighted even more strongly when they fail to cope with the message conveyed to them by the young man/angel inside the empty tomb. They too take flight, and fail to pass on to the disciples the good news and the instructions communicated to them.

John's version of the events offers a different perspective. Unlike Mark's story, it includes an encounter with the Risen Jesus. Magdalen's response is different. After some initial hesitation, she recognises the gardener as

Jesus, and her world is totally changed. She is overwhelmed with joy and affection, and embarks on a new mission, sent to announce the wonderful news to the rest of Jesus' band, news which reverberates around our own world to this day.

Taken together, these stories, I feel, reflect our experience. At times we are sad and downhearted, confused and fearful, content perhaps to be at a distance from Jesus and from the implications of following him. We struggle with it all. At other times, the dark shadows are dispelled, light breaks through, and we sense the closeness of Jesus. His presence inspires hope and meaning, and gives us the energy to say, *Yes* and reach out joyfully in mission. We feel that we can be bearers of good news, heralds of his Gospel, in the variegated tapestry of our particular world. There are times, maybe lengthy periods, when, though still in the shadows, we are called to hold out a helping hand, to utter an encouraging word, to offer a listening ear, to be of service to others. The narratives which we have considered can strengthen us, as they remind us that there is meaning in this pattern, a meaning caught up in the ultimate faithful love of God. In this we can put our trust.

# Chapter Seven – Conclusion

In the Introduction to this book, I suggested that a study of the encounters between Jesus and the *Little People* would reveal a great deal about Jesus and about the nature of genuine discipleship. As a final, brief chapter, I would like to summarise our main findings.

## Jesus

The Jesus who emerges from these pages is an attractive character, engaging, inspiring, at times discomforting too. For Mark, it is his authority which stands out.[1] His Jesus is the *stronger one,* engaged in overthrowing the domain of Satan. Through his exorcisms, healings, and raising the dead, Jesus introduces the Reign of God, and enables people to experience God's loving and transforming presence in their lives. The advent of this Kingdom is at the heart of his message. For Matthew, Jesus is the compassionate shepherd-guide of his people. For Luke, he is, above all, the one who searches out and saves the outcasts, the marginalised, the sinners. For John, Jesus the Word enfleshed, is light and life, the revealer of the Father's love, the bearer of God's life.

For me, as I reflect on this material, the many qualities and traits of Jesus merge into two: his freedom and his compassion. Jesus was thoroughly Jewish, brought up in that faith in the heart of a devout family. The religious atmosphere of his wide environment, with its traditions, its rich and varied expectations, its reverence for the Law, its pride in the Temple, and its love of the scriptures, soaked into his being and influenced him profoundly. He knew the religious heritage of his people and loved it. Yet he showed great freedom in regard to much that was central to it.

From the outset of his ministry, Jesus cuts through conventional barriers in order to reach out to people in need, people on the margins of religion and society. He ignores taboos and cramping legalism. He takes Simon's mother-in-law by the hand, and she a woman. He touches the leper, not only risking contagion, but incurring ritual defilement by doing so. He scandalously includes Levi, a tax gatherer, amongst his followers, and enjoys the subsequent celebratory party. His table-fellowship, his eating, drinking and sharing the company of *sinners*, is a powerful symbolic gesture, proclaiming a new and very different world. He takes the hand of Jairus' daughter, a young woman of marriageable age, raising her to new life, ignoring the ridicule of the neighbours. He speaks to the widow of

Nain, and incurs defilement by touching the bier on which her dead son is being borne to burial. He allows himself to be touched and anointed by the woman in the house of Simon the Pharisee and by the woman in the Bethany home of Simon the leper. He is comfortable in graciously accepting these expressions of thanks, esteem and affection. He causes raised eyebrows and incurs criticism because of his originality and disregard for convention. He is free to bring healing to Gentiles, people outside the boundaries of Israel; he is free enough to be inclusive. He allows women to be his disciples and his friends, to move around with him.

Jesus frequented the synagogue on the Sabbath, but on several occasions he healed on the Sabbath, contravening the normal interpretation of the Law. Observance of the Sabbath was one of the most typical and distinctive Jewish customs. It was a mark of the separateness of the Jewish people. The story of the man with the withered hand is a case in point. Jesus wasn't conducting a liberalising campaign; he just had different priorities. He reacted against the reversal of values which pedantic casuistry had brought about. People come first.[2] He is free to be true to himself, and to resist the pressures of religious leaders, of crowds and of his own disciples. Genuine freedom is frequently a threat to others.

Jesus is a man of great compassion. The verb is used in connection with the leper and the epileptic boy, and with the widow of Nain. Elsewhere it is used when Jesus teaches the crowds, and heals them, and feeds the hungry multitudes, and brings sight to the blind.[3] He is deeply concerned by the plight of the Galilean peasants. He is acutely aware of the leadership vacuum in Israel. In his dealings with people there is a gentleness and sensitivity about him, a concern for the individual as a person in need. He is moved by the pleas of Jairus and the centurion, immediately responding and moving to help. He is able to redirect Legion's enthusiasm to join and follow him. With the deaf-mute and the Bethsaida blind man, Jesus establishes a relationship, as he leads them apart and indicates his willingness to heal. With the woman long-afflicted with haemorrhaging, he refuses to accept anonymity, and establishes a rapport.

There is, I believe, another dimension to the compassion of Jesus. It is not only a personal emotional reaction to the suffering he encountered; it is a form of radical prophetic criticism.[4] Jesus' genuine concern highlights the inadequacies of the political and religious domination systems which were contributing to the pain, exploitation and oppression of the ordinary people.

Jesus was aware of the cynical indifference of the power brokers. In his compassionate outreach, he proclaimed and modelled an alternative way. In his teaching he was sketching the contours of a new world, where the structures and values and mores would be different. This he called the Reign of God. The compassion of Jesus posed a threat to the mindsets and domination systems of his day

I believe that both the freedom and compassion of Jesus derive from his relationship with the Father. His independence, strength, courage and self-possessed authority, stem from the fact that he knows the mind and heart of God, and that God is the unwavering focus of his being. God, whom he calls *Father,* is utterly central to his life. The Reign of God is his passion. His love for the Father to whom he constantly defers,[5] and for the people he encounters, is so strong and consuming.

Drawn into his circle, called to *be with* him and share his values and his mission, we are aware of the twists and turns of our life journey; we are conscious that we believe and don't believe, and that at times we stumble. Yet, the Jesus of the Gospel mirrors the Father in his faithfulness. Jesus is free enough and compassionate enough not to let go of us. And that is reassuring and heartening; it offers us the ongoing hope of growth and eventual transformation.

In a world which is not built on compassion, and which is in danger of becoming increasingly lacking in compassion, we are called to become genuinely compassionate people. This has far-reaching implications in our personal and professional lives, implications which can become costly. In a world which, in so many ways, seeks to curtail our freedom, we are called to know the meaning of inner freedom. That freedom which is derived from surrendering in trust to the Father of Jesus, and from seeking to be true to the values of the Kingdom. A reawakening of our call to be prophetic in our freedom and compassion is sorely needed, as individuals, as communities, as Church.

# The Little People

In the course of our reflections we have encountered a wide variety of *Little People.* Some are female, some male. Most are Jewish, a few are Gentiles. Most are numbered amongst the marginalised for various reasons: gender, ethnic origin, occupation, ritual impurity, the nature of their affliction. Yet, as I noted in the introduction, they play a major role in the Gospel story because in different ways they manifest key aspects of the Kingdom of God. Their responses to Jesus are implicitly compared and contrasted with the religious authorities and the Twelve. The two main areas in which they stand out as exemplars are their faith in the power, authority and kindness of Jesus, and their willingness to lose self and to serve.

In some of the stories both these aspects of discipleship occur. The classic case is the story of the paralysed man, whose friends manifest great devotion to him and to his welfare, going to extraordinary lengths to get him to Jesus. Their love and concern are quite remarkable; their commitment and ingenuity amazing. Their faith in the ability and willingness of Jesus to heal their friend is also very strong, strong enough to overcome the problem caused by the pressing crowd, and to take the risk of climbing onto the roof, making a hole in it, and lowering the man through. It is their faith, rather than that of the paralysed individual, which moves Jesus into action. Later, as Mark's narrative progresses, there are the people who take the deaf-mute to Jesus, and those at Bethsaida who bring to him a blind man. Again, they manifest concern for the welfare of their relative, friend or neighbour, and their seeking Jesus out and approaching him is an expression of their faith.

The distraught Jairus, the Syrophoenician woman and the father of the epileptic boy come to Jesus pleading for healing for someone close, for daughter or son.[6] As parents they are naturally deeply concerned about their dear one. In each case their initial faith in seeking Jesus out is tested further. When his sick child dies, Jairus is urged to believe in the impossible. The Gentile woman has to cope with a harsh comment from Jesus, but persists, showing insight and quick thinking. The father of the epileptic boy is challenged about the limited quality of his faith, and utters that moving plea for greater faith. In these three cases, Jesus accedes to the request of the parent. Matthew's centurion in a similar manner approaches Jesus seeking a cure for his servant. The faith of each consists in an awareness of personal poverty and need, a recognition of their dependence on Jesus and of his authority, and a trusting surrender to his compassion.

Other *Little People* come to Jesus seeking healing for themselves. Their situations are dire, hopeless and heart-rending. The leper ignores the rules and throws himself at Jesus' feet. The woman with the haemorrhage flouts custom and regulation and secretly touches his cloak.

Bartimaeus in his blindness realises that with the passing of Jesus amongst the journeying pilgrims an unexpected opportunity is presenting itself, an opportunity not to be missed. Ignoring the negative reaction of the crowd, he loudly repeats his plea. These three individuals take the risk of being rebuffed and rejected, given the cultural situation. They clearly believe that Jesus is capable of providing a cure; they hope that he is prepared to do so. Each meets a compassionate response which gives them new life.

In the case of Simon's mother-in-law, Levi, the man in the synagogue, Legion, Zacchaeus, the Samaritan woman and the widow of Nain the initiative rests with Jesus, as he reaches out to them and freely draws them into the transforming experience of the dawning Kingdom. Their presence in the story highlights the gift-like quality of God's saving intervention in Jesus, God's surprise, God's liberating and life-giving generosity.

In the second half of his Gospel, Mark's Jesus emphasises several times that his style is one of self-giving and service, as he talks about his coming passion. Jesus is not *into* domination, control, power, success, status; in this he is counter-cultural. Discipleship, therefore, demands a profound shift in mentality, the embracing of a revolutionary new value system and a different understanding of the nature of God. The inner group of disciples struggle with this. The religious and political leaders reject it. Some of the *Little People,* however, show perception and acceptance. In the opening phase of the ministry of Jesus, Simon's mother-in-law, once restored to health and vitality, heralds this message by immediately setting about serving Jesus, by providing him and his four disciple-friends with a meal. Levi throws a banquet for his outsider friends to celebrate what has happened to him. Legion wants to join Jesus as a follower, but then accepts Jesus' commission that he go to serve his people by proclaiming the *Good News* to them.

It is in the closing stages of the ministry and life of Jesus that the most significant examples occur. After receiving his sight back, Bartimaeus opts to follow Jesus on the way to Jerusalem, becoming a disciple. The poor widow gives her two small coins, everything she has and is, holding nothing back. The woman in Simon's house in Bethany likewise generously empties her alabaster jar as an expression of her love of Jesus, offering him the service of anointing his head. Their selflessness and generosity prepare the reader for Jesus' own self-giving on Calvary. During the passion, Simon carries Jesus' cross, such a powerfully symbolic act. We are informed about the women followers of Jesus who have served him throughout his ministry. Joseph provides Jesus with burial, and the women come with spices to the tomb with the intention of serving him by anointing his body. *These minor characters are examples of the paradox of suffering service as a manifestation of the power of the kingdom of God.* (Elizabeth Struthers Malbon)[7]

As readers we are drawn to these *Little People.* We recognise them as exemplars; they model what following Jesus is all about. The impact which they make is heightened by comparison with the rejection of Jesus and his way by the authorities, their blindness and hostility. Similarly, their response to Jesus contrasts with the failure of the Twelve to embrace Jesus' message and remain *with him.* At the end of Mark's Gospel the reaction of the women who visit the tomb, their fear and silence, aligns them with the inner circle of Jesus' disciples as *fallible followers.* The presence of the women among the followers of Jesus illustrates the inclusivity and openness of discipleship; their failure at the end highlights the challenge. The challenge of welcoming the Kingdom, journeying along the way of Jesus, living according to his values in trust and self-giving service, and proclaiming his message is left in the hands of the reader of the Gospel. You and I are aware that this is no easy task, but is in reality the only way to live.

Before drawing this book to a close, it is important, I believe, to remind ourselves that we have been examining Jesus and the *Little People* as characters in the Gospel narrative which Mark and the other Evangelists have composed and handed on. Our approach has been mainly literary; we have taken the text as it is, and analysed it as literature. In this way we have sought to highlight its theological message: what it is saying about Jesus and about discipleship. Scholars remind us of the gap that can exist between the Gospels and the historical Jesus, and also warn us against the dangers of blurring the edges between narrative and historical criticism. Nevertheless, I firmly believe that the basic traits of Jesus' character, style and activities which emerge from our reading genuinely reflect the way in which he was initially remembered, and the impact which he originally made. I am also convinced that the aspects of discipleship which are underlined truly express the way in which the following of Jesus was originally understood.[8]

# Endnotes
## Notes on the Introduction

1.  D Rhoads and D Michie, *Mark as Story* (Philadelphia, Fortress 1982), p101. In the second edition, 1999, co-authored with J Dewey, p98 and 116, this designation has been jettisoned in favour of the People: this category consists of the minor characters and the crowds. R A Culpepper, *Anatomy of the Fourth Gospel* (Philadelphia, Fortress 1983), p132-144, refers to *minor characters*. He sees them as vital to the fulfilment of the gospel's purposes (p106). See also E S Malbon, *In the Company of Jesus: Characters in Mark's Gospel* (Louisville, Westminster John Knox 2000), esp p189-225.

2.  Malbon, *Company,* p192.

3.  J D Kingsbury, *Conflict in Mark* (Minneapolis, Fortress 1989), p24-27.

4.  Mark normally uses the term *disciples* for the inner circle of *the twelve*; but he sometimes uses it also for the wider circle of Jesus' male and female followers. The *authorities* are opposed to Jesus. They comprise the religious leaders: scribes (the legal experts), Pharisees, Sadducees, chief priests (including Caiaphas personally) and elders; and the political establishment: Herod and his followers (Herodians), Pilate and the Roman soldiery.
    The authorities are consistently presented in a negative light. There are, however, exceptions: Jairus, the scribe who is *not far from the Kingdom of God*, and Joseph of Arimathea; and the Roman centurion. On exceptions see Malbon, *Company,* p157-165, and p195.

5.  Rhoads and Michie, p129. Malbon, *Company,* p193, notes their importance at the level of their responses to Jesus, and the comparisons and contrasts with other characters. They are models for appropriate attitudes and behaviours (p198).

6.  M T Winstanley, *Into Your Hands* (Homebush, St Paul's 1994), p51-68.

7.  See also 1:32-34; 3:7-12; 6:53-56.

8.  The parallels are found in Matt 14:34-36; Matt 4:23-25; Luke 4:44; 6:17-19.

9.  E S Malbon, *Mark's Jesus* (Waco, Baylor 2009), p17, notes that narrative characters *are known by what they say and by what they do, and by what others (the narrator and other characters) say and do to, about, or in relation to them.*

10. The NRSV is based on *The Greek New Testament* (United Bible Societies 1983).

11. Useful insights can be found in: M A Powell, *The Gospels* (Minneapolis, Fortress 1998); M J Borg and N T Wright, *The Meaning of Jesus* (New York, Harper Collins 2007); Catholic Bishops' Conferences of England & Wales, and Scotland, *The Gift of Scripture* (London, CTS 2005).

12. The Gospels were intended to be listened to rather than read. The ways in which the storyteller seeks persuasively to achieve this is called rhetoric; the branch of study exploring this is referred to as reader-response criticism.

13. Most Gospel commentaries provide a linear structural outline of the Gospel. Markan scholars realise, however, that Mark's storytelling artistry is complex; words like fugue and tapestry have been used in recognition of the interweaving patterns, repetitions and overlaps. See Rhodes, Dewey, Michie, p47; Malbon, *Mark's Jesus*, p24-43.

14. This area of study (form, source and redaction criticism) is fascinating; though literary, it is also strongly historical. Occasionally I shall refer to relevant issues, without lingering there. See J R Donahue & D Harrington, *The Gospel of Mark* (Collegeville, Liturgical Press 2002), p1-22.

15. In addition to the works of Rhoads and Mitchie and Culpepper, to which I have already referred, good introductions are:
M A Powell, *What is Narrative Criticism?* (Minneapolis, Fortress 1990);
E S Malbon, *Company*, p1-41;
J L Ressaguie, *Narrative Criticism of the New Testament. An Introduction* (Grand Rapids, Baker Academic 2005);
F J Moloney, *Mark: Storyteller, Interpreter, Evangelist* (Peabody, Hendrickson 2004), p31-37 .

16. Most of us want to know what exactly happened and what Jesus really said (we are questers for the historical Jesus). For a good summary and critique of academic *questing*, see J D G Dunn, *A New Perspective on Jesus* (London, SPCK 2005). He is particularly critical of too much emphasis devoted to what is written (the inadequacy of the *literary paradigm*), and the undervaluing of the role played by the original oral Jesus tradition. On historical issues connected with miracle stories, see particularly J P Meier, *A Marginal Jew* vol 2 (London, Doubleday 1994), especially p617-632. Borg, *Jesus,* (New York, Harper Collins 2006), p51, distinguishes between Jesus remembered and Jesus metaphorised.

17. See the treatment of these issues in Dunn, *A New Perspective*, p46-56, and R K McIver, *Memory, Jesus and the Synoptic Gospels* (Resources for Biblical Study 59; Atlanta, SBL 2011); his conclusions are found on p183-187.

18. B Byrne, *A Costly Freedom* (Collegeville, Liturgical Press 2008), pxvi, xx This is not to deny that before Mark the oral tradition had already developed narrative or kerygmatic blocks or sequences; see Dunn, *A New Perspective,* p124. Mark probably wrote soon after 70, the year of the destruction of Jerusalem by the Romans. A long tradition maintains that he wrote in Rome, and a majority of scholars still accept this view. Others suggest a place closer to Palestine, like southern Syria. Most commentaries on Mark deal with these issues in some detail.

19. This is the commonly accepted scholarly opinion. *Q* comes from the German *Quelle* meaning a source. It is possible that there were different versions of *Q*. Matthew and Luke probably wrote in the mid-eighties.

20. There is much discussion about the authorship of the Fourth Gospel. The long tradition which identifies three figures: John the son of Zebedee, the Beloved Disciple and the Gospel's author, is no longer generally held to be accurate. Today some scholars believe that a minor disciple during Jesus' ministry (later known as the Beloved Disciple) had an important role in the founding of the Johannine community and was the source of its tradition about Jesus. This tradition developed through decades of reflection, liturgical celebration, struggles and lived experience, and was eventually fashioned into our Gospel, probably at Ephesus, between 90 and 100 AD by an unknown but very gifted member of the community, himself a disciple of the Beloved Disciple. Another member of the community (usually referred to as *the redactor*) revised the text shortly afterwards, making a few additions. See R E Brown, *An Introduction to the New Testament* (New York, Doubleday 1997), p368-371; R A Culpepper, *The Gospel and Letters of John* (Nashville, Abingdon Press 1998), p29-41. For a recent study of the relationship between the Gospels, see P N Anderson, *The Riddles of the Fourth Gospel. An Introduction to John* (Minneapolis, Fortress, 2011).

21. *The Gift of Scripture,* p35 See also C R Koester, *The Word of Life* (Grand Rapids, Eerdmans 2008), p7; J D G Dunn, *Jesus Remembered* (Cambridge, Eerdmans 2003); R Bauckham, *Jesus and the Eyewitnesses* (Grand Rapids, Eerdmans 2006); R K McKiver, *Memory.*

22. See Borg, *Jesus*, p24-26, and 27-5.

# Notes on Chapter One

1.  I have found the following commentaries on Mark's Gospel helpful:
    H Anderson, *The Gospel of Mark* (London, Oliphants 1976);
    M E Boring, *Mark: a Commentary* (Louisville, Westminster John Knox Press 2006);
    B Byrne, *A Costly Freedom* (Collegeville, Liturgical Press 2008);
    C E B Cranfield, *The Gospel according to St Mark* (Cambridge, CUP 1959);
    R A Culpepper, *Mark* (Macon, Smyth & Helwys 2007);
    J R Donahue & D H Harrington, *The Gospel of Mark* (Collegeville, Liturgical Press 2002);
    W Harrington, *Mark* (Dublin, Veritas 1979);
    M D Hooker, *The Gospel according to St Mark* (London, A&C Black 1991);
    D McBride, *The Gospel of Mark* (Dublin, Dominican Publications 1996);
    G Martin, *The Gospel according to Mark* (Chicago, Loyola 2005);
    F J Moloney, *The Gospel of Mark. A Commentary* (Peabody, Hendrickson 2002);
    D E Nineham, *St Mark* (London, Penguin Books 1963);
    N T Wright, *Mark for Everyone* (London, SPCK 2001).

2.  Boring, p32, observes that the Greek word *archē* can also mean norm or rule; Mark's narrative provides the norm for the continuation of this proclamation in the mission of the Church.

3.  Mark uses *Gospel (euangelion)* seven times, whereas Matthew uses the term only four times. Luke and John do not use it at all, though Luke does frequently use the verb form.

4.  The noun *euangelion* is found only three times in the Septuagint (the Greek version of the Hebrew Bible, sometimes abbreviated as *LXX*). The verbal form is much more frequent; see Isa 52:7, and also 40:9; 41:27; 60:6; 61:1.

5.  Byrne, p22; also p6-7. The earliest Christian use of the noun is in Paul, who some 60 times uses it to convey in the form of a summary the meaning of the life, death and resurrection/exaltation of Jesus. Mark proclaims the Christ event in narrative form. See Donahue & Harrington, p14. *Apocalyptic* refers to a literary genre in which human beings are given revelations about cosmic transformations in the future, which help to interpret current situations on earth. The imagery is often vivid, and sometimes mysterious numbers are involved. See Brown, *Introduction,* p774-780.

6.  The Greek can indicate news *about* Jesus and news *from* him; Mark probably intends both meanings.

7.  Before Mark wrote, Jesus Christ had become a proper name (see Rom 1:1,4,6); here it is not used in that way.

8.  Moloney, *Gospel,* p31; see 2 Sam 7:14; Ps 2:7; 89:26-29; and Exod 4:22; Isa 63:16; Hos 11:1. The phrase *Son of God* is absent from some early manuscripts. Boring, p30 and Donahue & Harrington, p60, are amongst those who believe that it should be included.

9.  It combines Exod 23:20; Mal 3:1; Isa 40:3. Such composite quotations or fusions of texts are not uncommon in the Jewish tradition. Many commentators treat this as part of the Baptist sequence, verses 2-8; Moloney, *Gospel,* p27-30, divides these verses into three: 1-3 the authority of God; 4-6 the coming of the forerunner; 7-8 the voice of the Baptist. Boring, p33, presents 2-15 as the Markan *Prologue,* which sets the scene for the audience, providing them with a frame of reference and a perspective to understand the story; verses 2-3 are a discrete unit, a *Transcendent Prelude.*

10. Byrne, p26, notes the importance of this text, which opens second Isaiah (chapters 40-55) with his message of a liberation which would reverse the Babylonian exile, re-enacting God's foundational redemptive act in the Exodus. For Mark, this new Exodus is about to take place. Donahue & Harrington, p68, note the density of references to Isaiah in Mark's *Prologue.* S Voorwinde, *Jesus' Emotions in the Gospels,* (London, T&T Clark 2011), p62-63, stresses the link with Isaiah's new Exodus (40-66) as a fundamental perspective for Mark's Gospel: God as warrior-healer delivers his people from bondage, leads the blind along a new Exodus way, with Jerusalem as final destination. Jesus fulfils this expectation.

11. J Marcus, *Mark 1-8 Anchor Bible Commentaries,* Yale University Press 2007.

12. The word *Way* occurs 16 times in Mark; *the way of the Lord* leads to the cross and eventual vindication; this *way* becomes the path of discipleship.

13. See Meier, 2:19-63; Dunn, *Jesus Remembered*, p348-350.

14. Dunn, *Jesus Remembered,* p355. In John's Gospel his mission is to be a witness (1:6-9).

15. Isa 40:1-11. Several revolutionary liberation movements in fact symbolically originated there.

16. McBride, p29-30; Borg, *Jesus,* p118; Pagola, p78. Boring, p40, notes that already the reader is alerted to the tension between the Temple and the John/Jesus story.

17. See, for instance, Byrne, p28; Boring, p41. Dunn, *Jesus Remembered,* p353, sees this as a possibility. Moloney, *Gospel,* p33 and Meier, 2:48 do not agree, preferring to see it simply in terms of the garb of the desert nomad. The identification with Elijah is explicitly made by Jesus in Mark 9:11-13. Pagola, p80, observes that John wanted to remind the people of Israel's time in the desert before they entered the promised land; they were symbolically beginning again.

18. For a detailed discussion of the Baptist, see Meier, 2:19-223, here esp.42-56; N T Wright, *Jesus and the Victory of God* (London, SPCK 2000), p160-162; Dunn, *Jesus Remembered,* p339-379.

19. Isa 1:16: *Wash yourselves; make yourselves clean; remove the evil of your doings from before my eyes.* Ps 51:7: *Purge me with hyssop, and I shall be clean; wash me, and I will be whiter than snow.*

20. Joel 3:1-2; Ezek 36:25-27: *I will sprinkle clean water upon you, and you shall be clean from all your uncleannesses, and from all your idols I will cleanse you. A new heart I will give you, and a new spirit I will put within you...*

21. The quasi-monastic Qumran community were Essenes; they had no regard for the Temple, and practised the Law strictly. See Brown, *Introduction,* p76-77.

22. Donahue & Harrington, p63.

23. The prophets called for a wholehearted return to God. Jer 18:11: *Turn now all of you from your evil way, and amend your ways and your doings*; Isa 55:6-7: *Seek the Lord while he may be found, call upon him while he is near; let the wicked forsake their way, and the unrighteous their thoughts; let them return to the Lord, that he may have mercy on them, and to our God, for He will abundantly pardon*; Zech 1:4.

24. Meier, 2:53, argues strongly against this being a Markan or pre-Markan Christian creation. Dunn, *Jesus Remembered,* p359, notes that the Torah (Jewish Law) made provision for sins to be dealt with through the sacrificial system; John offered his own ritual as an alternative to the Temple. Borg, *Jesus,* p118, sees John as subversively bypassing the Temple. Unlike Matthew and Luke (who use the *Q* tradition), Mark does not provide us with further content of John's preaching. In John's preaching there was a strong note of judgement for Israel. His imagery is rich, powerful and daunting. It was probably a final warning to the current generation, rather than a warning of a final, universal cataclysm.

25. The *mightier one* (*ischyroteros*) is an attribute which is sometimes applied to God in the OT (2 Sam 22:31; 23:5; Ps 7:12; Isa 40:10; 49:25; 9:6 etc). In Job (22:13; 33:29; 36:22), *the mighty one* is a term for God. Here the phrase refers to a further, final agent in God's eschatological (end time) plan.

26. Dunn, *Jesus Remembered,* p357-361, describes John's baptism as a baptism of repentance and a baptism of preparation.

27. Ezek 36:25-27; Joel 3:1-5; Isa 43:25: *I, I am he who blots out your transgressions, and I will not remember your sins*; 44:3: *For I will pour water on the thirsty land, and streams on the dry ground; I will pour my spirit on your descendants, and my blessing on your offspring.*

28. Hooker, p39; Meier, 2:35; Dunn, *Jesus Remembered,* p369-371.

29. Meier, 2:131-137.
30. For the Infancy Narratives, see especially R E Brown, *The Birth of the Messiah* (London, Doubleday 1993); also M J Borg & J D Crossan, *The First Christmas* (HarperCollins, New York 2007); J Corley ed, *New Perspectives on the Nativity* (London, T&T Clark 2009); also Dunn, *Jesus Remembered*, p340-348; F J Moloney, *Beginning the Good News* (Homebush, St Paul Publications 1992), p73-100; *The Living Voice of the Gospel* (Dublin, Veritas 2006), p127-162.
31. On Matthew's Gospel I have found the following helpful:
W F Albright and C S Mann, *Matthew* (New York, Doubleday 1971);
F W Beare, *The Gospel according to Matthew* (Oxford, Blackwell 1981);
B Byrne, *Lifting the Burden* (Collegeville, Liturgical Press 2004);
Cabrido J A, *The Shepherd of Israel for All Nations A Portrayal of Jesus in the Gospel of Matthew: a Narrative-Critical and Theological Study,* (S T D diss, Pontifical Gregorian University, 2008);
W D Davis and D C Allison, *A Critical and Exegetical Commentary on the Gospel according to Saint Matthew* (London, T&T Clark 2004);
R H Gundry, *Matthew* (Grand Rapids, Eerdmans 1982);
D J Harrington, *The Gospel of Matthew* (Collegeville, Liturgical Press 1991);
C S Keener, *A Commentary on the Gospel of Matthew* (Grand Rapids, Eerdmans 1999);
J P Meier, *Matthew* (Dublin, Veritas 1980);
P S Minear, *Matthew, The Teacher's Gospel* (London, DLT 1982);
F J Moloney, *This is the Gospel of the Lord (Year A)* (Homebush, St Paul 1992);
E Schweizer, *The Good News according to Matthew* (London, SPCK 1976);
D Senior, *Matthew* (Nashville, Abingdon Press 1998);
N T Wright, *Matthew for Everyone,* 2 vols (London, SPCK 2002).
32. Matthew's community was composed of Jews and Gentiles; from the outset he has this mixed constituency in mind. Borg & Crossan, p25-53, maintain that the Infancy Narratives are neither fact nor fable; they are best understood as parable and overture, rich in theological significance, and a summary of what is to follow.
33. Letters of the alphabet are given numerical significance. David (=DWD) is 4-6-4, 14; the threefold repetition indicates that Jesus is the perfection of the Davidic line.
34. Matthew mentions four women in his genealogy, which is most unusual. Women of courage and initiative, they play significant roles in Israel's history. The four are probably Gentiles; and, like many of the males in the list, may be considered as sinners. Perhaps the main reason for their presence here is the fact that there was something irregular in their marriages, and yet their situation is caught up in God's saving design. This

is a preparation for the story of Mary. See Brown, *Birth,* p71-74; Moloney, *Living Voice,* p132-133.

35. Jewish matrimonial procedure entailed two steps. Firstly, betrothal took place, which was a formal exchange of consent in the presence of two witnesses. Usually this occurred when the girl was 12 or 13 years of age. The English term *engaged* does not accurately describe Jewish practice, because betrothal was considered a legally ratified marriage, and the **obligations** undertaken were binding. In fact, the man was known as husband immediately, and the woman passed from the authority of her father to that of the husband. Any infringement of marital rights was considered to be adultery. If the man died, the girl was treated as a widow. The second stage took place a year or so later, when the bride went to live with her husband in his home, and the marriage was consummated. See Brown, *Birth,* 123-124.

36. See Brown, *Birth,* p155-159.

37. This is the only instance in the New Testament when someone other than Jesus is called by this title.

38. Brown, *Birth,* p131. Matthew's Jesus later calls the people *my Church* (16:18). Cabrido, p129, stresses that in the OT *laos* is a specific term for a specific people.

39. Byrne, p24; see also 9:8; 18:12-35; 20:28; 26:28. Cabrido, p128, notes that the reader is reminded of God's saving activity throughout Israel's history.

40. Senior, p41.

41. Such quotations, often referred to as *formula quotations,* are a feature of Matthew's Gospel, which contains about 12 of them. Their purpose is to show that the New Testament is the fulfilment of the Old. It was a way of proving that God had foretold Jesus' career, and that everything, even minor details, was part of God's plan.

42. Matthew adapts the quotation, originally addressed to Ahaz in a situation of political and military crisis, to his own infancy context and his theological purpose. He concludes his Gospel with the Risen Christ promising to be *with* his disciples always, until the end of time.

43. In Judaism paternity was based on the man's acknowledgement of the child by giving it a name. Legal paternity was understood as real paternity. By exercising this right Joseph, son of David, becomes the legal father of Jesus, and in this way the child of Mary is drawn into the line of David.

44. The Greek is *tarassein.*

45. This recalls the response of Pharaoh at the news of the birth of Moses, as described by Josephus.

46. Davies and Allison, p24; Meier, *Matthew,* p11.

47. The verb for *come together* is *synagein;* Matt 26:3,57; 27:17,27,62; Ps 2:2. Matt 27:25: *His blood be upon us and our children.*

48. This quotation is not introduced by the usual formula; it is a conflation of Micah 5:1, 2 Samuel 5:2, and 1 Chronicles 11:2, with some adjustment. Rather than proclaimed by the narrator, the words are placed on the lips of the scribes. See Senior, p45; Brown, *Birth,* p186.

49. Beare, p79, notes that it is far from certain that the Jews of the time commonly held that the Messiah would be born in Bethlehem; the general view seems to have that expressed in John 7:27, that no one will know where he comes from. Davies & Allison, p20, likewise comment that it is uncertain as to what degree Jewish opinion looked to Bethlehem as the Messiah's birth place. After a very careful study, Meier, *Marginal,* 1:229, (also p350) tentatively concludes that Jesus may have been born in Bethlehem, but more likely in Nazareth, where he grew up and with which he was identified. He was known as a descendent of David. For the Nazareth option see also Dunn, *Jesus Remembered,* p345; Pagola, p55 fn2.

50. Brown, p215. The text is Hosea 11:1.

51. Moloney, *Beginning,* p94.

52. Meier, *Matthew,* p14. Matthew highlights this title in his version of the baptism (where it is made public), and the testing of Jesus. See M T Winstanley, *Lenten Sundays* (Bolton, Don Bosco Publications 2011), p7-18.

53. Brown, p220. Davies and Allison, p30, note that it was expected that the exodus/return paradigm would be repeated (Isa 4:3-4; Ezek 20:33-44; Hos 2:14-15). In the storyline there are echoes of Israel's journey to Egypt at the time of the first Joseph, the Exodus return under Moses, and entry into the land of promise under Joshua. There are very close parallels with the story of Moses. For the Evangelist, Jesus repeats the history of his people; he is the new Israel, the new Moses.

54. 31:15. The original quotation referred to Ramah, Rachel's burial place, near Bethel, NE of Jerusalem. There the exiles were assembled prior to their deportation. A different tradition, which Matthew follows, located her burial place near Bethlehem.

55. Byrne, p32 fn29.

56. The wording is almost verbatim Exod 4:19-20LXX. See Davies and Allison, p32-33. Jesus is the new Moses.

57. 4:15, quoting the prophet Isaiah 9:1-2.

58. Meier, *Matthew,* p16, considers this the most probable solution. (cf Judg 13:2-7; 16:17; Num 6:1-21; Isa 4:3)

59. Isa 11:1. See M L Coloe, *God Dwells with Us* (Collegeville, Liturgical Press 2001), p 171-174, for a strong case for the *branch* source; also B Pixner, *With Jesus through Galilee according to the Fifth Gospel* (Rosh Pina, Corazin Publishing 1992), p14-19.

60. Senior, p50.

61. Brown, *Birth,* p218.

62. Again see Brown, *Birth,* p235-470.

On Luke see:

B Byrne, *The Hospitality of God* (Collegeville, Liturgical Press 2000); G B Caird, *St Luke* (London, Pelican 1963); E E Ellis, *The Gospel of Luke* (London, Oliphants 1974); C F Evans, *Saint Luke* (London, SCM 1990);

J A Fitzmyer, *The Gospel according to Luke* (New York, Doubleday, vol 1 1981, vol 2 1985);

L T Johnson, *The Gospel of Luke* (Collegeville, Liturgical Press 1991); M Fallon, *Gospel according to St Luke* (Bangalore, Asian Trading Corporation 1997);

I H Marshall, *The Gospel of Luke* (Exeter, Paternoster Press 1978);

F Mosetto, *Lettura del Vangelo second Luca* (Rome, LAS 2003),

D McBride, *The Gospel of Luke* (Dublin, Dominican Publications 1991).

N T Wright, *Luke for Everyone* (London, SPCK 2001).

63. See the first chapter of M T Winstanley, *Don Bosco's Gospel Way* (Bolton, Don Bosco Publications 2002).

64. 1:50. Brown, *Birth,* p644, maintains that the canticles (now used daily as part of the Divine Office of the Church) probably originated amongst early Jewish Christians in Jerusalem, were taken over by Luke, adapted, and inserted into the infancy narratives because they fitted well with the characters to whom he attributed them. These, like the people who composed them, were *Anawim,* poor ones. Modern scholarship does not consider them to be compositions of Mary or Zechariah. Brown details the considerable OT background for the *Magnificat* on p358-360, and for the *Benedictus* on p386-389.

65. For an interesting alternative way of understanding the text of the Christmas story, see K E Bailey, *Jesus Through Middle Eastern Eyes* (London, SPCK 2008), p25-37.

66. 2:29-32; this hymn, known by its Latin opening words, *Nunc Dimittis,* has been used daily in the Church in Night Prayer (Compline) since the fifth century. Brown, *Birth,* p458, lists the Isaian passages which are echoed in the canticle: 52:9-10; 49:6; 46:13; 42:6; 40:5. The opening to the Gentiles anticipates the future preaching of the Gospel, and the story of Acts.

67. R E Brown, *The Gospel according to John* (London, Chapmans 1972), 2 vols, 1:18. Other useful works on the Fourth Gospel include:
C K Barrett, *The Gospel according to John* (London, SPCK 1978);
T L Brodie, *The Gospel according to John* (Oxford, OUP 1993);
W Carter, *John* (Peabody, Hendrickson 2006);
R M Chennattu, *Johannine Discipleship as a Covenant Relationship* (Peabody, Hendrickson 2006);
M L Coloe, *God Dwells With Us* (Collegeville, Liturgical Press 2001);
*Dwelling in the Household of God* (Collegeville, Liturgical Press 2007);
I de la Potterie, *The Hour of Jesus* (Slough, St Paul Publications 1989);
C H Dodd, *The Interpretation of the Fourth Gospel* (Cambridge, CUP 1968);

C R Koester, *Symbolism in the Fourth Gospel* (Minneapolis, Fortress 2003); *The Word of Life* (Grand Rapids, Eerdmans 2008);
R Kysar, *John's Story of Jesus* (Philadelphia, Fortress 1984); *The Maverick Gospel* (Louisville, John Knox Press 2007);
D A Lee, *The Symbolic Narratives of the Fourth Gospel* (Sheffield, JSOT 1994); *Flesh and Glory* (New York, Crossroad 2002);
R H Lightfoot, *St John's Gospel* (Oxford, OUP 1956);
B Lindars, *The Gospel of John* (London, Oliphants 1972);
F J Moloney, *The Gospel of John* (Collegeville, Liturgical Press 1998); *The Gospel of John, Text and Context* (Boston, Brill 2005);
R Schnackenburg, *The Gospel of John* (London, B&O vol 1 1968, vol 2 1980, vol 3 1982);
S M Schneiders, *Written That You May Believe* (New York, Crossroad 1999);
M W G Stibbe, *John Readings* (Sheffield, JSOT Press 1993).

68. See Brown, *John,* 1:521-523; Dodd, p274-277; Lee, *Flesh and Glory,* p32.
69. Sir 24:3; Wis 9:1-2.
70. Sir 1:1; Wis 9:9; Prov 8:27-30.
71. Eccles 2:13; Prov 4:18, 8:35; Sir 24:8-12; Prov 8:31; Sir 15:7; Bar 3:2.
72. Sir 24:8,11,23; Bar 3:36-4:1.
73. Brown, *John* 1:26-27, for example, prefers the former option, Barrett, p134, the latter.
74. In John's Gospel the term *world* is used in three senses: material reality, the theatre of human affairs, and the area which is in the power of evil.
75. The Greek is *eskēnōsen.*
76. Brown, *John* 1:32.
77. J D Kingsbury, *The Christology of Mark's Gospel* (Philadelphia, Fortress 1983), p60.
78. This point is made by McBride, *Mark,* p32.
79. Hooker, p45; Moloney, *Gospel,* p36; see Exod 2:11; Judg 19:1; 1 Sam 28:1. *In those days* highlights the eschatological (end-time) nature of Jesus' coming (Jer 31:33; Joel 3:1; Zech 8:23).
80. Boring, p44, stresses the Galilee/Jerusalem tension present in Mark's wider story; this journey from Nazareth to Judea is a foreshadowing of the later journey.
81. Donahue & Harrington, p65; Boring, p44.
82. Also referred to as the Lake of Gennesereth, a name derived from the Hebrew word for a lyre or harp, a connection inspired by its shape. In John's Gospel it is referred to as the Sea of Tiberias, which probably reflects a later designation linked with the Herodian city constructed on its shore.
83. See Meier, 1:301; Pagola, p56, suggests a smaller population of about 500.
84. Donahue & Harrington, p64; Pagola, p31-51.

85. This is also part of the message of the young man/angel to the women at the tomb. Scholars call this an inclusion. The one whom God raises from the dead is the same one who is declared by God to be his Son. The women are instructed to tell the disciples that Jesus is going ahead of them into Galilee. (See Kingsbury, *Christology,* p60-61). On Nazareth in the time of Jesus, see Borg, *Jesus,* p92-94; Pagola, p53-70.

86. Dunn, *Jesus Remembered,* p372. Luke does not explicitly mention the baptism, concentrating on the phenomena. In Acts 10:37-38 he omits a mention of the baptism, but refers to the anointing with the Spirit and power. In the Fourth Gospel the baptism is not described, but the Baptist witnesses to the descending of the Spirit and its remaining on Jesus; he testifies that Jesus is the Son of God. In Matthew John objects to baptising Jesus, but Jesus insists.

87. Mark's favourite link-word is *Immediately* (*euthys*), used 47 times; it conveys a sense of urgency and restless movement to the narrative.

88. cf. Gen 7:11; Ezek 1:1; Is 24:18; 63:11; Rev 4:1; 11:19.

89. Quoted by both Culpepper, p49, and Moloney, *Gospel,* p36; from Joel Marcus, *Mark 1-8* (New York, Doubleday 2000), p165.

90. Wright, *Mark,* p5.

91. Gen 1:2-3. Moloney, *Gospel,* p36, Byrne, p31 & Culpepper, p49, make this point.

92. Gen 8:11. Moloney, *Gospel,* p36 fn49, is open to this suggestion. Donahue & Harrington, p65, are of the opinion that Old Testament allusions do not reflect the language or situation of Mark.

93. Moloney, *Gospel,* p36 and Martin, p11.

94. Moloney, *Gospel,* p37.

95. Culpepper, p48, calls it a private or secret theophany or divine appearance, which declares Jesus' identity.

96. LXX Gen.22:2, 12, 16. Moloney, *Gospel,* p37. Voorwinde, p65 fn9, notes the veiled allusion to Abraham/Isaac; it is possibly an early pointer to the crucifixion.

97. Hooker, p45; she suggests that Mark's community would connect the baptism of Jesus with his death, and also with their own baptism.

98. Mark's word order is slightly different from that of the Psalm (LXX: *huios mou ei su;* Mark: *su ei ho huios mou*), and he adds *ho agapētos;* in this way the uniqueness of the relationship is emphasised.

99. Hooker, p47; see Exod 4:22; Deut 1:31; Ho 11:1.

100. Harrington, p6.

101. Dunn, *Jesus Remembered,* p374.

102. Voorwinde, p65; Culpepper, p50. Boring, p45-46, emphasises the link with Isaiah's Servant theology. Byrne, p31-32, accepts the allusion and its indication of representative suffering. Hooker, p48, does not accept any link to the suffering servant.

103. Isa 52:13-53:12.
104. Wis 2:12-20. Donahue & Harrington, p65. Hooker, p47, also refers to this Wisdom text, which sees the righteous person as a *child of God*.
105. Culpepper, p49. Kingsbury, p66-67, notes that the other designations of Jesus used in 1:1-13 (*Lord, mighty one, you*) are all in Jesus' capacity as Son. *Abba* is a familiar term for father (daddy); it seems to have been Jesus' characteristic way of addressing God.
106. Meier, 2:105; Moloney, *Gospel*, p36fn43; Dunn, *Jesus Remembered*, p350, 374; Boring, p44.
107. Culpepper, p48.
108. Dunn, *Jesus Remembered*, p350-351; Pagola, p86; Meier, 2:110-116.
109. Pagola, p87.
110. Meier, 2:114-115. See Ezra 9:6-15; Neh. 9:6-37.
111. Pagola, p299.
112. Dunn, *Jesus Remembered*, p376.
113. See, for instance, Borg, *Jesus*, p 120-122; Pagola, p297-298; the Jesus seminar too accepts a powerful religious experience in the context of his baptism. Borg, *Jesus*, p131-135, describes Jesus as a Jewish mystic, a Spirit-filled person.
114. Caird, *Luke*, p77. This view I agree with. Jesus' unusual choice of celibacy, a *eunuch for the sake of the kingdom of heaven* (Matt 19:12), seems to support this.
115. Meier, 2:109.
116. The verb (*exagein*) is also used frequently for Jesus' action in driving out the evil spirits. Matthew and Luke soften the verb to *was led* into the wilderness by the Spirit.
117. Dunn, *Jesus Remembered*, p379-382, believes that it is quite likely that Jesus did spend time in the desert, but the timing is uncertain – whether it took place immediately after the baptism or after John's removal from the scene.
118. See Moloney, *Gospel*, p38. The same verb *drive out* is used there.
119. See Winstanley, *Lenten Sundays*, p7-18 for Matthew, p117-128 for Luke. There is also the testing of Abraham (Gen 22; Sir 44:20) and of Job. Dunn, *Jesus Remembered*, p381, notes that the testing of the righteous has deep roots in Jewish tradition.
120. Deut 9:9,18; 1Kings 19:1-8.
121. Boring, p47.
122. Byrne, p35, considers this the more likely interpretation.
123. Moloney, Gospel, p39; Donahue & Harrington, p66.
124. Isa 11:6-9; 35:3-10; 65:24-25; Ezek 34:23-31; Hos 2:18: Ps 91.
125. Rhoads, Dewey, Michie, p82, maintain that Jesus is the victor; he has bound the strong one. They see later exorcisms as a consequence of this initial resolution of Jesus' conflict with Satan, a mopping-up operation.

126. Exod 14:19; 23:20,23; 32:34; 33:2.
127. 1 Kings 19:5-7.
128. Boring, p48.
129. See Byrne, p2-4.
130. It would seem that Jesus avoided the two major cities of Tiberias and Sepphoris, though he may as a young man have sought work in the latter when it was being rebuilt by Herod.
131. In John's Gospel he visits the city several times, which seems historically more likely. Meier, 1:352, speaks of frequent visits during his ministry.
132. With varying nuances see S Freyne, Jesus, a Jewish Galilean (London, T&T Clark 2004), p21; Culpepper, p48; Borg, Jesus, p120; Dunn, *Jesus Remembered*, p350; Pagola, p89; Boring, p44; Moloney, The Gospel of John, Text and Context (Boston, Brill 2005), p45-65.
133. Matt 11:9-11; Luke 7:26-28.
134. John 3:22-30. Moloney, Mark Storyteller, p49; Donahue & Harrington, p70. Dunn, *Jesus Remembered*, p351, takes it as a firm fact that the ministries of John and Jesus initially overlapped.
135. The verb is found in the Servant Song of Isaiah (52:13-53:12); in Paul it is shorthand for Jesus' passion and death. Mark uses it of Jesus 9:31; 14:10; 15:1,15; also for disciples 13:9-13. The verb is paradothēnai; it suggests God's design, God's presence in what is happening. John's execution by Herod is described in 6:14-29; he is Jesus' forerunner also in death.
136. Nineham, p68. Donahue & Harrington, p70, note the double nuance of *from* and *about* God. Most commentators prefer *from*.
137. Byrne, p40, notes the Isaian (exilic) framework and texts behind Jesus' words: Isa 40:9; 52:7; 61:1-2. Also Nineham, p68.
138. McBride, p38. The Greek kairos indicates a particularly significant and opportune point of time in God's design, whereas chronos denotes ordinary human time measurement.
139. Pagola, p104, notes Jesus' striking and challenging emphasis on the now. Moloney, Mark, Storyteller, p126, writes: *Scholars are in universal agreement that Jesus saw his mission as the establishment of the kingdom of God among men and women.* It is found in all the evangelists and in different literary forms: 13 references in Mark & Q, 25 in Matthew, six in Luke, two in John. It is found in parables, prayers, beatitudes, eschatological prophecies, miracle stories, requirements for entry, words concerning John the Baptist, and in summaries. It is almost always on the lips of Jesus. Outside the Synoptic Gospels it does not seem to have been widely used by either Jews or Christians in the early 1st century AD. The phrase is not used in Paul. All this can be explained only as reflecting Jesus' own usage and emphasis. See Meier, 2:237-243. Similarly Dunn, *Jesus Remembered*, p383-387: Jesus was remembered as speaking and preaching often on the subject; its centrality in his preaching is one of the

least disputable, or disputed, facts about him.

140. See Donahue & Harrington, p71; Hooker, p55; Boring, p51. Moloney, Gospel, p49 fn12, notes that the kingdom is not a static geographical place, but *a new situation in the lives of men and women unconditionally open to God, made possible by Jesus' teaching and person*. Dunn, Jesus Remembered, p388 fn31, refers to *the dynamic, personal presence of God, the sovereign activity of God*, quoting Chilton.

141. After a detailed study, Meier, 2:450-451, concludes that a number of Jesus' sayings and actions argue strongly for the view that at times Jesus spoke of the Kingdom as already present in some way in his ministry. The most significant sayings of Jesus about the Kingdom's presence contain reference to actions which communicate or symbolise that presence. For Donahue & Harrington, p71, it is the heart of Jesus' preaching in word and deed; for Malbon, Mark's Jesus, it is the dominant theme. Nineham, p68, observes that Mark has Jesus proclaim his ministry in the technical terminology of later Christianity; Mark sees this in essence as identical with Jesus' original proclamation and demand.

142. Borg, Jesus, p251-260; Pagola, p99.

143. Donahue & Harrington, p72; Hooker, p55-56. Brown, John, pcxix, writes that *In his ministry the reign of God was making itself manifest among men; and yet, as heir to an apocalyptic tradition, Jesus also spoke of a final manifestation of divine power yet to come. The obscurity of the Gospel references would indicate that Jesus had no clear teaching on how or when this final manifestation would take place.* Meier's conclusion, p348-351, is that Jesus understood the symbol of the Kingdom in terms of the imminent, definitive coming of God to bring the present state of things to an end and establish his full and unimpeded rule over the world and Israel; he emphasised the imminence of the kingdom's coming, but, unlike the apocalyptists, did not set any timetable. Future, transcendent salvation was an essential part of his proclamation of the kingdom. Also, Pagola, p119.

144. Dunn, *Jesus Remembered*, p466.

145. Byrne, p41. See Donahue & Harrington, p71.

146. Nineham, p69. Moloney, *Gospel,* p50, refers to a physical turning around and resuming the right path from which one has strayed, and a moral, spiritual turning around. Also Byrne, p41.

147. Byrne, p42. Boring, p51, sees belief as *an uncalculating obedience-in-personal-trust that involves one's whole life*.

148. Pagola, p100; Kingsbury, p134; W Kasper, Jesus the Christ (London, Burns & Oates 1976), p72-87; J Sobrino, Christology at the Crossroads (London, SCM 1978), p41-78; Hooker, p55; Meier, 2:243-253; Boring, p52.

149. Isa 33:22:43:15; Jer:8:19.

150. Exod 15:18; Ps 145:13.
151. Ps 47, 93, 96-99.
152. Ps 22:29; Jer 10:7; Amos 9:7; Ps 96:10; and, creation, Ps 95:3-5; 103:19; 18:1-48; 145:10-13.
153. Dunn, *Jesus Remembered,* p393-396, outlines the wide range of hopes and expectations for the future which may have been evoked by Jesus' kingdom proclamation: return from exile, renewed and abundant prosperity, the involvement of a particular (messianic) figure, a renewed covenant, the building of a new temple, the return of God to Zion, the future of the other nations, a climactic period of tribulation, cosmic disturbances, the defeat of Satan, final judgement. Pagola, p102, mentions a double hope: liberation from foreign oppression, and the establishment of justice, peace and fullness of life.
154. Ezek 20:33-37; Isa 25:6-9; 33:22; 26:21; Jer 25:30-31; Zech 2:11.
155. Isa 1-6; 11;1-9; 33:22; 52:7; 54:5; Mic 4:1-7; Zech 8:1f; 14;6-10; also Jer 8:7; 10:7; 46:18; 51:57 and Ezek 34.
156. Meier, 2:267.
157. Dunn, *Jesus Remembered,* p465-465. This is not to underplay the significance of his sayings about the future.
158. P Tournier, *Guilt and Grace* (London, Hodder & Stoughton 1962), p189.
159. Pagola, p114-117.
160. Such pre-industrial agricultural domination systems were normal at that time, and had been for centuries. Central features were: political oppression, economic exploitation, religious legitimation, and armed conflict. Basically a two class society emerged, politically and economically different: the wealthy and the peasant classes. See Borg, *Jesus,* p79-85.
161. Borg, *Jesus,* p105-108, notes that Jerusalem and its Temple were the sacred centre of sacred geography of the Jewish social world; it was the only place where sacrifices could be offered to God. God was present there in a special way. It was the centre of devotion and the destination of pilgrimages. It had an institutional monopoly of access to God. It was the focus of promise and hope for the future for Israel and the world. It was also the centre of the domination system, and of collaboration with Rome.
162. See Borg and Crossan, *The Last Week* (London, SPCK 2008), p1-30; Pagola, p31-38.
163. See Borg, Jesus, p186-187.
164. S Schneiders, *Religious Life as Prophetic Life Form* in The National Catholic Reporter, Jan 4-8, 2010.

# Notes on Chapter Two

1. Rhoads, Dewey and Michie, p77-97, analyse Mark's plot in terms of conflict: Jesus is in conflict with demons, illness and nature; with the authorities; and with the disciples. Malbon, *Company*, p17, also sees conflict as the key to Mark's plot.

2. 2:1-3:6; 11:27-12:37.

3. Some think that the first block is a pre-Markan collection, but Harrington and Hooker believe that Mark is responsible for bringing together and carefully arranging these stories which took place at different occasions in Jesus' life, not on one particularly bad day! See Harrington, p24; Hooker, p83; Nineham, p88. Byrne, p53-55, presents the carefully linked linear pattern of the first block, with its emphasis on Jesus' authority and its escalating hostility: sin/forgiveness; sinners/eating; fasting/not eating; eating/Sabbath; and also the chiastic or circular structure: miracle, eating, bridegroom, eating, miracle. Each controversy contains an important saying of Jesus, which serves a catechetical purpose. Rhoads, Dewey, Michie, p52-54, show how the outer and inner episodes form a ring around the central episode. Also Boring, p73; Malbon, *Mark's Jesus*, p110-111.

4. 3:22-30; 7:1-13; 8:11-13.

5. Moloney, *Gospel*, p60, fn68; Hooker, p83. Meier, 1:346-47, notes that although the Synoptic Jesus is in frequent conflict with the scribes, Pharisees and leaders of the synagogue, the lines of communication are still open, and at times positive; they were acceptable debating partners and sometimes sympathetic listeners. *But between Jesus, the Galilean peasant layman, who claimed charismatic religious authority outside the recognised channels, and the high priestly families of Jerusalem, whose power depended on their controlling the sacred centre of Judaism, the temple, there was only unrelieved hostility.* In chapters 1-10 the controversies are mainly between Jesus and the scribes and Pharisees. Twice the scribes are said to have come to Galilee from Jerusalem (3:22; 7:1), and so are linked with the Jerusalem leadership. The problem for the scribes and Pharisees is religious and concerns the attitude of Jesus to the tradition(s); the problem for the chief priests, scribes and elders in Jerusalem has a political twist and concerns Jesus' authority and influence over the people. As the story progresses, the level of conflict escalates. See Malbon, *Company*, p138-154.

6. Byrne, p52. He also observes that the hostility reflects not so much the interactions of Jesus' time, but several decades of growing estrangement between the nascent Church and Judaism. The conflict is not between Jesus and Judaism, but between the liberating challenge of the Kingdom and the kind of repressive, antihuman legalism to which any form of

religion, Christianity included, is prone. See also Donahue & Harrington, p97-98; Hooker, p96; Malbon, *Company*, p135.

7.   Donahue & Harrington, p103, note that in handing on this material Mark is presenting an accurate picture of the historical Jesus; such a discrediting practice would not have been created by the Early Church.

8.   1:16-20. Mark tends to refer to the harp-shaped (hence Chinnereth or Genesereth) stretch of water as the Sea (of Galilee), though it is really a lake, about 12 miles by 8.

9.   Levi does not appear in Mark's list of the Twelve; there is a James, son of Alphaeus, so they may have been brothers; this is Culpepper's preference, p83; also Martin, p43. In Matthew the one called is named as Matthew, in Luke Levi; Matthew is named in Mark's list of the Twelve. Levi and Matthew may be the same person with two names; Levi may be a disciple but not one of the Twelve (Martin, p44, adopts this view, which highlights the importance of *mere* discipleship); James and Levi may be the same person. Moloney, *Gospel*, p63-64, writes: *The need to have all the disciples explicitly called by Jesus in the list of the Twelve does not seem to have been a concern for Mark, however important it became for later Christianity*. See also Donahue & Harrington, p100-101. Hooker, p94, notes that Jesus' call is not limited to the Twelve, and Mark may have deliberately included this episode to make the point. Boring, p80, comments that Mark here presents Jesus' call as inclusive, and not limited to the Twelve; it includes *sinners*, and also women. I consider Levi to be one of the Little People, a minor character (see Malbon, *Company*, p43 and 214.)

10.  For Boring, p79, the Greek verb used (*anastas*) has overtones of resurrection language (*arose*).

11.  A point made by Martin, p44.

12.  Moloney, *Gospel*, p63-64.

13.  Donahue & Harrington, p101.

14.  Nineham, p99; Byrne, p58; Boring, p81.

15.  Hooker, p94.

16.  This story, the first of the five controversies in this section, we shall consider later in this chapter.

17.  Martin, p44, and Culpepper, p84, are of this opinion; also McBride, p54; Donahue & Harrington, p101; Byrne, p58. Hooker, p95, believes that it refers to Jesus, as the grammar of the Greek text implies. Wright, *Mark*, p21 shares this view. Nineham, p99, suggests that originally it may have referred to the house of Jesus, but that Mark probably understood it as Levi's house. In Mark, says Moloney, Gospel, p64, Jesus is found in the houses of others.

18.  Culpepper, p84; Boring, p81.

19. Culpepper, p84; McBride, p54-55.
20. Donahue & Harrington, p102. They were the spiritual leaders of the Jewish people in Jesus' day. They were not directly involved in Jesus' death. Later, after the destruction of the Temple in 70AD, it was their rabbinic movement which was central to the future of Judaism.
21. See Sir 38: 1-5.
22. In 10:45 he speaks of his having come *not to be served but to serve*; see also 1:38. McBride, p55, refers to Jesus holding a mobile surgery!
23. For this interpretation see Boring, p82. Dunn, *Jesus Remembered*, p528-532, makes the point that the self-perceived righteous people use sinner as a term of dismissal and exclusion. Such factional righteousness recognised covenant loyalty only if it accorded with its own terms and definitions.
24. Hos 14:4; Jer 3:22; 17:4; 30:17. See Harrington, p32.
25. Ps. 37 speaks of the righteous being rewarded and the wicked being punished; also Pss.Sol 17:23-25.
26. Donahue & Harrington, p104.
27. Boring, p82-83. He also observes that this scene in which Jesus shares table in a house with followers, including sinners, has overtones of inclusive Eucharistic celebrations in the Early Church.
28. Wright, *Jesus*, p274.
29. Jeremias J, *New Testament Theology* (London, SCM 1971), p116. Harrington, p32, notes that the basis of table fellowship is messianic forgiveness.
30. 5:1,15; 6:17,27,47,49; 7:29; 8:8-18; 9:35; 10:16,24,39; 11:28,31.
31. 5:30; 7:34.
32. See J R Donahue, *The Gospel in Parable* (Philadelphia, Fortress 1988), p148-151.
33. See Winstanley, Lenten Sundays, Year C, Sunday 4, p142-149.
34. See K E Bailey, Poet and Peasant and Through Peasant Eyes, (Grand Rapids, Eerdmans 1983), p161-169. Donahue, Parable, p154, believes, however, that the son's request was legitimate, even if inappropriate.
35. Fitzmyer, p1087-1090, however, believes that the father did not at this stage hand over the rest of the property to the older son; he remained master of the house and owner of the remaining property.
36. Donahue, *Parable*, p153, notes that far more Jews lived abroad than in Palestine.
37. *Against heaven and against you* is a typical Old Testament expression; see Exod 10:16.
38. The verb is *splanchnizesthai*; it occurs also in the parable of the Good Samaritan in Luke.

39. The slaughtering of an animal is a mark of the father's joy. Meat was not eaten often.

40. This too is quite contrary to cultural expectations; it would shock the hearers of the parable.

41. See P Tournier, *Guilt and Grace* (London, Hodder & Stoughton 1962), p189.

42. In terms of narrative characterisation, they form a group, the opposition.

43. Many commentators consider the story to be an amalgam of two originally independent units: a healing miracle following the classic scheme of complaint, request, cure, and demonstration of cure (1-5a, 11-12), and a saying about forgiveness (5b-10). An alternative view takes 1-5 in its entirety with 11-12, and so includes Jesus' word of forgiveness in the miracle story, and sees 6-10 as an interpolation by Mark himself or someone prior to him. This is the option I prefer; see Nineham, p91. Even if an insertion, 6-10 could record an incident which took place in connection with Jesus' claim; the scribal opposition would indeed be natural.

44. 1:40-45. We shall consider this story in Chapter 5.

45. The *house* is a favourite Markan setting; the term may also be a link with the house-churches of Mark's community.

46. Moloney, *Gospel*, p60; Byrne, p56; Donahue & Harrington, p93; Culpepper, p76; McBride, p51; Boring, p76, are of this opinion. Wright, Mark, p16-17, believes that the house belonged to Jesus. Normally, there were 3 or 4 families with small houses surrounding a common patio area.

47. The text says *the word,* which was a common early Christian technical expression for the proclamation of the Good News (often referred to as the *kerygma*); through missionary preaching the message of Jesus continues to be heard.

48. Lev 21:18; at Qumran the lame were not eligible for participation in the life of the community; see Donahue & Harrington, p93. Hooker, p85, notes that popular opinion regarded physical misfortune as the result of sin.

49. McBride, p51.

50. Donahue & Harrington, p93, translate this: *they tore open the roof over him, and pushing the debris aside....*

51. The term is *krabattos*.

52. Culpepper, p77, notes that Mark measures faith not by orthodoxy, but by its determination, courage and persistence.

53. This kind of verbal use is often referred to as the divine passive.

54. Moloney, Gospel, p61. Nineham, p93, suggests that perhaps originally Jesus was assuring the man of God's forgiveness, as Nathan did to David. Boring, p75, and 76-77, maintains that Jesus is going beyond such priestly and prophetic claims. Jesus is acting in God's place, forgiving sins, not just declaring that God has forgiven them. Malbon, Mark's Jesus, p152,

maintains that Jesus knows the forgiving and healing power of God and knows how to make it available to others; this availability is a consequence of the in-breaking rule of God.

55. Hooker, p86.
56. Hooker, p86.
57. Martin, p39.
58. Martin, p39, notes that in the OT sickness was often viewed as evidence of, or punishment for, sin. Jesus did not endorse this view, but saw both as the presence of evil. He was concerned for the whole person; the greatest need of this man was for forgiveness. Culpepper, p79, notes that just as sin and sickness were linked together in popular Jewish theology, in the OT healing and forgiveness are often associated too (Ps 41:4; 103:3; Isa 33:24).
59. Donahue & Harrington, p95.
60. Hooker, p86. Nineham, p91, views them as representative Jewish reactions to Christian claims that sins could be forgiven by and in the name of Jesus.
61. Culpepper, p79.
62. Mark 14:64.
63. Exod 34:6-7; 2 Sam 12:13; Isa 43:25; 44:2.
64. Nineham, p90; Harrington, p29; Donahue & Harrington, p95, note that charges of blasphemy were later made against the Christological claims of the Markan community.
65. See 1Sam 16:7; Ps 7:10; Jer 11:20; Sir 43:18-19.
66. Martin, p40; Donahue & Harrington, p95, see this as an implicit Christological claim; Culpepper, p79.
67. Hooker, p87.
68. Hooker, p87.
69. Moloney, *Gospel*, p62-63; see also Wright, Mark, p17.
70. J D G Dunn, *Jesus and the Spirit* (London, SCM 1975), p78.
71. Donahue & Harrington, p96; also Hooker, p87. Wright, *Mark*, p17, writes: *The paralysed man's healing points forward to the new life that Jesus himself will have in the resurrection, and will share with everyone who wants it.*
72. Hooker, p88.
73. Culpepper, p80.
74. Byrne, p57.
75. Donahue & Harrington, p96.
76. 7:34.
77. Bailey, *Jesus*, p239 and 241; Fitzmyer, p687, calls it one of the great episodes in the Lukan Gospel. Evans, p360, believes that style and language suggest that Luke was largely responsible for its present form.

Bailey believes that it was written before the composition of the Gospels, and most likely given to Luke in written form during his Jerusalem sojourn in AD 56-58; it records eyewitness testimony. Fitzmyer, p684, describes the story as conflated, but believes that it came to Luke in that way.

78. We shall reflect on Mark's version in a later chapter.

79. See M T Winstanley, *Symbols and Spirituality,* (Bolton, Don Bosco Publications 2007), p111-122.

80. Johnson, p128-29, argues strongly in favour of there being two separate incidents; Marshall, p304-306, is of the same view; likewise Culpepper, Mark, p482. Brown, John, 1:449-50, follows Benoit and others in maintaining that there were two incidents, with some passing over of details in the oral stage. Fitzmyer, p687, however, seems open to there being one original incident of an anointing during a meal, which took different forms as the tradition developed.

81. Wright, *Luke*, p90. Bailey, *Jesus*, p239, suggests a structure based on the typical prophetic template of 7 inverted stanzas with a climax at the centre: introduction (the Pharisee, Jesus, the woman), the outpouring of the woman's love (in action), a dialogue (Simon judges wrongly), a parable (at the centre), a dialogue (Simon judges rightly), the outpouring of the woman's love (in retrospect), conclusion (the Pharisee, Jesus, the woman).

82. Marshall, p314, and 306.

83. Caird, p114.

84. Bailey, *Jesus*, p242; Fitzmyer, p686-7, holds that the sinful woman comes to Jesus as one already forgiven by God, and seeking to pour out signs of love and gratitude; love is the consequence of her forgiveness.

85. Evans, p362, observes that it has to be presumed that she knew herself to be one of the company with whom Jesus associates, that he had already declared her sins forgiven, and that her actions were expressions of gratitude for this. Her actions can only be accounted for by something the story does not itself contain.

86. Fitzmyer, p688, thinks the invitation stemmed from the Pharisee's desire to honour an important person.

87. This is Bailey's opinion, Jesus, p242. M Fallon, *Gospel according to St Luke* (Bangalore, Asian Trading Corporation 1997), p153, adopts a similar negative line.

88. Mallon, p153, considers it a studied insult, and sees it as an expression of Simon's desire to humiliate him. McBride, p102, thinks that Simon has been polite according to the book, but has made no effort to make Jesus feel especially welcome. This is the view of Marshall also, p311.

89. Pagola, p151, states that this way of dining was reserved for special occasions. He believes that the banquet was held in front of the house,

where bystanders could listen to the conversation of the diners. The woman was probably a prostitute, not to be confused with Mary of Magdala or Mary of Bethany. Byrne, p74, makes the same point. Fitzmyer, p688, thinks the meal was a festive banquet, possibly a Sabbath meal after synagogue; also Marshall, p308.

90. See Caird, p114.
91. *From the time I came in she has not ceased to kiss my feet.* Bailey, *Jesus*, p244.
92. Johnson, p127, notes that *myron is an oil with a pungent scent; but there is in this story no connection with the burial of Jesus nor any suggestion that the oil is particularly expensive.*
93. Bailey, *Jesus*, p246.
94. Marshall, p308. Bailey, *Jesus*, p247, suggests that her tears are not because of her sins, but because of his humiliation. *She is in anguish because, before her eyes, this beautiful person who set her free with his message of the love of God for sinners, is being publicly humiliated.* Fitzmyer, p689, notes that traditionally the tears have been understood as tears of repentance; but she could have been weeping for joy at the realisation of the forgiveness she has already experienced.
95. Women were obliged to cover their hair in public. For a married woman failure to do so merited divorce. McBride, p103, notes that this was usually taken as a public signal that the woman was willing to negotiate a certain transaction.
96. Bailey, *Jesus*, p247.
97. Caird, p114.
98. Johnson, p127, notes that it is *axiomatic* that a prophet can see the heart; Jesus knows her heart and also Simon's. Fitzmyer, p689; also Evans, p362: Jesus shows prophetic discernment in knowing the Pharisee's inner thoughts. See 5:22; 6:8; 9:47; 11:17; 20:23.
99. Caird, p114. Mosetto, p165, suggests that Jesus' openness is itself profoundly prophetic.
100. Bailey, Jesus, p251, points out that this is a classical Middle Eastern idiom that introduces blunt speech which the listener may not want to hear.
101. Pagola, p151, notes that the creditor in the parable knows the suffering of those who cannot pay what they owe. 500 denarii is a large debt, the equivalent of a farm worker's wages for 2 years.
102. Bailey, *Jesus*, p254.
103. Marshall, p311.
104. Fitzmyer, p691, states that the application of the parable is not so much to contrast their deeds, as to stress the love manifested in them.
105. Bailey, Jesus, p257.
106. Johnson, p128, notes the use of the perfect passive, indicating what has

been done for her. Her expression of love *is not the basis for forgiveness, but the demonstration of it.* Also Byrne, p75; Fitzmyer, p692; Marshall, p304, 314.

107. Byrne, p75; Caird, p114-5, Marshall, p313, take this view also. Similarly Pagola, p152, who states that Simon sees in her the suggestive gestures of her profession; Jesus sees the tangible sign of God's forgiveness.
108. As with the paralysed man in Luke's version, 5:20.
109. Johnson, p128; see 8:12,48; 17:19; 18:41; Acts 15:11.
110. It picks up the Baptist's issue in 7:20, and anticipates Herod's question in 9:9.
111. Marshall, p304.
112. Johnson, p129.
113. Byrne, p76; McBride, p101, also stresses the contrasts.
114. Bailey, *Jesus*, p258. Mallon, p153, comments that Simon is exposed as the real sinner, too self-opinionated to realise it. But he has been offered the insight that would enable him to change.
115. For a discussion of his name, see Fitzmyer, p1223.
116. We will examine Mark's version of his cure in chapter five.
117. Evans, p660; Fitzmyer, p1222, also notes this.
118. Bailey, Jesus, p170.
119. Marshall, p694.
120. Bailey, Jesus, p175, suggests a *ring composition,* or inverted parallelism: Jesus comes; Zacchaeus, a rich man; the crowd (hostile); up a tree; Jesus' act of costly love (the central point); down the tree; the crowd (angry); Zacchaeus, money for others; Jesus' final word of love.
121. Bailey, Jesus, p176, suggests that the townsfolk would probably be planning to provide a banquet for him, and so would be disappointed.
122. Caird, p207. The Greek term is *architelōnēs.*
123. Evans, p662. Fitzmyer, p1223, observes that the implication is that his wealth came from his activity as a toll-collector. Jericho was an important border city.
124. Wright, Luke, p222, describes his situation extremely well; see Mallon, p283; McBride, p244.
125. 9:9, Herod said, *'John I beheaded; but who is this about whom I hear such things?' And he tried to see him.*
126. See Caird, p208; McBride, p244.
127. Byrne, p150.
128. Bailey, *Jesus*, p178; Fitzmyer, p1224, notes that NT Jericho had parks, avenues, and public squares where fine trees grew. Marshall, p696, points out that these oak-like evergreens (*sykomorea* or *ficus sycomoros* in Latin) are very different from our UK sycamores or planes.
129. Johnson, p285, notes that dei designates important turning points in

the story as directed by God; Marshall, p697, also sees the necessity as imposed on Jesus by God. Mosetto, p325, observes that the use of the verb *menō*, stay, recurs in the Emmaus story.

130. Johnson, p285, and Fitzmyer, p1224.
131. Bailey, *Jesus*, p181.
132. Caird, p208.
133. Some believe that this takes place inside the house at a meal; but that breaks the natural flow of the narrative. Marshall, p697, thinks it is probably outside in the presence of the people. Zacchaeus' words are not meant to sound like a boast.
134. Also Evans, p661; he notes, p663, that the Greek here does not convey any doubt. Bailey, Jesus, p181, notes that his words are exaggerated to indicate his sincerity, in traditional Middle Eastern style; his hearers would not expect him to fulfil what he says. He too seems to believe this took place at the evening banquet.
135. Marshall, p697; on p698 he expresses his view that the verb refers to the future.
136. Bailey, Jesus, p182, 185.
137. Johnson, p286, notes that the noun salvation is used only here after the Infancy Narrative; the verb, however, occurs frequently.
138. Fitzmyer, p1226 and 1222, also stresses the shepherd image and its background in Ezekiel. Further, he notes that the Son of Man title may have been added to an otherwise authentic saying of Jesus. Marshall, p695, makes the comment that the epitome of Luke's Gospel message is expressed here.
139. Fitzmyer, p1218.
140. Byrne, p151, notes this. Fitzmyer, p1220-21,1225, states that the verb expresses customary action; it need not be understood as a futurist present. The implication is that if he is guilty of extortion, it is not deliberate. Johnson, p285-6 and 257, says the verb is present progressive, indicating repeated, customary practice. Zacchaeus contrasts with the rich man in the earlier story (18:18-30).
141. Fitzmyer, p1221.
142. See also Ps 63:1; 143:6.
143. B.M. Metzger, *A Textual Commentary on the Greek New Testament* (London, United Bible Societies 1971), p220.
144. Bailey, *Jesus*, p230.
145. Brown, *John*, 1:335-336.
146. This is a slightly updated version of my *Lenten Sundays*, Year C, Sunday 5, p150-154.
147. Isa 55:1-3.
148. John 7:50-52.

149. Bailey, *Jesus*, p232-233.
150. Deut 22:23-24.
151. See John 18:31. I accept the view that the Romans usually kept to themselves the right to execution, especially in turbulent contexts like Judea.
152. See S Schneiders, *Religious Life as Prophetic Life Form* in The National Catholic Reporter, Jan 4-8, 2010.
153. Bailey, Jesus, p236. He also notes that Jesus upholds the sexual ethics of the biblical tradition but removes its penalty.

# Notes on Chapter Three

1. This central aspect of the Calvary scene and climax of the Gospel I shall leave until chapter 6.
2. The Johannine story of Jesus meeting the Samaritan woman is included in chapter 4.
3. Luke 9:51-56 (the villagers), 10:25-37 (the parable).
4. The mission of Jesus is to proclaim the good news and to overcome the power of evil. Those called to be disciples are to be *with Jesus* and *to be sent likewise to proclaim the message and to have authority to cast out demons* (3:14-15). Mark then presents Jesus teaching in parables, followed by a series of *mighty works:* the calming of the storm, the exorcism of Legion, the healing of the woman with a haemorrhage, and the raising to life of Jairus' daughter.
5. Hooker, p142.
6. Harrington, p67; Byrne, p95.
7. Nineham, p155.
8. Moloney, *Gospel*, p101; Martin, p112.
9. Meier, 2:650; Moloney, Gospel, p102; Harrington, p67. Hooker, p141-142, suggests that Mark may have combined two different accounts of the miracle. Byrne, p95 fn11, believes that Mark is presumably reliant on separate sources from which he has not put together a completely coherent account.
10. Donahue & Harrington, p169. Boring, p149, notes its lack of smoothness and consistency.
11. Moloney, Gospel, p102 fn156, suggests that it is Mark himself who has inserted the swine episode, making it the point of focus for the whole story. Meier, 2:650-653, notes that many additions and expansions to the core narrative have taken place over several decades thanks to literary activity and theological imagination. See also Boring, p149-150.
12. Moloney, *Gospel*, p102. He sees the story as establishing a beachhead for the coming of the kingdom among the Gentiles.
13. Moloney, *Gospel*, p102; Culpepper, p164. Harrington, p67, suggests a 4 act drama: the afflicted man, the swine, the fellow-countrymen, the man and Jesus. Similarly, Byrne, p95.
14. Some manuscripts have Gergesenes (a suggestion of Origen) because of its close proximity to the lake; others follow Matthew's Gadarenes (the city of Gadara is 6 miles from the lake).
15. Meier, 2:651.
16. Donahue & Harrington, p163; Culpepper, p165.
17. Nineham, p153, refers to Isa 65:1-4 as a passage which may have influenced the story; also Ps 68:6 (67:7); likewise Donahue & Harrington, p164; Culpepper, p164.

18. In 1:7 the Baptist speaks of *the more powerful one.* Later, Jesus states: *No one can enter a strong man's house and plunder his property without first tying up the strong man; then indeed the house can be plundered* (3:27).
19. Donahue & Harrington, p164; Hooker, p142; Martin, p106.
20. The verb is *proskynein.*
21. 1:24. Donahue & Harrington, p164, observe that the first exorcism on Jewish soil (1:24) is closely and deliberately echoed by the first in Gentile territory. There is a similar oscillation between singular and plural in the demon's/man's words.
22. Boring, p150.
23. It was a popular belief that to know someone's name gave power over the person. Boring, p150, suggests that the demon is attempting a reverse exorcism.
24. Harrington, p69; Donahue & Harrington, p165; Hooker, p143. Texts referred to include Gen 14:18-20; Num 24:16; Ps 114:14; Dan 3:26; 4:2; Acts 16:17. Gentiles confess the sovereignty of the God of Israel over the nations.
25. In Matthew 8:29 he says: *have you come to torment us before the time?* This makes the eschatological (end time) reference more explicit.
26. Nineham, p153.
27. Hooker, p143.
28. A Roman legion normally numbered about 6000 soldiers. Donahue & Harrington, p166, suggest that the term is a colloquial expression for a large number.
29. Moloney, *Gospel*, p103.
30. See, for instance, Nineham, p150; Meier, 2:651. McBride, p89, calls the swine a distraction.
31. Meier, 2:666 fn21. Abstinence from pork, like Sabbath observance, was a distinctive aspect of Jewish identity.
32. Donahue & Harrington, p166.
33. Nineham, p154; Moloney, Gospel, p104. For Byrne, p97, the demons return via the sea to their habitual abode in the underworld. In his version, Luke uses the word abyss, the primal ocean prison for powers opposed to God.
34. Some scholars suggest a socio-political dimension to the story, viewing it as a symbolic expulsion of the Romans; see Wright, *Mark*, p56. Boring, p151, observes that the story is not an allegory for liberation from the Romans, its scope is wider that that, but it could hardly have been read in Mark's time without political overtones. Donahue & Harrington, p166, are not convinced.
35. Byrne, p97, links the human transformation with the calming of the sea in the previous incident (4:39).
36. Nineham, p150; Byrne, p97; Martin, p111.

37. Moloney, *Gospel*, p105. Donahue & Harrington, p167, state that it is not fear but religious awe, as in 4:41.

38. 3:13-14: *he called to him those whom he wanted.....they were to be with him...*

39. Hooker, p145.

40. Hooker, p146.

41. Moloney, *Gospel*, p106.

42. Byrne, p98, notes that the first Gentile convert is the centurion at the cross; also Moloney, *Gospel*, p106.

43. Moloney, *Gospel*, p106.

44. Mark 3:14; John 13:8.

45. Culpepper, p181.

46. 6:1-6.

47. A Phoenician from Syria, rather than from Libya in N Africa.

48. Feeding (6:35-44 and 8:1-9); lake crossing (6:45-52 and 8:10); controversy (7:1-23 and 8:11-13); reference to bread (7:24-30 and 8:14-21); a healing (7:31-37 and 8:22-26).

49. In 7:24 and 31 the indications are explicit. The two stories probably existed separately in the earlier tradition; see Moloney, *Gospel*, p144; Meier, 2:660.

50. Boring, p206, reminds us of the 2 levels of the story: a woman seeking healing for her daughter, and the problems of Mark's Church, now predominantly Gentile.

51. The verb used here, rising up (anastas), is adopted by Mark when Jesus embarks on a significant new activity (1:35; 10:1); see Donahue & Harrington, p232; Byrne, p125. Boring, p207, observes that the verb is used of Jesus' resurrection; it is a subtle reminder of the realities of the post-Easter life of the Church. Some manuscripts add and Sidon (as in Matthew). Harrington, p104, notes that the region of Tyre included upper Galilee; Nineham, p 200, thinks it was Gentile only in a very limited sense.

52. For example in Isa 25:22 and Ezek 27:32. Boring, p209, notes that Tyre is presented there as the traditional enemy of the Jews, but, because it helped in the building of the temple, it was sometimes promised a part in eschatological salvation (Ezek 26-28; Joel 3:4-8; Amos 1:9-10; Zech 9.)

53. Boring, p209.

54. In Matthew's version (15:21-28) they are present and have a role in the story, urging Jesus to send the annoying woman away.

55. Hooker, p183.

56. McBride, p118, recalls that people from that area sought Jesus out in 3:8; also Donahue & Harrington, p233.

57. See 1:40 (the leper); 5:22 (Jairus) and 5:33 (the woman with the flow of

blood). Donahue & Harrington, p233 and 237, consider that the woman is a *Greek lady* of some social status, a landed property owner. Boring, p210, considers her a member of the wealthy urban class (the Greek words used for bed and table are an indication).

58. Harrington, p104, sees her as a representative of the Gentile world. Donahue & Harrington, p236, note echoes of the Elijah and Elisha cycles in 1 Kings 17:8-24; 2 Kings 4:18-37.

59. Moloney, *Gospel*, p146-147, observes that the saying, probably Jesus' own words, has the ring of a traditional proverbial saying. Culpepper, p238-239, suggests that the aphorism may have arisen out of hostility between Jews in Galilee and the more affluent Tyreans in connection with bread supplies in times of famine; see also Boring, p209. On p213 he points out that neither Jesus nor Mark created the metaphor.

60. Wright, *Mark*, p95. Matthew, whose version does not take place in a house, makes this explicit, for Jesus says: *I was sent only to the lost sheep of the house of Israel.* Isaiah included the nations in his view of salvation history: 2:2-4; 42:1; 60:1-3; 66:18-20. Paul's later practice was to preach first to the Jews, and then the Gentiles (Rom 1:16; 2:9-10; Acts 3:26; 13:46; 18:6). Donahue & Harrington, p233, suggest an allusion to the two feeding miracles (6:30-44; 8:1-10). Malbon, *Company*, p52, observes that Jesus' statement is undermined by his earlier healing of the Gerasene demoniac.

61. 6:30-44. For Boring, p211, the priority of Israel is maintained without excluding Gentiles.

62. Wright, Mark, p95, for instance.

63. Culpepper, p240. Boring, p210-211, dismisses such views.

64. Hooker, p182.

65. Hooker, p183; Moloney, *Gospel*, p147; Byrne, p126. Culpepper, p242, sees the word as possibly a confession; Boring, p214, as an acceptance of his authority; but for the reader, it is a Christian confession. Malbon, Mark's Jesus, p85, notes the deliberate and significant ambiguity.

66. Non-Jews allowed dogs into their homes; they were household pets rather than mongrel scavengers. Maybe in her experience the children deliberately threw them scraps; see Martin, p180.

67. Hooker, p183.

68. Nineham, p199.

69. In Matthew, Jesus' appreciation of her faith is strongly expressed: Great is your faith. Malbon, *Company*, p53, notes that it is her action in speaking up and speaking out (her *word*), not her faith alone or reasoning alone, that causes Jesus to change his mind and grant her request.

70. See Malbon, *Mark's Jesus*, p134.

71. Moloney, *Gospel*, p145, observes that in all the New Testament stories of

Jesus curing from a distance the aspect of wonder is lacking. He adds on p148, that all the stories (Matt 8:5-13; Luke 7:1-10; John 4:46-54) are the result of a Gentile request.

72. From the perspective of the Evangelist, the Gentile mission was a vibrant reality, and the Church was predominantly Gentile.

73. Hooker, p182.

74. Isa 49:6.

75. Moloney, *Gospel*, p147. Boring, p213, writes that the metaphor was intentionally crafted by the narrator to allow the woman to adapt it for her own (Markan) purpose. For the present the Jewish children are being fed; later the Gentiles will be included in the messianic salvation.

76. Hooker, p184.

77. Donahue & Harrington, p237.

78. Donahue & Harrington, p237.

79. See Eph 2:14.

80. Harrington, p105.

81. Luke is not the only Evangelist who pairs stories with male and female characters. In Mark, besides the current stories, there is a similar pattern with Legion and the twinned stories of Jairus' daughter and the woman with the haemorrhage.

82. Matthew 15:30-31 refers to dumb people, amongst others, being brought to Jesus and being cured; in Matt 11:5 there is a reference to the deaf hearing. Luke 11:14 refers to Jesus *casting out a demon that was mute; when the demon had gone out, the one who had been mute spoke, and the crowds were amazed.*

83. Moloney, *Gospel*, p149. Scholars view this story in parallel with the later cure of the blind man (8:22-26). Probably they were transmitted together; Mark is responsible for splitting them up for theological reasons, using them symbolically. The concluding verse, with its reference to Isaiah, may originally have been the conclusion to both. See also Meier, 2:691; Cranfield, p253-255; Boring, p215.

84. Meier, 2:711-12; Nineham, p203, comments that it was like travelling from Cornwall to London via Manchester!

85. Martin, p181-182.

86. Moloney, *Gospel*, p149; Byrne, p127. Boring, p216, suggests that Jesus is travelling through the region where Gentile Churches existed in Mark's day.

87. The Greek word used here (*mogilalos*) is unusual, found elsewhere only in Isaiah 35:6, where it translates the Hebrew for *stammerer* or *dumb*; see Nineham, p202; Moloney, *Gospel*, p149. Note also Isa 42:19; Exod 4:11: Who gives speech to mortals? Who makes them mute or deaf, seeing or blind? Is it not I, the Lord?

88. Moloney, *Gospel*, p149: the phrase is used of healing, not simply a

blessing. Nineham, p203, observes that the phrase came to be used as a metaphor for healing.

89. See also 5:37, 40; 8:23.
90. Meier, 2:712-13, notes the unusual and untypical string of symbolic or ritual-like gestures, almost magical. Luke and Matthew omit the story.
91. As in Mark 6:41 and John 11:41; Meier, 2:713, takes the sighing as an expression of prayer as well (see Mark 7:34); also Martin, p184; Boring, p217. Culpepper, p245, refers to a *prayer-sigh*.
92. According to Meier, 2:759 fn159, most exegetes think that the word is a relic from the Aramaic form of the Jesus tradition, and perhaps an actual word of Jesus. Donahue & Harrington, p240, stress that it is a word of power, not a magical incantation; similarly Culpepper, p245; Boring, p217.
93. Nineham, p204; Hooker, p186; Byrne, p128; Boring, p217. Not all commentators agree. The same Greek verb is used in Ezek 24:27: *on that day your mouth shall be opened to the one who has escaped, and you shall speak and no longer be dumb*. Meier, 2:714, concludes that the story reflects an event in Jesus' life.
94. Isa 35:5-6; the words *kōphon* and *mogilalon* of v32 are used in the LXX version; see Wis 10:21. See Moloney, *Gospel*, p151.
95. Harrington, p105; Culpepper, p243.
96. Gen 1:31; see Boring, p218.
97. 7:18.
98. Moloney, *Gospel*, p59-60, 150.
99. Matt 8:5-13; Luke 7:1-10; this is the only miracle story in the Q tradition which is developed at some length; it seems to be a mixed form: miracle story and pronouncement. See Meier, *Marginal Jew,* 2:718; 764 fn178. The Fourth Evangelist has a similar story involving a *royal official* and his son; this is situated in Cana, and has literary and structural ties with the earlier Cana incident, when Jesus changes water into wine at a wedding. See Winstanley, Symbols and Spirituality, p98. It is probably a variant of an original episode in Jesus' ministry. Moloney, *John*, p 153, 160-161, argues persuasively that this man is a Gentile, though not all agree (see Meier, 2:722).
100. Voorwinde, p16.
101. See Meier, *Matthew*, p79-81; D J Harrington, p115; Albright & Mann, p94.
102. Mark's version of the cure of Simon Peter's mother-in-law will be considered in the next chapter of this book, and his presentation of the cleansing of the leper in the subsequent chapter.
103. In Luke it is a delegation of Jewish elders who approach Jesus on his behalf. Meier, 2:721, notes that most centurions were ordinary soldiers who progressed through the ranks; the number of troops they commanded varied; it could be 30 or 60 men; they exercised more than

simply military duties, including building and diplomatic roles. Herod Antipas had a private army, probably mainly Gentiles, and adopted Roman military nomenclature. Harrington, p113, raises the possibility that the man could be retired.

104. *Lord* is polite and respectful; for Christian readers it would have greater significance. Matthew's Greek (pais) is ambiguous, perhaps reflecting earlier Aramaic ambiguity, and can mean servant or son; the Evangelist does not resolve the ambiguity. Most commentators and translations opt for servant. The versions of Luke (*doulos*), a servant, and John (*huios*), a son, reflect different interpretations. In Luke and John the problem is that the servant or son is near to death, in Luke with some unspecified illness, in John with a fever; in Matthew he is painfully paralysed, but not in danger of death.

105. Albright & Mann, p93.

106. Voorwinde, p19 notes that the centurion has authority because he is under (imperial) authority; Jesus is similarly under divine authority. Jesus is backed by God's authority.

107. Voorwinde, p18-19; Harrington, p113, takes this view; also Davies & Allison, p120. Senior, p98, follows most commentators in opting for the traditional opinion; also Schweizer, p213. Beare, p207, believes the view is over-subtle; in Matthew Jesus usually takes the initiative and sets his own course. Gundry, p143, rejects the indignant question idea. Meier 2:719 fn182, outlines in detail the issues involved, but concludes by disagreeing with the view. One strong reason is Jesus' immediate response to the marginalised leper in the previous incident, infringing the Law in the process; also, the centurion is not bargaining for an alternative, but is waiving the favour offered. The idea of Jesus going to the house was not part of the original request, and so cannot be a cause of indignation.

108. Also Mark 6:6; both here, and in Mark, Jesus' amazement is a response to the presence or absence of faith. Usually the verb (*thaumazein*) applies to other people: the disciples in Matt 8:27; 21:20; the crowds in 9:33; 15:31; the Pharisees in 22:22; Pilate 27:14. Matthew rarely refers to Jesus' emotions.

109. In Luke 13:28-29, this is a separate saying of Jesus, and is not linked with the miracle story; in Luke the reference to Israel precedes mention of the Gentiles, the reverse of Matthew. Meier, *Matthew*, p84 and Senior, p99, maintain that Matthew has added these verses from Q to the original healing story. The apocalyptic imagery of *outer darkness, weeping, and gnashing of teeth* are typical Matthaean judgement metaphors. Senior notes the view that in their original context these words may have applied to diaspora Jews responding to the Gospel more readily than those living in Judea. See also Davies & Allison, p121.

110. Isa 25:6-8; 49:12; Mal 1:11.
111. 12:15-21, quoting Isa 42:1-4; see Byrne, p77.
112. 24:14.
113. 15:24; see also 10:5-6.
114. 28:18-19.
115. Meier, *Matthew*, p84; Schweizer, p215-216.
116. Beare, p206.
117. Davies & Allison, p121.
118. Beare, p209.
119. Brown, *Introduction*, p 629, observes that between 70-80 percent of scholars are of the view that Paul was not the author.

# Notes on Chapter Four

1. The *Shema* is the name given to the prayer which was recited 3 times each day; the prayer consists of 3 OT quotations (Deut 6:4-9; 11:13-21; Num 15:37-41). The title (Shema) is derived from the Hebrew imperative singular *Hear*.

2. Pagola, p209-230.

3. Mallon, p155.

4. Fitzmyer, p695-98; Johnson, p131, refers to financial support.

5. Mosetto F, *Lettura del Vangelo second Luca* (Rome, LAS 2003), p169-170.

6. The town of Magdala (modern Migdal) is not mentioned in scripture apart from its link with Mary. Joanna's husband was probably the manager of Herod's estates. Nothing further is known about Susanna. Acts 13:1 suggests other links between Herod's court and the nascent Christian community.

7. Acts 1:14. Dunn, *Jesus Remembered*, p537, states that the prominence of women amongst Jesus' followers and his closeness to several must have raised a few eyebrows in polite society at the time. Jesus saw no deficiency in their status as women or in their innate capacity for service and ministry.

8. Meier, 2:707.

9. Some scholars view 1:21-34 as a model day in Jesus' ministry; he preaches and casts out devils in the synagogue, heals Simon's mother-in-law, and later heals many people; through the presence of Jesus, God's power breaks through into the lives of needy people. The centrepiece is the current episode.

10. Culpepper, p57-58. He discusses the excavations; also Martin, p26; McBride, p45.

11. Byrne, p46, believes the house setting is highly symbolic; it announces the consecration of the domestic church which is a feature of this Gospel. Rather than Temple and synagogue, gatherings in simple homes will be the place where the Risen Lord will be at home with his healing and life-giving power. Also Boring, p66.

12. Martin, p25. See also Meier, 2:754, fn135. Boring, p66, takes the illness as life-threatening.

13. 1Cor 9:5.

14. Byrne, p46; Boring, p66.

15. Donahue & Harrington, p82.

16. Byrne, p47; Donahue & Harrington, p82.

17. Byrne, p47.

18. Moloney, *Gospel*, p55.

19. Culpepper, p58; Meier, 2:754-55; Martin, p25. The verb is egeirein.

20. McBride, p46.
21. Moloney, *Gospel*, p55.
22. 9:33-37.
23. 10:35-45.
24. 15:41. See Culpepper, p59; Byrne, p47.
25. In terms of Mark's narrative this is the first incident in which Jesus' revolutionary attitude to women is encountered. Because of the way I have ordered the material in this book, we have met it earlier.
26. See Winstanley, *Symbols*, chapter 8.
27. We have reflected on this episode in chapter 3.
28. Some scholars think that the original events happened in this way. Others believe that they happened and were narrated separately, before being brought together either by Mark himself (Hooker, p147; Boring, p157) or an earlier redactor of the cycle of miracle stories. See also Meier, 2:778.
29. See also 3:19-35, 6:6b-29, 11:12-25, 14:1-11, 14:53-72. Other terms to describe this literary technique, which is not a Markan invention, are insertion, intercalation, interpolation, dovetailing, interweaving; see Boring, p157.
30. Wright, Mark, p58.
31. Byrne, p99.
32. Meier, 2:845 fn30; Culpepper, p171. Large cities would have more officials and greater functional differentiation.
33. The only other person named in a Markan miracle story is Bartimaeus. For Malbon, *Company*, p157-159, Jairus is one of three Jewish religious leaders who is presented positively. Also Boring, p158.
34. It is the diminutive, *thygatrion*.
35. Nineham, p160; Harrington, p75-76; Hooker, p148; Martin, p115; Culpepper, p172. Boring, p157, notes that in the biblical world to be sick was already to be in the grasp of death, and to be healed was to be restored to life. Resurrection imagery is present.
36. In the text there are 7 participles describing her condition.
37. Boring, p157, lists many aspects: Jairus is named, male, a synagogue leader, a parent, who approaches Jesus in public for healing for his daughter, he asks Jesus to touch her. The woman is nameless, poor, excluded from synagogue, concerned about her own living death, approaches Jesus surreptitiously, touches Jesus. But both have faith.
38. Donahue & Harrington, p174; Boring, p159.
39. Lev 15: 25-30. See Moloney, *Gospel*, p107; Hooker, p148; Martin, p116.
40. Byrne, p100, observes that the term *unclean* suggests that her condition has placed her within the grip of the demonic world; metaphorically she is within the tombs.

41. Donahue & Harrington, p180; Boring, p159. Martin, p116, points out that according to Lev 20:18 sexual intercourse was forbidden.

42. The phrase *the things concerning Jesus* can also mean the religious truth about Jesus and his work, as in Luke 22:37; 24:19; 24:27; Acts 18:25; 23:11; 28:31. See Nineham, p160; Harrington, p72. Her faith stemmed from the testimony of other people.

43. Malbon, *Mark's Jesus*, p84, considers that she makes a bold move of gaining access to the power of the in-breaking rule of God that is available through Jesus, and it is successful.

44. Hooker, p149: in the LXX *dynamis* is used primarily for God's power. Donahue & Harrington, p175, link this with 1:7 and 1:10, Jesus as the Spirit-endowed prophet. Nineham, p161, prefers the translation: t*he power proceeding from him* (i.e. his messianic power of healing) had gone forth.

45. Moloney, *Gospel*, p108. Donahue &Harrington, p175, refer to human fragility in the presence of divine power. She is not *afraid* because she has been found out. Byrne, p101, takes this as a Christological confession.

46. McBride, p91. Donahue & Harrington, p176, note the link between faith and salvation; saving faith describes the confidence and boldness whereby people surmount obstacles to come to Jesus.

47. Meier, 2:709; Hooker, p149.

48. The verb is *parakouein*.

49. 9:2; 13:3; 14:33. Andrew joins them in 13:1.

50. Donahue & Harrington, p177; Boring, p161.

51. Wright, *Mark*, p62. For details of mourning practices, see Donahue & Harrington, p177; Culpepper, p177. For Boring, p162, given that the dead were often buried on the day they died, the funeral has already begun.

52. Meier, 2:844 fn26c.

53. In the OT Elijah and Elisha go alone (1Kings 17&19,23; 2 Kings 4:33, 36-37), as does Peter in Acts 9:40.

54. *Talitha* is affectionate for *lamb*. The *young lady* (*korasion*) of the translation can be used for a girl approaching marriageable age. *Koum* or *kum* is the common word for *Get up.*

55. Here and 7:34, the story of the deaf-mute, which we considered in the previous chapter. The Greek verb (*egeirein*) for arise is used for the resurrection of Jesus in 14:28; 16:6; the verb for got up (*anistēmi*) is likewise used of Jesus in 8:31; 9:9,31; 10:34. *The density of language about death and resurrection here is evidence that the Markan readers are to see this narrative as a foreshadowing of Jesus' resurrection and of their own awakening from the sleep of death.* (Donahue & Harrington, p178).

56. The original Aramaic was understandable by the witnesses; and Mark translates it for his readers; its use has nothing to do with unintelligible magic formulas, as has sometimes been suggested.

57. Repeated in 16:8.

58. The command is probably a Markan addition, another example of his secrecy motif.

59. Wright, *Mark*, p64-65.

60. Moloney, *Gospel*, p111. For Byrne, p103, the meaning of the raising can only be grasped by those who are being schooled in belief in Jesus' own resurrection, which is never to be separated from his death. Boring, p163, also emphasises the links with Jesus' resurrection.

61. *koimasthai* or, as here, *katheudein*.

62. Hooker, p148.

63. Harrington, p75.

64. Hooker, p147-150.

65. Meier, 2:756, thinks that it may have been a factor which brought the stories together originally.

66. Moloney, *Gospel*, p111.

67. Hooker, p150. Boring, p158, lists the contrasts and parallels between the two.

68. E S Fiorenza, In Memory of Her, (New York, Crossroad 1983), p122-124; see Donahue & Harrington, p181; Byrne, p102.

69. Verses 28, 30, 31.

70. Moloney, *Gospel*, p111; Byrne, p103.

71. See Winstanley, Lenten Sundays, Year B, Sunday 6, p113-116.

72. Moloney, *Gospel*, p245, states that Mark is responsible for placing these traditions in the temple context. The first series of controversies is found in 2:1-3:6; see earlier in chapter 2 of this book.

73. These two groups are united in the decision to destroy Jesus in 3:6.

74. Along with Jairus and Joseph of Arimathea, this scribe is a member of the Jewish religious establishment who is favourably presented by Mark. He is an exception to the stereotype.

75. Hooker, p294, notes that not all scribes were guilty of hypocrisy, but warnings about the behaviour of particular scribes tended to become sharpened later into blanket condemnation of the whole party in the bitter conflict between the Church and the Jewish authorities.

76. Donahue & Harrington, p362, 365; Boring, p350. A description of the ideal is found in Sir 38:24-39:11. See the strong critique in Matt 23. Mark may have made a selection from a larger tradition. Luke locates the critique in a different context (chap 11).

77. Mark speaks of their long, flowing outer garment, and their preference for the synagogue seats in front of the ark containing the sacred scrolls, which faced the rest of the congregation. See Byrne, p194; Hooker, p295; Moloney, *Gospel*, p245.

78. Hooker, p295; Boring, p351.

79. 12:41-44; Luke 21:1-4. Matthew does not include the story. It is difficult to decide whether Mark joined the two passages, or whether this had already occurred in the tradition; see Moloney, *Gospel*, p 246. Byrne, p193, notes that the two episodes form something of a diptych showing contrasting portraits of behaviour inspired by religion. Also Donahue & Harrington, p364.

80. Nineham, p334, suggests that this was originally a Jewish parable which Jesus took over in his teaching and which was later transformed into an incident in his life.

81. Martin, p335; Culpepper, p428.

82. Donahue & Harrington, p363.

83. Exod 22:22; Deut 10:18; Isa 1:17; Jer 7:6; 22:3; 49:11; Ezek 22:7; Zech 7:10; Mal 3:5. The exploitation of widows, or failing to care for them, were serious religious offences.

84. Jesus uses the *Amen* formula to introduce his comment. Donahue & Harrington, p364, suggest that Jesus may have been able to tell from the sound of the metal coins reverberating off the receptacle. Boring, p352, notes that the Greek can mean that she gave more than any other individual, or more than all of them together.

85. Moloney, *Gospel*, p247; also Martin, p336.

86. 1:16-20; 2:13-14.

87. 8:34-9:1; 9:33-37; 10:41-45.

88. Nineham, p334-35; Moloney, *Gospel*, p247-48; Harrington, p195. From a structural angle, this episode leads into the farewell discourse of Jesus (the eschatological discourse) in which Jesus foretells how his followers will also have to suffer and give their lives. (See Malbon, *Company*, p217.)

89. Donahue & Harrington, p365; Martin, p336. The original article was by A G Wright, *The Widow's Mites: Praise or Lament? – A Matter of Context,* CBQ 44 (1982), p256-265.

90. McBride, p199-200.

91. Culpepper, p430.

92. Byrne, p195 fn39, maintains that this interpretation is more suited to the Lukan version than to that of Mark; he opts for the exemplar view. Malbon, *Company*, p176 and 54-55, finds Wright's view unconvincing; she believes that his contextual focus is too narrow. Boring, p352, does not support a Temple polemic.

93. Malbon, *Company*, p172-188. She observes, p178-179, that the first action of Jesus in the Temple, in driving out the buyers and sellers, points to the end of the Temple. His final action in the Temple, which is his reaction to the widow's action, points to his own end. The two ends are closely interrelated in Mark.

94. See G.A. Yee, *Jewish Feasts and the Gospel of John* (Collegeville, Liturgical Press 1989), p60-65; Moloney, John, p194.

95. Commentators generally see 14:1 as the beginning of Mark's passion; most believe that Mark used and adapted a fairly extensive pre-Markan narrative. See Boring, p378; Moloney, *Gospel*, p275-276.

96. This indicates the priestly aristocracy who had positions of power over Temple and treasury (Donahue & Harrington, p385). They are the official opposition. People and leadership are contrasted. The Pharisees, who last featured in the story in 12:13, play no further role. See Boring, p379-381.

97. The Greek can also be rendered as not in the presence of the festival crowds. In this case Judas makes it possible for the arrest to take place away from the crowds.

98. Nineham, p370. Mark uses this intercalation or literary sandwiching device equally effectively when describing the Last Supper. See also Donahue & Harrington, p389; McBride, p217.

99. Hooker, p325. So, in all probability, this event happened on the Wednesday of that final week.

100. The story is told in very similar words in Matthew 26:6-13. John has an alternative form in 12:1-8, situated in Bethany at Passover time. Here the woman is named as Mary, the sister of Lazarus; she anoints the feet of Jesus. For a full treatment of this, see Winstanley, Symbols and Spirituality, chapter 7. At this point in his story, Luke omits the incident. Earlier in his narrative in a different context, he describes an anointing by a sinful woman; this we discussed in chapter 2.

101. Byrne, p217.

102. Donahue & Harrington, p386.

103. Nineham, p374. Hooker, p328, suggests that the jar was an *alabaster*, a type of jar, and not necessarily made of alabaster.

104. Ointment jars used in anointing the dead were often broken and left in the tomb.

105. This is Moloney's assumption, *Gospel*, p281; for Culpepper, p485, Jesus' response makes more sense if addressed to the disciples. Matthew makes this explicit; in John it is Judas who complains. The verb is used also of the complaining of the disciples when James and John make their request for the top jobs in the Kingdom (Mark 10:41). Boring, p382, 384, believes that the objection does not come from the disciples, but, as in 2:18-20, from people outside his circle.

106. Nineham, p372.

107. The Greek is *kalon ergon*

108. Deut 15:11 says T*he needy will never be lacking in the land; that is why I command you to open your hand to the poor and needy kinsman in your*

*country.* Jesus shows his concern for the poor in 10:21-22.

109. The words are a further passion prediction. See Jesus' comment in 2:19-20 about the limited time in which the bridegroom is present.
110. Harrington, p 214.
111. Donahue & Harrington, p388, refer to Jesus as a dead man walking. Hooker, p330, believes that this comment was added to the original story, probably by Mark, who saw her action as symbolic, foreshadowing Jesus' coming death.
112. Nineham, p372, 375.
113. Hooker, p330.
114. 2 Kings 9:1-13; 1Kings 1:38-40. Harrington, p 215. Moloney, *Gospel*, p282, states that the woman has recognised that Jesus' death is near, and has provided a royal anointing that prepares his body for burial.
115. Hooker, p328. Culpepper, p482, notes the irony of it all. Malbon, *Company*, p181, comments on the irony of the poor widow's gift taking place in the doomed Temple, and the anointing of Jesus in a leper's house at the hands of a woman rather than a priest; also p202.
116. See Moloney, *Gospel*, p281; Donahue & Harrington, p390. Byrne, p218 fn11, does not share this view; Boring, p383 fn81, rejects the messianic anointing idea.
117. Hooker, p328.
118. Mark 8:35; John 12:25.
119. The two incidents are carefully paired by Luke. We reflected on Matthew's version of this story in the previous chapter. Although found only in Luke, the story about the widow of Nain is not a Lukan creation, but is derived from his special source material, which he has edited. Meier, 2:797, notes that the anchoring of the story in the obscure Galilean town of Nain (now shown by archaeology to have had a gate), as well as the presence of some possible semitisms in the text, argues for the origin of the story among Jewish Christians in Palestine. With some hesitation, he inclines to the view that the story goes back to some incident involving Jesus at Nain during his public ministry. Mark, Luke and John have each only one story of Jesus raising someone from the dead. Meier acknowledges the influence of the Elijah-Elisha stories and the story of Jairus' daughter on the way Luke's story is written.
120. 7:22
121. McBride, p.95, refers to a crowd following life and a crowd following death.
122. Also Fitzmyer, 1:658; Johnson, p.118; Evans, p.346.
123. Marshall, p.285; Wright, *Luke*, p.83. See earlier in this chapter in the story of Jairus' daughter.
124. McBride, p96.

125. This is the first time that Luke uses the title Lord for Jesus, a title common in the Early Church; it is appropriate in this life-giving context, and becomes a distinctive feature of the narrative of this Gospel. See Johnson, p118; Fitzmyer, 1:659; McBride, p96; Marshall, p285. Luke also uses the technical verb for compassion (splanchnizesthai) in 2 parables, as he describes the reaction of the Samaritan and of the father of the two lost sons (10:33; 15:20).

126. Moloney, *This is the Gospel of the Lord* (C) (Homebush, St Paul Publications 1991), p134.

127. This phrase echoes 1Kings 17:23, the story of Elijah and the son of the widow of Zarephath; there are a number of parallels and verbal echoes. The other OT instance of raising someone to life is the case of Elisha and the Shunamite woman's son (2 Kings 4:32-37). The two prophets pray fervently to God; Elijah stretches himself over the child three times. Jesus simply speaks a word; he is in a different league. See Voorwinde, p127. Luke tells the story with deliberate echoes of these prophets: thus Wright, Luke, p83; Fitzmyer, 1:659; Mosetto, p156; Johnson, p120; Evans, p346.

128. Byrne, Hospitality, p70.

129. 1:68.

130. Fitzmyer, 1:660.

131. Caird, p109.

132. McBride, p96.

133. 9:51. References to the journey punctuate the next ten chapters.

134. In Mark (12:28-31) it is Jesus who answers the scribe's question; he does so by giving two separate commands, love of God and love of neighbour. In Luke the two aspects form one unified commandment.

135. Donahue, Parable, p134-135. He describes this story as a parabolic narrative.

136. Marshall, p451, notes the view that she may have been a widow. Byrne, p102, sees her as the dominant figure.

137. Perispaomai. See 1Cor 7:35. Johnson, p173, observes that her being overwhelmed is an objective fact, not a case of neurotic obsessiveness. Wright, Luke, p130, points out that the main problem is that Mary is behaving like a man, crossing an important social boundary; the kitchen was the space where women belonged.

138. 12:13; see 15:28-29.

139. 8:14; see 12;29; 21:34.

140. The verbs are merimnaō and thorybazō.

141. McBride, p142; Byrne, p103.

142. Caird, p150.

143. Johnson, p175. Several commentators stress that active and contemplative styles of spirituality are not being compared or evaluated here.

144. Donahue, Parable, p136-137, linking the story of the sisters with the parable of the Good Samaritan.

145. 8:21; 11:28;12:47.

146. Byrne, p103.

147. Fitzmyer, 2:892, notes that a diakonia that bypasses the word is one that will never have lasting character.

148. For bibliography see chapter one.

149. This chapter is an updated version of Symbols and Spirituality, p25-45.

150. John uses the term sign to designate the miracles of Jesus.

151. John 2:1-12 to 4:46-54.

152. The Christology of the Fourth Gospel is high; yet the humanity of Jesus is also very evident.

153. Gen 33:19; 48:22; also Josh 24:32. Genesis mentions the land, not the well. The targums (Aramaic translations) and rabbinic literature link traditions about the well to Jacob; Jacob is a well-giver, produces miraculous flowing water; the well was the gift of God. See Coloe, God Dwells with Us, p91-92.

154. Bailey, Jesus, p201-202, states that the capstone was 18 to 20 inches thick, and 5 feet across, with a hole in the centre for lowering the bucket. The capstone prevents dirt from getting into the well, and children from falling in. It also provides a working surface.

155. Gen 24:10; 29:1; Exod 2:16-22. See also Hagar, also a foreign woman, in Gen 16 & 21. Schneiders, Written, p135-136, 141, suggests that the symbolic theme of Jesus as the bridegroom, introduced at Cana and continued by the words of the Baptist (3:29-30), continues here. Jesus comes to woo and claim Samaria as part of the new Israel, the Christian (and Johannine) community.

156. Bailey, Jesus, p202.

157. Coloe, God Dwells, p87.

158. Coloe, God Dwells, p87.

159. Brown, John, 1:170; Bailey, Jesus, p203.

160. The term Jew is used in the Fourth Gospel in different ways: in a neutral sense, for the people who follow the Mosaic Law; in a positive way, for those who respond to Jesus (4:22; 11:19,31,36,45; 12:9,11); and negatively and polemically, for those who are against Jesus, mainly the religious leadership, the representatives of unbelief. These nuances are to be understood against the background of the Johannine community's painful struggle with Judaism following the destruction of the Jerusalem Temple.

161. Bailey, Jesus, p205.

162. Coloe, God Dwells, p92-93, notes that it is possible to translate the phrase as: If only you knew the gift of God who is speaking to you. Jesus is the

primary gift (For God...gave his Son). Jesus is giver and gift.

163. See Ps 42:1-2a; 63:1; 143:6.

164. See Coloe, God Dwells, p90; Jesus' invitation is inclusive in religious terms and in gender; autos is generic.

165. Eternal life is a term which John frequently uses; it means the life of the above, the life of God. Believers come to share this life now in the present. This kind of life will continue beyond the grave.

166. The etymology of Jacob is supplanter. He is now being supplanted by Jesus. See Coloe, God Dwells, p86, fn4.

167. Moloney, *John*, p118.

168. Maybe she is looking for a husband in Jesus.

169. Some scholars (like Dodd) interpret the five husbands symbolically, as indicating the gods and cults brought into Samaria by the foreign colonists from five cities (or nations) who were introduced into the country by the Assyrians. This is an indication of Samaria's infidelity to the Mosaic covenant. Jesus' words constitute a prophetic denunciation of false worship. See Schneiders, Written, p139-140. But the book of Kings names 7 gods, not 5; also John does not normally use allegorisation. Barrett, Brown, Lindars, Moloney, Schnackenburg and Lee see no need for this symbolic view, and interpret Jesus' revelation of her past literally.

170. Stibbe and Brodie are also open to this bridegroom interpretation.

171. Coloe, God Dwells, p97-99.

172. Coloe, God Dwells, p99 fn 54. In her structure, this is the central section; Jesus is the new Temple of God; true worship can only happen in him.

173. Deut 27:4-7. See Coloe, God Dwells, p101.

174. Coloe, God Dwells, p112.

175. Bailey, Jesus, p210.

176. See Deut 18:18, I will raise up for them a prophet like you from among their brethren, and I will put my words into his mouth, and he shall speak to them all that I command him.

177. Exod 3:14.

178. Moloney, *John*, p130. See Isa 52:6; 41:4; 43:10; Coloe, God Dwells, p102.

179. Lee, *Symbolic Narratives,* p83-86. Other scholars interpret the Greek question as hesitant; the woman is uncertain about the identity of Jesus; her faith has grown but is still only partial; she has not understood his words about true worship and his self-revelation as I am. See Moloney, John, p130-131,135. Coloe, God Dwells, p106, takes the indication of doubt (mēti) as due to the fact that she is a woman, and has an irregular marital background which would disqualify her as a witness. The mēti is a rhetorical device which allows the villagers to hear her words as an invitation and make their own journey of faith. Her role is to be a catalyst.

180. 1:37-41.

181. It seems unlikely that Jesus himself engaged in ministry in Samaria. The story legitimates the early Christian mission to Samaria, mentioned in Acts 8:4-25, and the presence and equality of Samaritans in the Johannine community. Bailey, Jesus, p214, notes that Herod had built a temple on the western edge of the city of Samaria (which he had rebuilt) in honour of the Emperor Augustus, and erected a large statue there. The temple could be seen from Caesarea Maritima. He wonders whether the title Saviour of the world was applied to him by Jesus' time, and whether the Samaritans are affirming Jesus as the genuine alternative.

182. Coloe, God Dwells, p107.

183. Coloe, God Dwells, p113.

184. Prov 9:1-5; 13:4; 16:22; 18:4; Isa 55:1; Sir 15:3; 24:21, 23-25.

185. Barrett, p233.

186. 1:18.

187. 1:17. Light and bread are also symbols of the revelation which Jesus brings.

188. See Brown, John, 1:178-8; Schnackenburg, 1:426; Lee, Symbolic Narratives, p76-78.

189. Isa 44:3; 32:15; Joel 2:28; Ezek 36:25-27.

190. The verb is hallomai. Judg 14:6; 15:14; 1Sam 10:10; 17:13.

191. 7:37-39.

192. 19:28-37.

193. Acts 2:38; 8:20; 10:45; 11:17; see Heb 6:4.

194. Coloe, God Dwells, p94, sees a third interpretation: the living water refers to the new Temple.

195. Bailey, Jesus, p212. See his chapter on Jesus and Women, p189-199.

196. See Seamus Mulholland OFM, Jesus and the Samaritan Woman: a Model for Discipleship, in Spirituality 67 (Dublin, Dominican Press 2006), p 211-214.

197. See Mark 10:1-12. Pagola, p221, observes that patriarchal marriage was not part of God's plan. There is no place for structures of male superiority and female submission in God's reign.

198. Mark 10:35-45; Luke 22:24-27; see Winstanley, Symbols, chapter 8.

# Notes on Chapter Five

1. We first met the controversies in chapter 2.

2. Moloney, *Gospel*, p 47-48,57 incorporates it in a wider section; Donahue & Harrington, p91, see it as an appendix.

3. Culpepper, p61.

4. The NJB refers to a virulent skin disease. The term would include psoriasis, lupus, ringworm, favus. Leprosy, now known as Hansen's disease, was found in India in 600BC. It had become a common disease by Greek and Roman times, and may have begun to appear in Palestine by the time of Jesus. Voorwinde, p69 fn17, is of the view that the leper cured by Jesus could have been suffering from leprosy as we know it, (also Donahue & Harrington, p88). On the other hand, he could have been afflicted with one of the skin diseases described in Lev 13-14, whose symptoms are not consistent with modern leprosy.

5. See Lev 13:45-46.

6. See also Donahue & Harrington, p88.

7. I find the JB translation preferable here. Donahue & Harrington, p89, see an implicit Christology in the request. They prefer the translation: *you have the power*...which emphasises that Jesus is the stronger one.

8. Better *Be cleansed!* This is a divine passive, indicating that it is God who effects the cure.

9. Voorwinde, p71. Moloney, *Gospel*, p58, notes that as in his touching Simon's mother-in-law, Jesus here shows his lack of concern for the purity traditions, a theme developed later. Technically, this is referred to as a prolepsis.

10. Culpepper, p62, thinks that *moved to anger,* though a weaker reading, is the more difficult, and may be the more original; also Boring, p70; Moloney, *Gospel*, p58 fn56, sees this as the best reading; also Byrne, p49. Meier, 2:748, does not think the arguments are conclusive. Donahue & Harrington, p89, hold that the weight of the best manuscripts, and the fact that copyists have not altered other passages that present Jesus as angry, suggest the compassion reading as authentic. Jesus appears as compassionate in two other healing narratives and in curing the possessed boy.

11. Moloney, *Gospel*, p58 fn56. Byrne, p50, suggests that a cure like this could attract the kind of enthusiasm which would threaten the true direction of his mission (as illustrated in the previous incident in the narrative).

12. Num 12:10-15; 2 Kings 5:1-14.

13. Voorwinde, p71. He sees Jesus in Mark as the divine Warrior-Healer figure of the New Exodus of Isaiah.

14. The verb is *embrimaomai.* In classical literature it can mean to bellow or snort; here it means to insist on something sternly. See Culpepper, p63.

Donahue & Harrington, p89, translate as with a deep groan.

15.  See Martin, p33; Moloney, *Gospel*, p58; Byrne, p50 fn19. Voorwinde, p72, follows Lane in holding that Jesus is infuriated with the leper because he foresees his disobedience. Boring, p71, disagrees.

16.  Moloney, *Gospel*, p58-59.

17.  Moloney, *Gospel*, p59-60, notes that the so-called messianic secret is a Markan literary and theological feature that reserves the answer to the mystery of the person of Jesus, Christ and Son of God, until the story comes to its climax. Commands to silence during the story direct the reader towards the conclusion – Jesus the crucified one.

18.  Donahue & Harrington, p91.

19.  Culpepper, p63.

20.  This happens in parallel fashion in Matthew's cure of the two blind men (9:30). The language of proclaiming and word corresponds to the terminology of the early Christian mission.

21.  Voorwinde, p74; Martin, p35; Byrne, p50.

22.  Donahue & Harrington, p91.

23.  In form-critical categories, it is thus as much a pronouncement story as a miracle. (Hooker, p106; Boring, p92). Malbon, *Company*, p198, comments that the conflict theme overwhelms the healing narrative.

24.  Wright, *Mark*, p30.

25.  For this see Meier, 2:682-683. The Sabbath issue is raised in connection with Jesus healing people in the Fourth Gospel also: see 5:16; 9:16.

26.  Martin, p56; Culpepper, p98; Voorwinde, p75. For Mark the synagogue is a place of misunderstanding and opposition.

27.  See 1:21.

28.  Meier, 2:682. Donahue & Harrington, p115, believe that the Greek suggests a longstanding malady, perhaps from birth. Hooker, p108, observes that the noun used (cheir) can also refer to the whole arm.

29.  McBride, p61.

30.  Byrne, p65. The verbs are *paratēreō* and *katagoreō*.

31.  Hooker, p107.

32.  The verb is *egeirein*, (*Get up* rather than *Come forward*, as in the above translation); it is used of restoring to health and also restoring to life (resurrection); see 2:9-12; 5:41; 10:49.

33.  Voorwinde, p77, observes that Jesus is skilfully using the device of synonymous parallelism, saying the same thing twice: do good/save life; do evil/kill.

34.  Luke (6:6-11) follows Mark fairly closely. In Matthew's version (12:9-14) Jesus asks: *Suppose one of you has only one sheep and it falls into a pit on the Sabbath; will you not lay hold of it and lift it out?* A similar question,

quoting a child or an ox rather than a sheep, is found in Luke's story of a Sabbath healing of a man with dropsy in the house of a Pharisee (14:1-6). The issue of healing on the Sabbath is found earlier in Luke 13:10-17, when Jesus cures a crippled woman in the synagogue and is criticised by the synagogue leader. On that occasion Jesus points out that people take their ox and donkey to water on the Sabbath!

35. Harrington, p37.

36. Nineham, p109-110.

37. The verb form for *angry* is strong. Jesus also looks around in anger when visiting the Temple later in the ministry (11:11). The verb translated *grieved (syllypoumenos)*, found only here in the New Testament, is likewise strong; it can also mean *feel sorry for* (as in Ps 69:20; Isa 51:19LXX).

38. Hooker, p107. The prophet Jeremiah frequently laments Israel's *hardness of heart* (Jer 3:17; 7:23; 9:13; 11:18; 13:10; 16:12; 18:12; 23:17); it indicates resistance to God's plan. Culpepper, p99, and Boring, p95, refer also to Pharaoh in Exodus. The disciples are criticised in these terms in Mark 6:52 and 8:17. Nineham, p111, observes that such blindness was seen as a punishment by God for the sin into which men were led by the supernatural forces of evil. Jesus' attempts to cure such blindness were all part of his struggle against the forces of evil.

39. Voorwinde, p79-80.

40. Hooker, p108; Byrne, p65.

41. The two groups are mentioned together again in 12:13. Boring, p92, notes that in order to execute an offender, the religious authorities in Galilee needed the support of Herod. The word *destroy* occurs again in 11:18 in connection with the plot of the priests and scribes against Jesus.

42. Nineham, p110, observes that these conflicts are typical of the grounds on which eventually the religious and secular authorities combined to destroy Jesus. Boring, p96, sees this story as a dramatic foreshadowing of what will happen later in Jerusalem

43. Culpepper, p301, notes the parallel with the exorcism of the Gadarene demoniac. This demon, however, is silent. There are also parallels with the raising of Jairus' daughter. Moloney, *Gospel*, p182-183, believes that elements directed at the disciples have been inserted into the traditional story of a cure, resulting in a mixed form of healing and teaching/instruction. This may explain the odd features. Boring, p276, observes that the focus is not on the exorcism but on discipleship, faith and prayer. Byrne, p149, suggests that the rambling, complex nature of the story may be an indication that Mark is relying on more than one tradition. Donahue & Harrington, p280, emphasise that the story is an exorcism, not a healing.

44. See also 5:21,24; 6:34; 8:1; 12:37.

45. Some interpreters (including Hooker, p222-223) think there may have

been something unusual about Jesus' post-transfiguration appearance, akin to that of Moses on descending from Sinai. Boring, p273, suggests that the crowd's amazement is mentioned here rather than at the end of the story because Mark wishes to focus there on a different point.

46. In the text the identity of the them is unclear. I have opted for the disciples, though it could refer to the crowd. The scribes have no further role in the story.

47. Culpepper, p303.

48. Donahue & Harrington, p277-278.

49. Voorwinde, p93, discusses this at some length; Byrne, p149. For Mark it is clearly a case of demonic possession.

50. Martin, p227; Moloney, *Gospel*, p183, emphasises the disciples' lack of faith, though Jesus will not in fact abandon them; Culpepper, p304, considers them as representative of their generation. Donahue & Harrington, p278, detect a hint of Jesus' sense of his approaching death. Boring, p275, notes similar phraseology expressing God's exasperation in Num 14:11; Deut 32:20.

51. *Panta dynata (all things are possible)* occurs three times in Mark (9:23; 10:27; 14:36), and only once elsewhere in the NT.

52. Moloney, *Gospel*, p184; for him Jesus is the model of belief; Hooker, p224; Boring, p274; Rhoads, Dewey, Michie, p107. Voorwinde, p92, sees this interpretation as possible, but believes it makes more sense to see it as a challenge to the doubting man; likewise Byrne, p148 fn31, who maintains that the power which Jesus possesses is in virtue of his status as God's Son and Messiah, not in virtue of any faith relationship to God. Donahue & Harrington, p278, suggest that Jesus is criticising the disciples and the father.

53. Moloney, *Gospel*, p185, fn58, sees the man as a contrast to the disciples, not as paralleling their limited faith; Mark exploits the gap between them; they do not turn to Jesus in their need. Malbon, Mark's Jesus, p86, sees Jesus' words as for the disciples as much as the father.

54. Donahue & Harrington, p279.

55. Voorwinde, p92. For Boring, p275, he both believes, and does not believe.

56. The reference to the gathering of a crowd, as if for the first time (despite 9:14), which spurs Jesus into action, is obscure. Voorwinde, p94, thinks that Jesus does not wish this difficult exorcism to become a public spectacle. Donahue & Harrington, p279, refer to the possibility of a riot.

57. Also 1:31 (Simon's mother-in-law); 5:41 (Jairus' daughter), where the same three verbs are used.

58. Moloney, *Gospel*, p185; see Culpepper, p307; Martin, p230; Donahue & Harrington, p279-280. Voorwinde, p95, notes the two typical resurrection verbs (*egeirein, anistēmi*); the miracle is not only an exorcism but a

direct pointer to the resurrection of Jesus. He quotes Lane in noting that it is through Jesus' death and resurrection that Satan's power can be definitively broken.

59. A house is often the setting in Mark for private instruction (3:20; 4:10-12, 33-34; 7:17; 9:33; 10:10; 7:24).

60. Some manuscripts add *and fasting*; this is generally regarded as a later scribal addition.

61. Byrne, p.150. For Boring, p.275, prayer and faith are two sides of the same coin.

62. Moloney, p.182-186, emphasises the failure of the disciples and their lack of faith, in this whole section.

63. John 11:26,40. Malbon, *Mark's Jesus,* p86, calls the father's statement an emblem of the dynamic process of faith.

64. John 9:1-41 develops a wonderful drama in his description of the healing of the man born blind, and his journey into the insight of faith; see Winstanley, Symbols, chapter 4; Lenten Sundays, Year A, Sunday 4, p44-56.

65. Feeding (6:35-44 and 8:1-9); lake crossing (6:45-52 and 8:10); controversy (7:1-23 and 8:11-13); reference to bread (7:24-30 and 8:14-21); a healing (7:31-37 and 8:22-26).

66. Donahue & Harrington, p257, add that it is *pivotal* because it provides a bridge; also McBride, p130. Meier, 2:691, speaks of a *Janus-like quality.*

67. Culpepper, p263. He observes that five different verbs for see are used in the scene. Hooker, p197-198 and Moloney, *Gospel*, p163, believe the parallels may be the result of Mark's editing; the two stories are not doublets. Meier, 2:691, suggests that this story may have already been shaped as a twin narrative in the pre-Markan tradition; Mark's main contribution was the pivotal place he gave it in the Gospel structure.

68. Martin, p.197; Moloney, *Gospel*, p.162,fn236.

69. McBride, p.128, believes that recent archeological surveys have confirmed this.

70. It happens often that a person in need is brought to Jesus by friends or relatives: 1:32; 2:3-5; 6:55; 7:32.

71. 7:32

72. Boring, p233; he refers to Jer 31:32; Isa 42:6-7 and Isaiah's new Exodus imagery.

73. Donahue & Harrington, p257.

74. See Meier, 2:693.

75. Meier, 2:739 fn57. According to Donahue & Harrington, p256, the Greek verb anablepein implies that the man had lost his sight, and was now recovering it; also Byrne, p138 fn3. As well as regain sight, the verb can mean *look up.*

76. The three verbs are *diablepein, apokathistēmi,* and *emblepein,* each with a

different nuance. The rare word *tēlaugōs* (*clearly from afar*) indicates the completeness of the cure. (Moloney, *Gospel*, p164 fn244).

77. This is also the view of Donahue & Harrington, p.257. Moloney, *Gospel*, p.164, notes that Jesus is not a messianic miracle-worker; his identity will be revealed on the cross. Some manuscripts have: Tell no one in the village. Harrington, p.117, McBride, p.129, and Nineham, p. 219, prefer this.

78. Moloney, *Gospel*, p.164.

79. Jesus predicts his passion and vindication three times (8:31; 9:31; 10:33-34); each is followed by evidence of the disciples' failure to understand, and by definite teaching from Jesus concerning the nature of discipleship.

80. 16:7

81. McBride, p.168-169.

82. Moloney, *Gospel*, p208.

83. Harrington, p174; though Nineham, p285, suggests that possibly the man was originally nameless, and later came to be identified with Bartimaeus, a man known in the Early Church.

84. 2 Sam 7:12-16; 1Chr 17:11-14; Ps 89:29-38; especially the Psalms of Solomon, from 50BC. See Culpepper, p353; Meier, 2:689-90; Martin, p281; Moloney, *Gospel*, p209; McBride, p170. Nineham, p282, maintains that this is the first public and unrebuked recognition of Jesus as Messiah; Jesus endorses it by healing the man.

85. Hooker, p253.

86. 11:10; in this context this is a false messianic expectation. See Winstanley, *Lenten Sundays*, Year B, Sunday 6, p114-116.

87. 12:35-37.

88. Meier, 2:687. Boring, p305, maintains that the title Son of David is for Mark a misunderstanding of Jesus' true identity. Malbon, *Mark's Jesus*, p89, observes that Bartimaeus is still blind when he calls Jesus Son of David. Jesus ignores the title.

89. Moloney, *Gospel*, p209.

90. Moloney, *Gospel*, p210.

91. epitimaō: 1:25; 3:12; 4:39; 8:30; 9:25; 10:13 (when the disciples rebuke those bringing children to Jesus).

92. Culpepper, p354, notes that he stands amongst those who show faith under duress: the paralytic's four friends, Jairus, the woman with a haemorrhage, the Syrophoenician woman, and the father of the epileptic boy. Bartimaeus' faith is persistent.

93. Culpepper, p352.

94. 1:18,20; 2:14; 10:21,28. Culpepper, p354, notes the 3 uses of call in v.49, suggesting that this is also a call story. The garment may represent that which the disciple leaves behind to follow Jesus. Similarly, Martin, p283;

Hooker, p253; Wright, p143; Byrne, p170; Boring, p305-306. Meier,2:734 fn33, disagrees because the formal invitation is lacking. Boring, p306, detects a hint of baptism; he throws aside the garment of his old self.

95. The verb (*sōzein*) often refers to both healing and salvation; see Nineham, p286.
96. Moloney, *Gospel*, p211.
97. Moloney, *Gospel*, p211.
98. Hooker, p253.
99. Culpepper, p355; also Meier 2:686: *more importantly for Markan symbolism he follows Jesus on the way, that is, on the way of the cross, the way the disciples followed in fear, the way every true disciple must follow.*
100. Meier, 2:687. This is true, but the actual encounter is not recorded by Mark.
101. Nineham, p283, maintains that the words *faith*, *save*, *follow*, and *way* are used with their full religious meaning.
102. In Matthew's version, in which two blind men are cured, this is specifically highlighted (20:34).

# Notes on Chapter Six

1. Lev 24:14; Num 15: 35-36; both texts use *exagein* (*lead out*), as does Mark; 1Kings 21:13; Acts 7:58 (Stephen).

2. D. Senior, *The Passion of Jesus in the Gospel of Mark* (Wilmington, Glazier 1984), p116, gives only the first alternative.

3. R.E. Brown, *The Death of the Messiah* 2 vols (London, Chapmans 1994), 2:915.

4. Moloney, *Gospel*, p318; Culpepper, p548; McBride, p250. It is perhaps unwise to identify Rufus with the man of that name found in Romans 16:13, since this was a common Roman name; Paul refers to his mother, but not his father. Alexander is a Greek name. Matthew and Luke mention Simon, but omit the reference to his sons.

5. Nineham, p422. The issue is whether this was the Passover or its eve (as in John). Boring, p423, states that the text does not mean *from a field*, as some suggest.

6. *If any want to become my followers, let them deny themselves and take up their cross and follow me* (8:34). The verb is *airein*. Luke's phrasing highlights this more clearly; Simon carries the cross *behind Jesus* (23:26; 14:27).

7. The Fourth Evangelist omits the Simon incident altogether, probably for theological reasons, because he presents Jesus during the passion as totally and majestically in control.

8. Byrne, p240.

9. An allusion to Amos 8:9-10: *on that day, I will make the sun go down at noon, and darken the earth in broad daylight*. Moloney, *Gospel*, p325, observes that the eschatological nature of the prophecy indicates that the final intervention of God into human affairs has arrived, with universal implications.

10. Moloney, *Gospel*, p328. The sense of final abandonment and obedient self-gift is powerful; the cry is linked with the final battle with evil.

11. Byrne, p245. McBride, p257, notes that the high priest tore his clothes; now God vindicates Jesus by tearing the temple veil.

12. Byrne, p245-47.

13. Brown, *Death*, 2:1111, notes a third veil, the precinct veil, situated in the Tabernacle at the entry to the sacred compound. Mark may not have known the Temple details. For this discussion, see Brown, *Death*, 2:1109-13.

14. Brown, *Death*, 2:1111. This is the view of Byrne, p244; Martin, p439; Moloney, *Gospel*, p329; Senior, Passion, p126.

15. 11:15-19.

16. 13:1-2.

17. 14:57-58; 15:29; 12:10-11.

18. Brown, *Death*, 2:1100-1102, 2:1135. Senior, Passion, p127-128, sees the tearing of the veil as primarily a sign of judgement; also Culpepper, p561-562, who provides a good summary of Mark's presentation of Jesus' opposition to the Temple.

19. Byrne, p246-47, detects an allusion to the expiatory rites connected with the Jewish day of atonement, and links this with Jesus' words over the cup at the Supper.

20. Eph 2:14; Donahue & Harrington, p452; Nineham, p430. Hooker, p378, observes that this may refer to the barrier in the Temple beyond which Gentiles were not permitted to pass.

21. 15:44. Mark uses the loan word from Latin, *kentyriōn*; Matthew and Luke prefer *hekatontarchēs*.

22. Brown, *Death*, 2:1144-45; Donahue & Harrington, p449. Byrne, p245 fn20, states that it was not the sight of the curtain being rent which prompted the centurion's reaction. In Matthew it is the accompanying signs and wonders which give rise to faith.

23. Hooker, p378; Nineham, p431; McBride, p257; Senior, *Passion*, p129. Moloney, *Gospel*, p330, stresses that it is the way in which Jesus breathes his last, crying out to God in loud desperation and screaming in final agony, that leads the centurion to make his confession.

24. 14:62; 15:9-15.

25. Donahue & Harrington, p449: *Only at his death on the cross is the true identity of Jesus as the suffering Messiah and God's Son revealed.* The past tense, was, underlines this (Brown, *Death*, 2:1151).

26. Culpepper, p564.

27. Boring, p434. Malbon, *Company*, p202, maintains that the centurion is portrayed as knowing what he was saying; in *Mark's Jesus,* p123, she maintains that he is sincere rather than sarcastic; he is an exception amongst the Roman characters.

28. Hooker, p378; Moloney, *Gospel*, p330. For a detailed discussion, and the same conclusion, see Brown, *Death*, 2:1146-52.

29. 1:1; 1:11; 9:7.

30. 3:11; 5:7.

31. Brown, *Death*, 2:1150, concludes that Mark's audience in 70AD would not make a distinction between their creedal statement and the meaning of the centurion's affirmation in 30/33. Boring, p434-435, maintains that the centurion's confession is correct but inadequate; it is only in the light of the resurrection that it can be said that Jesus is the Son of God.

32. 13:10. Senior, Passion, p131, emphasises the fact that the centurion is Gentile and an outsider. Culpepper, p564-565, likewise; he traces the Gentile theme across the Gospel narrative.

33. Mary of Magdala's name occurs in all accounts. The other Mary is usually

thought to be the mother of James the son of Alphaeus, one of the Twelve (3:18), though Brown, *Death*, 2:1017, 1154 fn33, believes that she is the Mary of Clopas in John. Matthew (27:56) identifies Salome as the mother of the sons of Zebedee. Brown, *Death*, 2:1016, offers a comprehensive table of the women's names in the various Gospels at Calvary, the burial and the empty tomb. Boring, p437-438, observes that the only other mention of James and Joses is in Mark 6:3, where they are listed amongst the brothers of Jesus; perhaps in an oblique and subtle way Mark intends us to believe that this Mary is Jesus' mother. Mark has presented one good scribe, one good Roman, and will present one good Sanhedrin member; perhaps he wishes also to portray one good family member. Donahue & Harrington, p449, see this as a tempting possibility.

34. Luke also mentions this earlier in his narrative (8:1-3); see chapter 4. Also Matt 27:55-56; Luke 22:49,55; 24:10.

35. Jesus calls disciples to *follow* (1:16-20; 2:13-14), and to *be with him* (3:3:14). They are called to *serve* (10:45).

36. See Moloney, *Gospel*, p331; Brown, *Death*, 2:1155. A smaller group of women within a larger group parallels the three close companions of Jesus amongst the Twelve.

37. Moloney, *Gospel*, p332, and fn.289; he insists that the words be given their full Markan meaning; also Donahue & Harrington, p449; Martin, p442-443; Pagola, p224; Senior, *Passion*, p131; Malbon, *Company*, p58. Brown, *Death*, 2:1156, thinks that Mark would consider them as disciples, though probably did not think of them when using that term in the ministry of Jesus.

38. See Pagola, p224-227, on women as disciples; their ongoing presence would be a source of scandal, but they are considered by Jesus as *sisters* in his new family, on a par with the *brothers* (Mark 3:35).

39. Senior, Passion, p131. Byrne, p248 fn27, suggests that they are a faithful foil to the absent inner male trio – Peter, James and John.

40. 14:37; 10:45. See Byrne, p248.

41. Brown, *Death*, 2:1158; he links this view with the portrayal of their role in the two subsequent scenes.

42. 14:54; Moloney, Gospel, p332. Malbon, *Company*, p60-67, notes the surprising fact of women disciples, and the reversal it expresses; but they are depicted as fallible followers.

43. 6:29.

44. Brown, *Death*, 2:1212. Dunn, *Jesus Remembered*, p781, observes that the tradition of Jesus' burial is one of the oldest pieces of tradition we have (1Cor 15:4).

45. Moloney, *Gospel*, p333, suggests that this fact has disappeared from Mark's calculations.

46. Brown, *Death*, 2:1212-13; Culpepper, p568. The Romans often left executed criminals to rot or be devoured by animals or birds. Jewish attitudes were very different; they were extremely careful about funeral rites, even for suicides and enemies. It is unlikely that Pilate would have given Jesus' body to his friends or followers; having committed himself to public action, he would have had to be apprehensive about the possible idolising of Jesus by his followers and about the severity of the emperor in matters relating to treason. See Brown, *Death*, 2:1206-11. Hooker, p380, comments that it makes little sense for Joseph to avoid desecration of the Sabbath by burying Jesus on another holy day (if Friday was the Passover).

47. Nineham, p434.

48. 14:64. Brown, *Death*, 2:1213-14; Culpepper, p569. Donahue & Harrington, p453, suggest that possibly Mark exaggerates the scope of the meeting and the unanimity of the verdict which led to Jesus' death.

49. See Moloney, *Gospel*, p333; Nineham, p434; Hooker, p381; Martin, p444; Brown, *Death*, 2:1216. The phrase can apply to pious observers of the Law. Earlier (14:34) the good scribe is described as being *not far from the kingdom of God.* Donahue & Harrington, p456, link him with this scribe in being examples of the best in the religious tradition of Israel. For Luke Joseph is *a good and righteous man,* a Sanhedrin member *who had not agreed with their plan and action.* Wright, Mark, p220, maintains that he must have been a secret supporter of Jesus, which is the view of John 19:38. For Matthew (27:57) he is *a disciple of Jesus.* Perhaps he was a later convert (Byrne, p250). In favour of a burial of Jesus by the Jews, see Acts 13:27-29; John 19:31; GPet 6:21.

50. Deut 21:22-23. The Jews usually buried the dead on the day of death if possible, though not on the Sabbath.

51. Brown, *Death*, 2:1216; Martin, p445.

52. Byrne, p249; Donahue & Harrington, p454; Senior, *Passion*, p133. Pilate would probably not have allowed a disciple to take the body.

53. Pilate also *wondered* in 15:5 at the silence of Jesus.

54. Hooker, p381.

55. For further details about tombs and burial practices, see Brown *Death*, 2:1247-51; Martin, p446; Dunn, *Jesus Remembered*, p834-835. John 20:5 also suggests a horizontal tomb.

56. 1Kings 13:21; Jer.22:19; 26:23. The *Mishnah*, which dates from 220AD, is the Hebrew written version of the oral traditions of Israel.

57. Brown, *Death*, 2:1249. Matthew (27:60) states that Joseph used his own tomb; perhaps because of the haste Joseph was prepared to have his own tomb used as a temporary receptacle until the Sabbath was over. Moloney, *Gospel*, p335, notes that this kind of burial was not for the common people.

58. Senior, Passion, p133. For Malbon, *Company*, p203, he suffers and serves by bearing the expense, the labour and the risk of burying Jesus' body.

59. Hooker, p381; Moloney, *Gospel*, p333.

60. Brown, *Death*, 2:1243-44.

61. Byrne, p249-250.

62. The text could indicate that Mary was the daughter of Joses, rather than the mother.

63. Brown, *Death*, 2:1218; Culpepper, p571; Martin, p447. Byrne, p249, suggests that they fulfil the function of the two or more witnesses required by the Law (Deut 19:15). Donahue & Harrington, p455, note that the imperfect tense of the verb suggests the women *took in everything from start to finish*.

64. Some scholars have thought that Mark's original ending was lost, the final section of the scroll being worn away or detached; others that he was prevented by sickness or death from continuing as he had intended. But most now feel it best to assume that he ended where he wanted to end, in spite of the bad Greek! See Byrne, p253; Nineham, p439-442; Senior, Passion, p135; Dunn, *Jesus Remembered*, p826 fn7. Moloney, *Gospel*, p339-341 discusses this in detail, concluding that the original Gospel ended at 16:8. Wright, *The Resurrection of the Son of God* (London, SPCK 2003), p616-624, argues strongly that Mark did continue beyond 16:8, so that Jesus' prophetic words would be fulfilled; Matthew probably filled out his schematic form.

65. There (15:47) the second Mary is said to be the mother of James the younger and Joses. At the burial there is no mention of Salome, and the Mary is named as the mother (or daughter) of Joses. Mark makes no attempt to harmonise his lists. Hooker, p.383, suggests that he was probably reproducing different independent traditions; Culpepper, p.584.

66. Byrne, p.254, calls this a highly evocative allusion, a dawn ripe with promise of renewed creation. In similar vein Moloney, *Gospel*, p.343, sees light now dawning as God enters the story. Mark's two time references are not consistent; he often uses duplicate time expressions, the second more precise than the first. Culpepper, p.585, notes the view that they set out in the dark, but that it was light when they arrived. Reference to t*he first day of the week* reflects early Christian practice of meeting together on the Lord's Day.

67. This is Luke's view also; in John, since Jesus received a lavish burial as befits a king, the purpose for Magdalen's visit was simply to mourn.

68. Boring, p.443.

69. But, as Nineham remarks, p.443, those who collected and handed on the traditions were presumably well aware of local customs, attitudes and conditions. See also R.E. Brown, *A Risen Christ in Eastertime* (Collegeville,

Liturgical 1991), p.12,fn9.

70. R.H. Fuller, *The Formation of the Resurrection Narratives* (London, SPCK 1972), p54, and R.E. Brown, *The Virginal Conception and Bodily Resurrection of Jesus* (London, Chapman 1974), p121 fn203, maintain that this detail of the rolled back stone may be very ancient, and belong to the earliest form of the tradition. The perfect tense of the passive verb suggests that the effect of the rolling away of the stone would last forever. Also Boring, p444.

71. Boring, p444, links this verb (anablepein) with its use in 8:24, where it is used for the preliminary and partial healing of the blind man of Bethsaida. Unlike Bartimaeus, they do not attain full sight within Mark's narrative.

72. Matt 28:2 and Luke 24:23 interpret it this way. See Moloney, *Gospel*, p345; McBride, p262; Brown, *Death*, 1:299-300. The simplest account of the Empty Tomb is that reflected in John: see later in this chapter. The emptiness of the tomb did not give rise to resurrection faith. It was the appearances of Jesus to his disciples which gave rise to faith, as well as providing the explanation why the tomb was empty. In passing on the tradition it was necessary to insert an explanation. An accepted literary manner of doing so was to put the message on the lips of an angel. Then the Empty Tomb narrative becomes the vehicle for the proclamation of Easter faith: *he has been raised*. This is the text which we are now considering. See Brown, *Bodily Resurrection,* p123.

73. See 9:15; 14:33.

74. The reference to the *young man*, which recalls the *young man* of the arrest scene who fled away naked, may be a hint of God's power to reverse also the failure of the disciples. See Moloney, *Gospel*, p345-46. Not all scholars agree with this connection.

75. Kingsbury, Christology, p153; Brown, *Risen Christ*, p13-14. See 1:23; 10:47; 14:67.

76. The perfect tense (*estaurōmenon*) is used here, indicating a past event which continues: Jesus' identity remains the *crucified one.* The second verb (*ēgerthē*) is aorist tense (past definite), as in Rom.6:4; 7:4; 8:34; 2Cor.5:15. It expresses the act of passing from death to life. Paul uses the term crucified rather than died in 1Cor.1:23; 2:2; Gal.3:1; 5:24; it is found also in Acts 2:36; 4:10.

77. 14:27; in that verse the verb see is not used, though it is perhaps implied. (Byrne, p256).

78. Probably this time the verb (*proagein*), here in the present tense, means that Jesus is preceding them, will get there first.

79. Nineham, p448.

80. Anderson, p358. Byrne, p258, suggests that Mark wishes to emphasise that resurrection faith was not the result of the empty tomb or the women's

testimony, but because the disciples *saw* the Lord.

81. Hooker, p387; Martin, p452.

82. Hooker, p387. Malbon, *Company*, p204, observes that these three women are better designated as fallible followers, like the male disciples.

83. Moloney, *Gospel*, p349. Brown, *Risen Christ*, p16-17, suggests that some in Mark's community may have failed under persecution, and could find encouragement in the failure of the male disciples. Others may not yet have been tested; like the women they may fail if they are overcome with fear. Discipleship involves suffering. Wright, Mark, p221-224, argues that Mark probably did write a conclusion in which the women told the disciples, and Jesus appeared to them, and gave them a commission. As it stands, however, we are invited to fill in the blank. Dunn, *Jesus Remembered*, p830 fn13, suggests that the effect is to relativise the role of the women and reinforce that of the disciples as primary witnesses of and for the resurrection.

84. Moloney, *Gospel*, p348-354.

85. Boring, p449. Dunn, *Jesus Remembered*, p832-833 fn26, similarly: It is part of Mark's genius that he leaves his story open at the end, open for the congregations who hear it being read to carry it on from what they know happened thereafter and what they know from personal experience is still happening.

86. This section is a slight adaptation of chapter 11 in Winstanley, *Symbols and Spirituality.* For further bibliography see the section on John in chapter 1.

87. John 19:38-42. The garden of burial becomes the garden of life. The setting evokes the creation narrative in Genesis (Gen 2:15-17; 3:8; 3:15), and the Canticle of Canticles (3:1-4). The theme of Jesus as King is prominent in the Johannine passion, especially in the Roman trial, and the polyglot notice fixed to the cross. Jesus reigns from the cross. The action of Joseph and Nicodemus, as they emerge from the shadows into the open, is an indication of the beginning (the *gathering*) of the new community.

88. Lee, *Flesh and Glory,* p220-226.

89. Koester, *Symbolism*, p68.

90. Here we touch a solid core of early Christian tradition in its simplest form. Some take Mary's use of the plural we as an indication of the presence of other women with her, as in the Synoptic tradition. John has omitted them because he prefers to have Jesus encounter individuals. Moloney, *John*, p518-519, 522, maintains that Mary is associating the two male disciples with her lack of faith at this stage in the story. Awareness of an empty tomb does not automatically lead to resurrection faith. Something more is needed.

91. See also Luke 24:24.

92. The journey or race to the tomb fits awkwardly into the narrative. The Evangelist is modifying earlier traditions by inserting the passage about the

two disciples into the Magdalen story. He wishes to locate the Beloved Disciple, the source of the Johannine tradition and a founder member of the community, in this important setting. There is considerable scholarly debate about the quality of the Beloved Disciple's faith. Some understand it as full resurrection faith, reached without an appearance of the Risen Jesus, a model for later disciples like us. For we, like him, do not see; we can, however, unlike them, understand the scriptures. His faith is based on his interpretation of the face veil, folded and left on one side, recalling the veil of Moses and/or that of Lazarus. Other scholars maintain that his failure to communicate his faith to Mary, and the fact that the two disciples return to the place where they were before, point to a faith which is only partial. The disciple is aware that a mysterious action of God is involved, but he does not yet fully understand its import.

93. See Brown, *Bodily Resurrection,* p106-107 fn177; the pattern was first advocated by C.H.Dodd.

94. Schneiders, *Written*, p192-201.

95. De la Potterie, p210.

96. 1:38. Jesus also asks this question in the garden (18:4). *Seeking* Jesus is an important concept in John (6:24-26; 13:33). There may also be an echo of the imagery of the bride seeking the spouse in the Song of Songs (3:1-3).

97. An alternative view suggests that Mary, grieving and confused, is still in control. She wants information; she will solve the problem, set things right, and do it herself.

98. John 10:3-5,14-15,27; Isa 43:1. Lee, *Flesh and Glory,* p223, notes the importance of the double naming (*Mary, Rabbouni*); names in the ancient world evoke identity, presence and relationship.

99. Lee, *Flesh and Glory,* p224.

100. De la Potterie, p212-213.

101. The language of ascension in the text is confusing. Whilst Moloney, *John*, p529, considers Jesus to be in the midst of a process not yet concluded, Brown, *John*, 2:1014-15, believes that this is not a reference to a time sequence at all, as if Jesus is *in between* resurrection and ascension. *It is a theological statement contrasting the passing nature of Jesus' presence in his post-resurrectional appearances and the permanent nature of his presence in the Spirit.* Schneiders, Written, p198-199, translates Jesus' words about ascension as a rhetorical question (*Am I as yet not ascended?*), expecting a negative answer: he is indeed ascended, and glorified, and therefore will be encountered in the community, not in his earthly body. As far as Mary is concerned in the narrative, Jesus has not yet ascended to the Father. Whilst Mary realises that he is risen, she hasn't yet realised that he is glorified. See also Schneiders, *The Resurrection of the Body in the Fourth Gospel* in J R Donahue, ed, *Life in Abundance*

(Collegeville, Liturgical Press 2005), p183.

102. See Moloney, *John*, p518-529.
103. Mary, woman of faith, key witness, is a foundational member of the Johannine community. Schneiders, *Written*, p201, describes her as symbolically both the Johannine community encountering its glorified saviour, and the official witness to that community of what God has done for it in the glorification of Jesus.
104. See J V Taylor, *A Matter of Life and Death* (London, SCM 1986), p62.

# Notes on Chapter Seven

1. His power (*exousia*).
2. See Winstanley, *Come and See* (London, DLT 1984), p62-73.
3. Mark 1:41; 6:34; 8:2; 9:22; Matt 9:36;14:14; 15:32; 20:34; Luke 7:13.
4. See W Brueggemann, *The Prophetic Imagination*, (Augsburg, Fortress Press 2001), p88.
5. Malbon, *Mark's Jesus,* p173-194, refers to deflected Christology; Jesus attempts to deflect attention and honour from himself to God.
6. In the first part of the Gospel (1:1-8:21) the *Little People* are suppliants, who manifest faith in Jesus' healing power (and so are exemplars too). In the central section (8:22-10:52) there are three suppliants, whose stories have symbolic reference to discipleship. In the third section (11:1-16:8) they model service and sacrifice, and recognise aspects of Jesus' identity. See Malbon, *Company*, p200-205.
7. Malbon, *Company*, p203.
8. See the conclusions of Dunn, *Jesus Remembered*, p881-884. He emphasises the initial (pre-Easter) impact of Jesus on his early disciples, and the role of oral tradition and community tradition in which core content is stable and details varied. In *Memory, Jesus and the Synoptic Gospels* (Atlanta, SBL 2011), R K McIver studies recent research into personal and collective memory. In the light of this he addresses the Synoptic Gospels, and concludes that the eyewitness memories behind the Gospel accounts represent a generally reliable record of what Jesus said and did. Collective memory only rarely contains information which is not related to actual events. His conclusions are found on p183-187.

# Bibliography
## MARK

Anderson H, *The Gospel of Mark* (London, Oliphants 1976)

Boring M E , *Mark A Commentary* (NTL Louisville & London, Westminster John Knox 2006)

Byrne B , *A Costly Freedom* (Collegeville, Liturgical Press 2008)

Cranfield C E B , *The Gospel according to St Mark* (Cambridge, CUP revised 1977)

Culpepper R A, *Mark* (Macon, Smyth & Helwys 2007)

Donahue J R & Harrington D H, *The Gospel of Mark* (Collegeville, Liturgical Press 2002)

Harrington W, *Mark* (Dublin, Veritas 1979)

Hooker M D, *The Gospel according to St Mark* (London, A&C Black 1991)

Kingsbury J D, *Conflict in Mark* (Minneapolis, Fortress 1989); *The Christology of Mark's Gospel* (Philadelphia, Fortress 1983).

McBride D, *The Gospel of Mark* (Dublin, Dominican Publications 1996)

Malbon E S, *In the Company of Jesus: Characters in Mark's Gospel* (Louisville, Westminster John Knox 2000); *Mark's Jesus. Characterisation as Narrative Christology* (Waco, Baylor University Press 2009)

Martin G, *The Gospel according to Mark* (Chicago, Loyola 2005)

Moloney F J, *The Gospel of Mark. A Commentary* (Peabody, Hendrickson 2002); *Mark, Storyteller, Interpreter, Evangelist* (Peabody, Hendrickson 2004)

Nineham D E, *St Mark* (London, Penguin Books 1963)

Senior D, *The Passion of Jesus in the Gospel of Mark* (Wilmington, Glazier 1984)

Wright N T, *Mark for Everyone* (London, SPCK 2001)

# MATTHEW

Beare F W *The Gospel according to Matthew* (Oxford, Blackwell 1981)

Byrne B *Lifting the Burden* (Collegeville, Liturgical Press 2004)

Cabrido J A *The Shepherd of Israel for All Nations. A Portrayal of Jesus in the Gospel of Matthew: a Narrative-Critical and Theological Study,* (STD. diss., Pontifical Gregorian University, 2008)

Davis W D and Allison D C, *A Critical and Exegetical Commentary on the Gospel according to Saint Matthew* (London, T&T Clark 2004)

Keener C S, *A Commentary on the Gospel of Matthew* (Grand Rapids, Eerdmans 1999)

Kingsbury J D, *Conflict in Mark* (Minneapolis, Fortress 1989)

Meier J P, *Matthew* (Dublin, Veritas 1980)

Moloney F J, *This is the Gospel of the Lord (Year A)* (Homebush, St Paul 1992)

Senior D, *Matthew* (Nashville, Abingdon Press 1998)

Wright N T, *Matthew for Everyone* 2 vols (London, SPCK 2002)

# LUKE

Byrne B, *The Hospitality of God* (Collegeville, Liturgical Press 2000)
Caird G B, *St Luke* (London, Pelican 1963)
Ellis E E, *The Gospel of Luke* (London, Oliphants 1974)
Evans C F, *Saint Luke* (London, SCM 1990)
Fallon M, *Gospel according to St Luke* (Bangalore, Asian Trading Corporation 1997)
Fitzmyer J A, *The Gospel according to Luke* (New York, Doubleday, vol.1 1981, vol.2 1985)
Johnson L T, *The Gospel of Luke* (Collegeville, Liturgical Press 1991)
Marshall I H, *The Gospel of Luke* (Exeter, Paternoster Press 1978)
Moloney F J,*This is the Gospel of the Lord (C)* (Homebush, St Paul Publications 1991)
Mosetto F, *Lettura del Vangelo second Luca* (Rome, LAS 2003),
McBride D, *The Gospel of Luke* (Dublin, Dominican Publications 1991)
Tuckett C.M, *Luke* (Sheffield, Academic Press 1996)
Wright N.T, *Luke for Everyone* (London, SPCK 2001)

# JOHN

Anderson P N, *The Riddles of the Fourth Gospel. An Introduction to John* (Minneapolis, Fortress, 2011).

Ashton J, *Understanding the Fourth Gospel* (Oxford, Clarendon 1991).

Barrett C K, *The Gospel according to John, 2nd ed.* (London, SPCK, 1978).

Brodie T L, *The Gospel according to John. A Literary and Theological Commentary* (Oxford, OUP 1993).

Brown, R E, *The Gospel according to John, 2 vols.* (London, Chapmans 1972); *The Community of the Beloved Disciple* (1979); *The Death of the Messiah, 2vols.* (London, Chapmans 1994).

Byrne B, *Lazarus* (Collegeville, Liturgical 1991)

Carson, D A, *The Gospel according to John* (Leicester, IVP 1991).

Carter W, *John* (Peabody, Hendrickson 2006).

Chennattu R.M, *Johannine Discipleship as a Covenant Relationship* (Peabody, Hendrickson 2006).

Coloe M L, *God Dwells With Us* (Collegeville, Liturgical 2001); *Dwelling in the Household of God* (Collegeville, Liturgical 2007).

Culpepper, R A, *Anatomy of the Fourth Gospel* (Philadelphia, Fortress 1983); *The Gospel and Letters of John* (Nashville, Abingdon 1998).

Dodd C H, *The Interpretation of the Fourth Gospel* (Cambridge, CUP 1968).

Donahue J R ed , *Life in Abundance* (Collegeville, Liturgical 2005).

Doohan L, *John, Gospel for a New Age* (Santa Fe, Bear 1988).

Haenchen, E, *John, 2 vols.* (Philadelphia, Fortress 1984).

Harvey A E, *Jesus on Trial. A Study in the Fourth Gospel* (London, SPCK 1976).

Jones L P, *The Symbol of Water in the Gospel of John* (Sheffield, SAP 1997).

Koester C R, *Symbolism in the Fourth Gospel* (Minneapolis, Fortress 2003); *The Word of Life* (Grand Rapids, Eerdmans 2008).

Kysar, R, *John's Story of Jesus* (Philadelphia, Fortress 1984); *The Maverick Gospel* (Louisville, John Knox Press 2007).

Lee, D A, *The Symbolic Narratives of the Fourth Gospel* (Sheffield, JSOT 1994); *Flesh and Glory* (New York, Crossroad 2002).

Lightfoot R H, *St John's Gospel* (Oxford, OUP 1956).

Lindars B, *The Gospel of John* (London, Oliphants 1972).

Marsh J, *St John* (London, Penguin 1968).

Martyn J L, *History and Theology in the Fourth Gospel* (New York, Harper & Row 1968).

McPolin J, *John* (Dublin, Veritas 1979).

Meier J *A Marginal Jew, vol 2* (New York, Doubleday 1994).

Moloney F J, *Belief in the Word. Reading John 1-4* (Minneapolis, Fortress Press 1993); *Signs and Shadows. Reading John 5-12* (1996); *The Gospel of John* (Collegeville, Glazier 1998); *The Johannine Son of Man* (Rome, LAS 1976); *The Gospel of John, Text and Context* (Boston, Brill 2005).

de la Potterie I, *Mary in the Mystery of the Covenant* (New York, Alba House 1992); *The Hour of Jesus* (Slough, St Paul 1989).

Pryor J W, *John: Evangelist of the Covenant People. The Narrative and Themes of the Fourth Gospel* (London, DLT 1992).

Schnackenburg R, *The Gospel according to St John vol 1* (London, Burns & Oates 1968), vol 2 (1980), vol3 (1982).

Senior D, *The Passion of Jesus in the Gospel of John* (Leominster Gracewing 1991).

Schneiders S M, *Written That You May Believe* (New York, Crossroad 1999).

Smalley S S, *John Evangelist and Interpreter* (Exeter Paternoster 1978).

Smith D Moody, *The Theology of the Gospel of John* (Cambridge, CUP 1995).

Stibbe M W G, *John. Readings* (Sheffield, JSOT Press 1993); *John's Gospel* (London, Routledge 1994).

Talbert C H, *Reading John a Literary and Theological Commentary on the Fourth Gospel and Johannine Epistles* (London, SPCK 1992).

Winstanley M T, *Symbols and Spirituality* (Bolton, Don Bosco Publications 2007).

Yee G A, *Jewish Feasts and the Gospel of John* (Collegeville, Liturgical 1989)

Zevini G, *The Gospel according to John, 2 vols* (Rome, LAS 2009).

# OTHER BIBLIOGRAPHY

Winstanley M T, *Into Your Hands* (Homebush, St Paul's 1994); *Don Bosco's Gospel Way*

Bailey K E, *Jesus Through Middle Eastern Eyes* (London, SPCK 2008);

*Poet and Peasant and Through Peasant Eyes,* (Grand Rapids, Eerdmans 1983)

Bauckham R, *Jesus and the Eyewitnesses* (Grand Rapids, Eerdmans 2006)

Borg M, *Jesus* (New York, Harper Collins 2006);

M J Borg and N.T Wright, *The Meaning of Jesus* (New York, Harper Collins 2007);

M J Borg & J D Crossan, *The First Christmas* (New York, Harper Collins 2007); The Last Week (London, SPCK 2008)

Brown R E, *An Introduction to the New Testament* (New York, Doubleday 1997); *The Death of the Messiah 2vols* (London, Chapmans 1994); The Birth of the Messiah (London, Chapmans 1993); *A Risen Christ in Eastertime* (Collegeville, Liturgical 1991); *The Virginal Conception and Bodily Resurrection of Jesus* (London, Chapmans 1974)

Brueggemann W, *The Prophetic Imagination*, (Augsburg, Fortress 2001)

Catholic Bishops' Conferences of England & Wales, and Scotland, *The Gift of Scripture* (London, CTS 2005)

Corley J ed, *New Perspectives on the Nativity* (London, T&T Clark 2009)

Donahue J R, *The Gospel in Parable* (Philadelphia, Fortress 1988)

Dunn J D G, *Jesus and the Spirit* (London, SCM 1975); Jesus Remembered (Cambridge, Eerdmans 2003); *A New Perspective on Jesus* (London, SPCK 2005)

Fiorenza E S, *In Memory of Her* (New York, Crossroad 1983)

Freyne S, *Jesus, a Jewish Galilean* (London, T&T Clark 2004)

Fuller R H *The Formation of the Resurrection Narratives* (London, SPCK 1972)

Jeremias J, *New Testament Theology* (London, SCM 1971)

Kasper W, *Jesus the Christ* (London, Burns & Oates 1976)

McKiver R K Memory, *Jesus and the Synoptic Gospels* (Resources for Biblical Study 59; Atlanta: SBL, 2011)

Meier J P, *A Marginal Jew,* 3 vols (London, Doubleday 1991, 1994)

Pagola J A, *Jesus: An Historical Approximation* (Miami, Convivium 2011)

Powell M A, *What is Narrative Criticism?* (Minneapolis, Fortress 1990)

Ressaguie J L, *Narrative Criticism of the New Testament.* An Introduction (Grand Rapids, Baker Academic 2005)

Rhoads D and Michie D, *Mark as Story* (Philadelphia, Fortress 1982); 2nd edition with Dewey J, 1999.

Schneiders S M, *Religious Life as a Prophetic Life Form* in the National Catholic Reporter, May 2010.

Sobrino J, Christology at the Crossroads (London, SCM 1978)

Taylor J V, A Matter of Life and Death (London, SCM 1986)

Tournier P, Guilt and Grace (London, Hodder & Stoughton 1962)

Voorwinde S, Jesus' Emotions in the Gospels (London, T&T Clark 2011)

Winstanley M.T., *Into Your Hands* (Homebush, St Paul's 1994); Don Bosco's Gospel Way (Bolton, Don Bosco Publications 2002); Lenten Sundays (Bolton, Don Bosco Publications 2011)

Wright N T, Jesus and the Victory of God (London, SPCK 1999); The Resurrection of the Son of God (London, SPCK 2003)

# Don Bosco Publications – Other Titles

CHRISTMAS & ADVENT SWATCH by DAVID O'MALLEY

SALESIANS – CONTEMPLATIVES IN ACTION by MICHAEL J CUNNINGHAM

SWATCH JOURNEY THROUGH LENT by TONINO PASSARELLO & DAVID O'MALLEY

SWATCH & PRAY by DAVID O'MALLEY

SCHOOL ETHOS & CHAPLAINCY by DAVID O'MALLEY

THE CHRISTIAN TEACHER by DAVID O'MALLEY

CHRISTIAN LEADERSHIP by DAVID O'MALLEY

ORDINARY WAYS by DAVID O'MALLEY

PRAYERS TO START MY DAY by DAVID O'MALLEY

PRAYERS TO CLOSE MY DAY by DAVID O'MALLEY

TRUST THE ROAD by DAVID O'MALLEY

VIA LUCIS (HARDBACK) by DAVID O'MALLEY

STARTING AGAIN FROM DON BOSCO by IAN MURDOCH

SERVING THE YOUNG by JAMES GALLAGHER

KATIE COMES TO MASS (HARDBACK) by KATHLEEN PEARCE

BOOK ROSIE GOES TO CHURCH (HARDBACK) by KATHLEEN PEARCE

DVD ROSIE GOES TO CHURCH by KATHLEEN PEARCE

CHLOE AND JACK VISIT THE VATICAN (HARDBACK) by KATHLEEN PEARCE

| |
|---|
| GOOD NEWS IN THE FAMILY (HARDBACK) by KATHLEEN PEARCE |
| MEMORY GAME |
| OUR COLOURFUL CHURCH YEAR (HARDBACK) by KATHLEEN PEARCE |
| 101 SAINTS & SPECIAL PEOPLE  by KATHLEEN PEARCE |
| TREASURE WITHIN by MICHAEL J CUNNINGHAM |
| LET YOUR HEART PRAY by MICHAEL J CUNNINGHAM |
| LOST AND FOUND by MICHAEL J CUNNINGHAM |
| A TIME FOR COMPASSION by MICHAEL J CUNNINGHAM |
| WITHIN & WITHOUT by MICHAEL J CUNNINGHAM |
| SEAN DEVEREUX by MICHAEL DELMER |
| GOD OF MANY FACES by  MARGARET  RENSHAW |
| MAMMA MARGARET by TERESIO BOSCO |
| SYMBOLS and SPIRITUALITY by MICHAEL T WINSTANLEY |
| LENTEN SUNDAYS by MICHAEL T WINSTANLEY |
| DON BOSCO'S GOSPEL WAY by MICHAEL T WINSTANLEY |
| TEACHER, TEACH US TO PRAY by WINIFRED ACRED |
| DON'T ORGANISE MY TEARS by TONY BAILEY |
| BOSCO Z BOOK |
| THE WITNESSES by WINIFRED ACRED |